GOETHE
POET AND THINKER

For

BARKER FAIRLEY
Pioneer, Master and Friend

GOETHE
Poet and Thinker

ESSAYS BY

ELIZABETH M. WILKINSON AND L. A. WILLOUGHBY

EDWARD ARNOLD

First published 1962
By Edward Arnold (Publishers) Ltd
41 Maddox Street, London W1
Reprinted 1970

Reprinted by photolithography in Great Britain
by Bookprint Limited, Crawley Sussex

Preface

These essays were written, one in collaboration and all in consultation, in the years immediately following World War II, most of them in connection with the Bicentenary celebrations of 1949. The obligation this imposed to come to terms with Goethe, and from an English point of view, lends them, we feel, a certain unity and continuity. Though the Volume makes no pretence to either a fully-rounded picture or a complete appraisal—there is, for instance, no single essay on Goethe's fiction, though several references to it by the way—it does present a balance between poet and thinker. And in its examples of 'close reading', and of translation as a mode of interpretation, it is, we think, still in line with present-day trends of literary criticism. We do not, of course, suggest that this is our last word on Goethe. It would be a sad reflection on both the process of scholarship and our own powers of growth if it were. On the other hand, we feel no inclination to deny what we then wrote. For, as Goethe told Eckermann, an author will write differently at different stages of his life, even as he himself becomes different; but this is not to say that either he or his work becomes better: 'The main thing is that he should try to see and feel truly at every stage, and express what he thinks as clearly and unambiguously as possible. Then his work, at whatever stage it was written, will stand, however much the author himself may change and develop'.

All the essays, with the exception of that on *Faust*, have appeared before in English, and are reprinted here with little alteration. Except in the one on 'Steigerung', which is largely semantic, we have usually translated longer quotations in prose but left verse in German. We have removed more flagrant overlapping, but not hesitated to retain repeated discussion of recurrent key-concepts in Goethe's thought, and even drawn attention to this by cross-references in the Notes. These have been severely simplified, and relegated, along with authorship and provenance of each essay, to the end of the Volume. For our acknowledgments to, and exchanges with, earlier scholars we must therefore refer the interested reader to the original publications. Our thanks are due to the editors of these for permission to reprint, and above all to Mrs. Joyce Crick for reading the proofs and preparing the index.

E.M.W
L.A.W

University College London
28 August, 1961

A*

Table of Contents

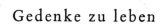

Gedenke zu leben

I. The Living Goethe

IF we hail Goethe as Europe's greatest man as well as Germany's greatest poet, we have first and foremost in mind the magnitude and multiplicity of his achievements. For he was not only a poet, but many things besides: painter, scientist, statesman, philosopher, critic, theatre manager, minister of education, in charge of the state silver mines. To all these things he devoted abounding energy and in each achieved such success as would satisfy any ordinary man. The multiplicity of his activities is only matched by the diversity of his poetic style: he is the world's master of the short lyric—as simple as Burns, as magical as Keats, as incantatory as Coleridge, as philosophically profound as Wordsworth, equally at home in mysterious symbolism and in urbanely ironic detachment. He vies with Homer, emulates Sophocles, rivals Martial and embraces Hafiz. He can move with ease among all the forms and styles of literary tradition: from the Shakespearean bustle of *Götz* to the Racinian grace of *Tasso;* from the apparent looseness of dithyrambic odes to the distilled perfection of the *Roman Elegies;* from the classical harmony of *Iphigenie* to the profusion of styles which goes to make up the baroque richness of *Faust, Part Two.* He can bring to life types as disparate as Götz in *Götz von Berlichingen* and Eduard in the *Wahlverwandtschaften.* He could move from heaven to hell and back again to heaven as in his Divine Tragedy of *Faust,* and leave out not one phase of human experience in the earth between, as he drew on any mythology and on any philosophic or scientific knowledge which would serve his vast poetic purpose. He is the last encyclopaedic mind and the last universal man, the last Greek among the Europeans. The immediate debt we owe to him, says Oscar Wilde, is greater than the debt we owe to any man since Greek days.

But he is also the first of the moderns—so modern that Carlyle was perhaps right when he said that it might well be more than a thousand years before the impact of his influence made itself fully felt. And when we say that he has living meaning for us today, we think not so much of the magnitude of his achievements, nor even of their multiplicity.

Such phenomenal many-sidedness is something that happens rarely, something that makes him a unique figure of history, to be admired but beyond emulation. We think rather of the way he was able to integrate his varied and often conflicting potentialities, so that he was not only wide and rich, but whole. His living meaning emerges not so much from our contemplation of the finished product of what he became but from the record of his struggle to achieve it. It is as a representative of modern man, faced with problems which are still essentially the problems of our time, and coping with them more successfully than anyone else whose life is on record, that his inspiration is vital to us today, equally vital whether our talents are great or small, whether we have little to integrate or much.

The problems which faced him were less acute than they have since become, but at bottom they were the same. Born in the post-Newtonian age, he stands at the dawn of modern society with its technological background, and shares in the beginning of our world of specialization with its over-emphasis of intellect at the expense of emotion and sense. He had experienced in his own person the vital phases of political development, from the patriarchal aristocracy of the *ancien régime*, through the anarchism of the French Revolution, to the tyranny of one-man rule under Napoleon, on to the liberal-conservative state of which he was the protagonist. He had seen with apprehension the coming of the demagogic spirit and the subjection of the people to the masses; he foresaw the dangers of commercialism and totalitarianism. Above all he was exposed to all those dualisms which have rent and torn Western man since Plato and St. Paul so uncompromisingly severed mind from matter and the spirit from the flesh. In our modern age of dissociated and frustrated human fragments he stands out as the nearest approach to a complete man. And he was able to be and remain this despite what was in some ways a severe handicap: the handicap of being a poet. For this means that he was a man possessed not only of an infinitude of vision but of a hypersensitive, even irritable, organization, prone by nature to turn molehills into mountains and, as Keats puts it, to let 'the smallest vexation grow in five minutes into a theme for Sophocles'. Yet he did not sacrifice activity to vision, nor permit his sensitivity to make him shy away from his fellow creatures. He was never the difficult, temperamental artist, too sensitive for the practical routine of mundane matters; nor was he an intellectual recluse who despised the life of the senses and the good things of the earth. Far from it: he lives in a large house, eats well and drinks well, and enjoys good company and good talk. His tastes are disconcertingly bourgeois, he has a healthy respect for money, drives hard bargains with his publishers and is proud of his good middle-class stock: 'Wo kam die schönste Bildung her, Und wenn sie nicht vom Bürger wär?' He is a constant, and sometimes uncomfortable, challenge to modern man to strive, despite all difficulties within and without, towards a society of more completely integrated human beings. More than one hundred and fifty years ago Goethe's great contemporary, Friedrich Schiller, recognized that the repression and violation of individual human nature which Western civilization increasingly demands was a state of affairs bristling with dangers. The solution for him, unlike Rousseau, lay not in a return to nature, but in the reconciliation of natural impulses with those impulses which tend towards civilization. This, as he saw it, was the central problem of our modern world, and it still remains the central problem today. Civilization means, inevitably, much denial of natural impulse. But a life which goes against natural impulse beyond a point is likely to result in such cumulative stress and strain as may well threaten the very basis of civilization. What Goethe was able to do more successfully than most people was to harness his instinctual drives into fruitful creative activity, to reconcile high intellectual and moral endeavour with the least possible violation of the natural man in him. And he did it by the most complete acceptance of the fact that man is part of nature, nature as modified by reason, consciousness and conscience—but nevertheless *nature*. Anticipating the evolutionists he saw the whole of creation as an ascending ladder of existence, of which man is the highest point, nature become conscious of itself. His Faust surveys the ordered progression of living things with a sense of kinship with the humblest of them:

> The ranks of living creatures thou dost lead
> Before me, teaching me to know my brothers
> In air and water and the silent wood.

Elsewhere Goethe set out the evolutionary process in scientific form. But the measure of how much this knowledge was an integral part of his mind and being is that it could thus find expression in some of his finest verse. For him there is no sharp break anywhere in nature, no point at which something wholly different and opposed in character supervenes. The qualitative difference which clearly exists between man and the lower forms of life comes about, in his view, through a gradual intensification and differentiation of the same original characteristics. Hence mind and matter are not mutually exclusive opposites, but different aspects of one and the same thing. And this means that for him the laws which apply in the natural world also apply, in modified form, in the world of mind and spirit, in the sphere of characteristically human behaviour. Nor are God and nature in any way opposed. As a very young man he observed that to discuss God apart from nature is as difficult and perilous as if we were to separate the soul from the body. 'We know the soul only through the medium of the body and God only through the medium of nature.'[1] This is no Romantic apprehension of God in Nature through ecstatic contemplation—though it may include that. It is a reasoned conviction which his scientific studies confirmed. And as an old man he can still ask: 'Was wär' ein Gott, der nur von aussen stiesse?'

> What were a God who moved things from outside
> And let the universe upon his finger ride?
> Him it befits to move it from within
> Himself in nature, nature all in him,
> So that what in him moves and dwells and lives,
> Full proof of his great power and spirit gives.

It was through this clear recognition of the interpenetration of nature and spirit in all aspects of life that Goethe was able to achieve what he did. It accounts for the organic impression we receive from all he was and made, from the body of his thought, which grew rather than was intellectually composed, from his life as much as from his work. If those ruthless denials of impulse and potentiality, which are the very condition of civilized life, did not warp him or whittle him down, or result in the breakdowns and frustrations which seem to be the price so many have to pay for civilization, it is because he yielded to the rhythms of nature wherever possible and submitted to natural laws wherever and whenever they are in place.

The law of nature which most of us find hardest of all to accept is that everything in the universe is in flux and change. The whole inclination of the human mind is towards permanence and stability; we cling stubbornly to what we have, hark back with nostalgic longing to the past, and our deepest fears are of the unknown and the future. But Goethe was so much in tune with natural process that the realization that nothing persists or is truly at rest, that even what we call inanimate nature fluctuates in movement—'nur scheinbar steht's Momente still'— even this knowledge does not disturb him. When he writes in *Dauer im Wechsel*, one of his loveliest poems: Seize the fruits of the earth in haste, for the harvest time is scarcely over when the new shoots spring; with every shower of rain thy valley is changed and in this self-same stream thou wilt never swim again—this is not the lament of a Romantic poet over the transitoriness of all earthly things, but a willing recognition that nothing stands still.

> Willst du nach den Früchten greifen,
> Eilig nimm dein Teil davon!
> Diese fangen an zu reifen,
> Und die andern keimen schon;
> Gleich, mit jedem Regengusse,
> Ändert sich dein holdes Tal,
> Ach, und in demselben Flusse
> Schwimmst du nicht zum zweitenmal.

When he writes: And you yourself, the eyes with which you see the world are not the same eyes with which you looked upon it yesterday, these lips that kissed, this foot that climbs the crag, this hand that turned to comfort, the whole structure of your being is different now from what it was—this is not the Psalmist's stern reminder that 'in the midst of life we are in death', that 'man's days are as grass, the wind passeth over it and it is gone'; it is the same willing acceptance that man too is subject to the universal law of change and transformation.

Hence Goethe does not waste his energy in trying to halt the inevitable flow of nature's process. His desire for permanence does not emerge in petrifaction, in attempts to hold fast to what he has become, to perpetuate relationships in their original form, to go on writing in the same style, or to hang on to the characteristics of one stage of his life when moving on into another. That trait which has been so often noted and deplored in him, his readiness to turn his back on a place or a person, to cut his losses, is undoubtedly due to his infallible sense for the moment when the end of a phase of growth had been reached. And it was the same in his poetry: he outgrew anacreontic playfulness, the fury of his *Sturm und Drang* gave place to reflective classicism, and where with most poets this might well have been the end, he goes on to a symbolism which takes up into itself all his earlier Romantic and Classical tendencies. And to his eightieth year he retains the power to write short lyrics which blend intensity of subjective experience with objective apprehension in a magic simplicity. And almost to the end of his life, too, he retains the courage to lay himself open to new experience, to risk again the pain and disturbance of losing himself by falling in love. He himself never ceased to live out the famous admonition of one of his most famous poems: 'Stirb und werde!' 'Death', he had written earlier,[2] 'is the artifice of life to go on producing life', and the constant dying which is necessary if one is to change and become, if one is to go on growing to the end, this he never shunned. It is the old paradox of 'losing one's life to gain it'. It is not by avoiding the painful uncertainty of change and growth that our desire for permanence is to be fulfilled. The only permanence is in the sum of remembered experience, and in the cumulative body of human thought and art. It was by thus putting permanence where it belongs, and submitting in actual experience to the natural law of change, that Goethe developed his miraculous power to undergo constant transformation, a power which has been the admiration and envy of some of his most perspicacious admirers such as Paul Valéry and André Gide.

Two other fundamental laws of nature which Goethe accepted completely and lived out in even the smallest details of his daily life are what he called the law of polarity and the law of compensation. The law of polarity he perceived at work everywhere in the universe as a constant alternation of opposites exemplified in the force of attraction and repulsion which is inseparable from matter. Polarity is manifest in the very forms of the universe, in the rhythm and pulsation of life: day and night, summer and winter, up and down, breathing in and breathing out. Each of these complements the other, and only together do they constitute a unity. Through the acceptance of this polarity he was able to reconcile many oppositions in the human sphere which have often seemed so conflicting as to be counted mutually exclusive: God and the world, mind and matter, sense and reason, love and hate, contemplation and activity, the real and the ideal, subjective and objective, conscious and unconscious, analysis and synthesis—no one of these is complete without its opposite pole. The law of compensation was equally fundamental to his thought. It was a conviction, gained from the study of the morphology of plants and animals, that there is no gain without a corresponding loss, no progress except at the cost of some regress. The higher animals have gained in the power to control their environment, but they have lost correspondingly in their power of adaptability. And since this law holds throughout nature so he sees that it must hold and be accepted in the human sphere. There are, he told Eckermann,[3] advantages at every stage of life, but also the corresponding disadvantages. On no account, therefore, would he wish at eighty to return to the stage of development he had reached at forty. Again, to wish for the fulfilment of all our potentialities is to ask the impossible. To pursue one path means giving up another. To say that he accepted this law of nature does not mean that it always came easy to him. It took him the first forty years of his life to accept the fact that he would never make more than a mediocre artist with brush or pencil, and that he had much better stick to his medium of language and find fulfilment as a poet. But by realizing that in thus giving up other possible developments of his talents he was acting in tune with nature and not against it—to get *one* fine rose buds must be pruned away—he avoided embitterment and frustration. He realised that he was but bowing to the inevitable, and it was in this sense that the word *Entsagung*, renunciation, became the corner-stone of his practical philosophy. It is often misinterpreted negatively as 'resignation'. But it is rather a willing acceptance of the limits set by the unalterable laws which govern the human no less than the natural order of the universe. It is absurd, he once said,[4] to expect a force to limit *itself*. It can only be limited by another force: 'Ein Gott kann nur wieder durch einen Gott balanziert werden'. Hence in a healthily functioning personality one impulse is held in check by another, the frustration of the one offset by the fulfilment of the other, and the balance of the whole thus self-regulating. And so, too, in a healthily functioning society. Mere theoretical reflection, says Goethe,[5] can easily lead us astray here, for it is prone to make false generalizations from some particular instance. For example, people often say that each man acts from self-interest, that love is but a form of egoism. 'As if', Goethe goes on, 'nature were not so constituted that the aims of the individual, far from conflicting with the whole, do but serve to maintain it . . . as if I could ever further the welfare of another without its flowing back upon me.' For the welfare of others is by no means to my disadvantage, and it is but rarely that I am called upon to achieve it by some self-sacrifice of my own. It was in this sense that Goethe could describe renunciation as the sum of man's earthly wisdom.[6] And the limitations which apply to human behaviour also apply to human knowledge. Goethe had learned from Kant that there are things unknowable through the senses. But realist that he is he does not indulge in speculation about this unknowable, about the 'Ding an sich'. Man's task is not to ask the Why and the Wherefore of nature—these are not scientific questions— but patiently to explore the How,[7] and Goethe finds fault with one contemporary scientist for transgressing the inevitable limitations of scientific knowledge and encroaching upon the province of poetry and religion.[8] To pause in awe before the unknowable is for him the supreme act of piety—'Wir heissen's: fromm sein'.

All this implies a conception of human behaviour which is realistic in the sense of being realizable. Goethe does not, like some idealistic philosophers, set up standards which are so impossible of fulfilment that we are constantly discouraged by our sense of failure. He always en-

visages the possibility of rising to the heights—in earlier life he spoke
of building the pyramid of his existence as high as possible.[9] But we
note that it is a pyramid, something with a broad firm basis, and the
building is to be done gradually, step by step. This may mean yielding
to violent impulses and learning through disaster that they must be
curbed; it may mean being thrown violently from one extreme of
experience to the other. But it is only through the *practice* of life that
we can learn to swing easily between the poles of our existence, and
achieve a balance which still vibrates with fruitful tensions. Reason must,
of course, take a hand in directing and guiding human development;
but there is no forcing the pace. Goethe conceives of personality as an
organic growth, subject to its own unalterable rhythms. Like any organism its growth depends on constant interaction with its environment,
and the criterion of its health lies in the proper functioning of the
various tendencies within the organism and in its power to respond
appropriately to the varying stimuli which come to it from without.
It is all a question of the right response at the right moment. Even the
most perfect virtue becomes a fault when practised out of season, just
as the most excellent talent becomes a danger if it gets out of hand
in the harmonious functioning of the whole personality.

But because Goethe's philosophy of life is realistic it does not mean
that it is easy to practise or even to accept. It makes few concessions to
weakness and none to sentimentality. They are hard truths he has to
propound, unpalatable to many. It is not easy to accept his insistence
that nature is as important as nurture, that though environment can of
course foster or inhibit its unfolding there is an unalterable basis of
personality from which there is no escaping: 'So musst du sein, dir
kannst du nicht entfliehen.'[10] Yet this is a truth with which modern
science is more and more inclined to agree. Again, he is realistically
convinced of the inequality of man, without repining and without
cynicism. Men are not born equal and it is useless to pretend that they
are. 'The majority', he declares,[11] 'the masses, are bound to be absurd and
wrong-headed, for they are lazy, and error is always much easier than
truth.' Such sayings as this have earned him the reputation of being
arrogant and a snob. There was certainly no false modesty in his estima-
tion of his own worth, physical and spiritual, none of that tiresome
self-denigration which hides insecurity and resentments. And it is a moot
point whether it is not perhaps less arrogant to accept, as he did, that
he was what he was as much by grace as by effort. Again it has caused
him to be regarded as a reactionary in progressive circles because he was
uncomfortably suspicious of the wisdom of democratic methods in the

carrying out of practical projects. He was liberal enough concerning the great principles of democratic government, but he was all for the authority of experts in working out the details. 'Men are united by convictions', he writes,[12] 'but divided by opinions . . . The former constitute a simple unity in which we come together, the latter a multiplicity in which we are dispersed.'

Despite its asperities Goethe's thought is eminently practical just because it is rooted in activity. Common *action*, he always insisted, is the best kind of union between men, a bond far more powerful than ideas, and the best solace too, in time of trouble. Don't seek to solve your problems by going away into a corner and brooding over them. Rather get busy and 'whatever thy hand findeth to do, do it with thy might'. For Goethe thought and action are inseparable, one of the great polarities of existence. 'Both must pulse through life as unceasingly as breathing-in and breathing-out. Like question and answer neither should exist without the other.'[13] It was in fact this ruling belief in activity which provided Goethe with the best argument for individual survival after death: 'The conviction of a life after death', he told Eckermann,[14] 'comes to me from my own sense of activity. If I work without ceasing to the end of my life here, nature is bound to find me another form of existence when this one can no longer contain my spirit.'

It is, perhaps, this close connection of thought and action which makes it so difficult to transmit the 'feel' of Goethe to those who do not know his writings intimately. Both the poet Hans Carossa and the philosopher Karl Jaspers recently expressed the view that the best way to celebrate his Bicentenary was not by lecturing or talking about it, but by persuading people to sit down and read him. And this is undoubtedly true. But it is only after long reading that one begins to feel his power. The individual passage rarely takes us by storm, unless we are so steeped in both his thought and his style that each word gets its full value. The difficulty is not just that his thought is scattered about in his conversations and correspondence. Even when these scattered fragments are collected and arranged, as they have been by Emil Ludwig and Hermann Weigand in convenient anthologies, this still does not put the essence of his wisdom across. With most thinkers one gets the gist of the matter through summary or paraphrase. But the unique thing about Goethe is that he *is* what he thinks, and *is* it before he thinks it, or at least before he formulates it. All his scientific studies, for instance, only serve to confirm what he already intuitively knew about himself and the universe. The difference between him and his friend, Schiller, is that Schiller puts forward the *ideal* of an integrated personality, but this ideal is something very different from what he himself actually was. Goethe *was* that integrated personality. And this shows in his style. The conceptual formulations of his thought do not account for the cumulative weight of its effect. For the thought, whether he translates it into concepts or not, is so assimilated into his activity, even into the activity of his writing, that it emerges in the very form of what he says, in the very inflections of his language, both poetry and prose. The lover of Goethe will often turn to him in stress of mind. But not merely in order to find comfort and consolation for the transitoriness of all existence, nor again to discover what Goethe himself would have done in a similar situation. Rather to be brought by the forms of his language to the fundamental forms of being. These sentences of his, which so often contain within themselves a paradox or an opposition, correspond to the tensions of life. But they do not leave them unresolved. For the contraries are held within the embracing unity of the sentence, and imperceptibly, cumulatively, they effect a unification of opposites in us. And it is a language which never turns us in upon ourselves and our own problems, but inescapably leads us out into the objects of the world around us. Not at all because he is a 'descriptive' writer, but because his language, often by its very syntax, gives as much value to the object outside as to the subject which perceives it.

This is some indication why lovers of Goethe find it so difficult to explain to others just what he means to them. As the Dutch poet, Verwey, puts it, Goethe is for them a part of their being, almost a secret. And the life they draw from him is not to be got by any short cut, but only by direct contact with his own abundance of life. It is not only that he had by nature an abundance of vitality, but that he believed in life as a value. We hear much today about the loss of values in the modern world. Perhaps the cause is that we have lost our sense of this, the most fundamental of all values, the value of life. Goethe did not scorn the other great values: goodness, truth, beauty, freedom, duty and service. But each and all depend for their existence upon the overriding value which is life. No one of them may be elevated to the purpose of life, for 'the purpose of life', he never tired of insisting,[15] 'is life itself'. Nor was he ever unmindful of the rôle of death in life: not for nothing is the 'Die and Become' of his *Selige Sehnsucht* quoted in and out of season. But living is the task to which we are called. And if in *Wilhelm Meister* he deliberately offered as a counterpoise to the mediaeval *memento mori* his own humanist 'Gedenke zu leben', it was in no spirit of *carpe diem* but as a solemn warning to be *mindful* to live. The emphasis falls with level stress on both parts of the injunction—as it does in the last, hard-won, line of the infinitely sad and infinitely beautiful love-poem, *Der Bräutigam*, which he wrote when he was rising eighty:

Wie es auch sei, das Leben, es ist gut.

II. Goethe's Poetry

THERE was a time, and not so long ago, when Goethe's poetry meant very little to me. It carried none of the tender associations of childhood. I came to it late, and from a language richer in great poetry than any in the world, and the difficulties I encountered are, I think, shared by many of my countrymen. For us Goethe's poetry is very much an object outside us, couched in an alien medium. This situation has its advantages and disadvantages. Distance may make us see the object more clearly, unobscured by purely personal associations, may make us alive to nuances which long familiarity is inclined to take for granted. But, on the other hand, unless its peculiar quality strike us at once with forcible impact, we may well pass it by with indifference and forego the arduous joy of discovery. I was, of course, enchanted by songs I had first come to know through famous musical settings: by the evocative power of 'Kennst du das Land, wo die Zitronen blühn?' or the nostalgic poignancy of

> Nur wer die Sehnsucht kennt,
> Weiss, was ich leide.

I was compelled by the rhythmic incantation of *Erlkönig, Der Fischer* or

> Meine Ruh ist hin,
> Mein Herz ist schwer,
> Ich finde sie nimmer
> Und nimmer mehr.

And later on I was impressed by the mysterious oracular wisdom of

> So musst du sein, dir kannst du nicht entfliehen,
> So sagten schon Sibyllen, so Propheten;
> Und keine Zeit und keine Macht zerstückelt
> Geprägte Form, die lebend sich entwickelt.

But there remained all the same a vast body of Goethe's poetry which I dutifully admired because I was told it was great, but which made no deeper impact at all. In the words of Elephaz the Temmanite, the hair of my flesh did not stand up as I read it; no shiver went down my spine; I experienced no contraction of the throat, no gathering of tears to the eyes—in short, none of those physical symptoms which, according to A. E. Housman,[1] are the unmistakable signs of the impact of pure poetry. I found here neither that sheer magic which 'entangles us in a web of thoughtless delight', and which is characteristic of some of the finest lyrical achievements of our own Romantic Age, that pure utterance of song,

> The same that oft-times hath
> Charm'd magic casements, opening on the foam
> Of perilous seas, in faery lands forlorn.

Nor did I find the organ roll of Milton's sonorous sublimity, nor yet again that enticing obscurity which, especially to the young, so often spells profundity and can provoke us to go in search of hidden meanings in the poetry of a Rilke, a Valéry or a T. S. Eliot. By contrast with these, some of what I should now call Goethe's most poetical utterances seemed to me plain statements of unvarnished fact, simple to the point of obviousness.

Take, for instance, that most perfect of his short poems, 'Über allen Gipfeln', rightly acknowledged to be one of the lyrical gems of world literature. There is in it not a simile, not a metaphor, not a symbol. Three brief, simple statements of fact are followed by a plain assertion for the future. In word-for-word translation it becomes almost trite and has hitherto resisted any rendering into English which could win recognition of its beauty:

> O'er all the hill-tops
> Is rest,
> In all the tree-tops
> You sense
> Scarcely a breath;
> The little birds hush in the wood.
> Wait,—soon
> You too shall rest.

'Is *that* all there is to your Goethe?' our friends are inclined to say. To which we very properly make reply that the original German exhibits a perfect union of sound and sense. We point to the immediacy with which language here conveys the hush of evening:

> Über allen Gipfeln
> Ist Ruh.

In the long *u* of 'Ruh' and in the ensuing pause we detect the perfect stillness that descends upon nature with the coming of twilight.

> In allen Wipfeln
> Spürest du
> Kaum einen Hauch.

The gentle expiration of breath in 'Hauch', and in the echoing 'auch' of the last line, has often been compared to that last sighing of the wind as it dies away in the trees. While the indispensable syllable *e* in 'Vögelein' and 'Wald*e*' makes the sixth line a lilting lullaby which inevitably evokes the rocking movement of rest 'in the tree-tops':

> Die Vögelein schweigen im Walde,
> Warte nur, balde
> Ruhest du auch.

Here, we might conclude, when trying to convey the wonder of this poem to a friend ignorant of German, here the verse does not *describe* the stillness of evening, it has as it were become the stillness of evening.

This is perfectly right and true. But have we exhausted the meaning of this poem, indeed have we indicated its specifically Goethean quality at all, if we depict it thus as a perfect evocation of *Abendstimmung*? The power to evoke mood, by language in which sound is inseparable from sense, is after all equally characteristic of a Verlaine, a Keats, or of a Tennyson at his best, indeed of most Romantic poets. That Goethe's poem often *is* experienced simply in this way is suggested by the fact that it is frequently misquoted as 'Über allen *W*ipfeln ist Ruh', as though the suggestive sound of the words were all that mattered, as though it were immaterial whether *Gipfel* or *Wipfel* comes first. This is of course not so. It is absolutely essential, it is indeed the heart of the poem's meaning and the feature which stamps it as peculiarly and specifically Goethean, that *Gipfel* should precede *Wipfel*. For the order of the natural objects named here is not arbitrary. It is not dictated purely by the mood of this wanderer as he stands, a human being over against nature, and lets his eye range across the evening landscape, seeing in its stillness an *analogy* of the peace which will one day tranquillize his own troubled breast. Nature here is no mere background for human needs and desires, something outside and around man, other than himself and ever to be sought in nostalgic longing. Nor is the order of the objects determined purely by the requirements of aesthetic composition, an order of the outward appearances of nature as perceived by the senses. It is an order of the inner processes of nature as known by the mind, an organic order of the progression in nature, from the inanimate to the animate, from the mineral, through the vegetable, to the animal kingdom, from the hill-tops, to the tree-tops, to the birds, and so at last to man. The poet-wanderer here is not embracing Nature in the Romantic way. He is, of necessity, by the very order of the poem, embraced within it, as the last link in the chain of being. We are not surprised to learn that this poem was born in those years when Goethe's mind was preoccupied with the study of rock formations, when, as he tells us in that master-piece of German prose, his essay *On Granite*,[2] he sat 'auf einem hohen nackten Gipfel' and surveyed the landscape, and pondered the continuity in the forms of nature, the relation between the human heart, the youngest, most complex, labile, easily moved and most completely vulnerable of all her manifold phenomena, and granite, the oldest, 'dem ältesten, festesten, tiefsten, unerschütterlichsten Sohne der Natur'. It is all there, distilled, in the brief compass of eight short lines of a pure lyric. And yet there is no statement of these profound and complex thoughts in conceptual form. He does not say here explicitly, in so many words: this is the evolutionary order of nature—as he will say it explicitly in his two scientific elegies, *The Metamorphosis of Plants* and the *Metamorphosis of Animals*. Here, in this lyrical poem, his understanding of natural process has been so completely assimilated into the forms of language, that it is communicated to us directly by the order of the words, or by such a fine nuance as the modulation from 'Gipfeln' to '*W*ipfeln'. For this is not just a pleasant musical assonance—though it is that too. The idea of metamorphosis, the evolving of the animate out of the inanimate, the natural principle of infinite variety within an embracing unity, all this has here moved out of the orbit of mere intellectual knowledge into that of the poetic imagination, has been so completely 'imagined' by the poetic mind, that language itself, the poet's medium, has taken on this very form. The change of a single letter in a word which is otherwise the same reflects those imperceptible changes which mark the slow evolution of one form of nature out of another. And yet to say 'reflects' seems inadequate. For, to adapt Coleridge,[3] words are here elevated into process, and living process too.

Only when we have said all this, and more, have we conveyed the peculiarly Goethean quality of this *Wanderers Nachtlied*. There is, as Mr. I. A. Richards would say,[4] an 'inside' to this poem. Its ideas, its thoughts, are not all expressed with prominence, displayed to the casual

gaze as in 'an Exhibition of Poetic Products'. Some of them are, to use
another phrase of Coleridge, 'expressed but darkly'. But that does not
mean that they are dim or vague. Nor again does it mean that this is
a 'difficult' poem in the sense of being syntactically obscure or esoteric
in its symbolism. It means that Goethe hides his depth where Hugo von
Hofmannsthal said the poet should hide it—on the surface.[5] The simplicity, the apparent obviousness, the plainness of statement, is deceptive.
A world of meaning is hidden in it, and the only way to find it is to
concentrate on the poem without averting the gaze. That is what Goethe
at his most characteristic demands of us—nothing less. This is not to
say that the personal associations the poem may call up in us do not
enrich our experience of it. For the English reader it may well evoke
those words of incomparable consolation from the Book of Common
Prayer: 'Until the shadows lengthen, and the evening comes, and the
busy world is hushed, the fever of life is over and our work done.'
But to let such associations invade us too completely as we read, means
to move away from the poem itself without having savoured its essential
quality or penetrated to its precise meaning.

It would be difficult to find in literature a lyric of such brevity
containing so much profundity of thought. What is so amazing about
it, is that 'subjective' and 'objective' experience are here completely
fused. The evocation of mood, the projection of man's longing for
peace on to nature, the tenderness of the diminutive 'Vögelein' with its
reminiscence of the folk-song, all these are not at all at odds with—they
are entirely consistent with—the 'objective' presentation of natural
process. It is all said at once: the appearances of Nature are rendered,
but also the organic relation between them; man's mind is shown as the
final link in the chain of creation, Nature become conscious of itself,
but it also takes its proper place within nature. It does not stand outside
or over against it. A fine stylistic point is of importance here. The end
of the poem is often said and sung like this:

> Warte nur, balde
> Ruhest auch *du,*

a transposition characteristic of our Western subjectivism. It gives a
prominence to *du,* to the subject, which it does not have at all in the
poem as it stands. In the line

> Ruhest du auch

it is impossible to emphasize *du* except by a violation of metrical stress, and it is to do violence to the meaning and quality of the whole poem to force it out of its naturally unstressed position.

We have here the clearest evidence that Goethe's reconciliation of the subject-object dualism was no intellectual *tour de force* but his way of being. A man's conscious opinions, his intellectual convictions and philosophical beliefs, do not always express him; they may well disguise him. But his style, the images he chooses, his recurrent turns of phrase, the structure of his syntax, the order he adopts, these betray him unmistakably. A poem such as 'Über allen Gipfeln' has clearly been organized at the deepest levels of the mind. The proof of this is not that it sprang spontaneously to the poet's lips in exactly the form we have it now. It was in fact considerably touched up. At one time it was to begin 'Über allen Gefilden', and what I have called the indispensable *e* in 'Vögelein' is a later addition. The proof lies rather in the complete assimilation of experience into language without the intervention of conceptual thought. At the deepest level of Goethe's thought the subjective and objective modes are quite evidently harmonized. One and the same poetic formulation can give expression to both the subjective feeling of the human heart and the objective knowledge of the human mind. When in later life he speaks in philosophical terms of the reconciliation of subject and object, he is not so much overcoming a dualism he has felt in himself, as coming to terms with the difference between his own mode of experiencing and the dominant trend of Western thought.

A comparison may prove illuminating, comparison with a poet who is typical of Western frustration and torn disunity, heir to each and all of our dualisms, and overwhelmingly subjective. The comparative method in criticism is beset by all manner of snares and pitfalls. Coleridge has made us chary of it by his stricture that 'a fondness for judging one work by others argues a vulgar taste'.[6] But he has also encouraged its legitimate use, 'not for the idle purpose of finding which of the things compared is the better, but in order to see and understand the difference'. The two poems I have in mind are sufficiently alike in theme for their characteristic difference to be thrown into sharp relief. They are both lovely of their kind. Heine's evokes a summer evening at dusk, vaporous and cool, a golden moon against a blue sky; by the stream a cricket sings, the water stirs, and the wanderer hears a splashing and the breathing of the lovely elf as she bathes there, arms gleaming in the light of the moon:

Dämmernd liegt der Sommerabend
Über Wald und grünen Wiesen;
Goldner Mond am blauen Himmel
Strahlt herunter, duftig labend.

An dem Bache zirpt die Grille,
Und es regt sich in dem Wasser,
Und der Wandrer hört ein Plätschern
Und ein Atmen in der Stille.

Dorten, an dem Bach alleine,
Badet sich die schöne Elfe;
Arm und Nacken, weiss und lieblich,
Schimmern in dem Mondescheine.

The order here is that of pictorial and dramatic composition. The natural objects are selected and assembled so as to give maximum effect to the focal point of the scene: the gleaming arm and shoulder of the girl. In the background wood and meadows are misty as dusk falls; in the foreground the moon's rays are concentrated with spot-light effect on the whiteness of the limbs. It is a masterly use of mistiness and light, almost in the manner of the French Impressionists. Cricket and wanderer are only introduced to enhance the dramatic discovery of the bathing girl. The first person pronoun, I, does not appear in this poem; the wanderer's thoughts, feelings, responses are not mentioned. But subjectivity prevails all the same. Not one of these objects is there for its own sake, that we may contemplate its essential nature. The poet uses them, arranges and disposes them, for his dramatic intention as surely, though not as obviously, as when in that other, even more famous, poem he lets a fir-tree in the icy north dream of a palm-tree in the burning south.

Goethe's poem is not a description of evening; it is not a rendering of a static scene at all. Characteristically it is a rendering of a process: the coming into being of evening.

Dämmrung senkte sich von oben,
Schon ist alle Nähe fern;
Doch zuerst emporgehoben
Holden Lichts der Abendstern!
Alles schwankt ins Ungewisse,
Nebel schleichen in die Höh';
Schwarzvertiefte Finsternisse
Widerspiegelnd ruht der See.

Nun am östlichen Bereiche
Ahn' ich Mondenglanz und -Glut,
Schlanker Weiden Haargezweige
Scherzen auf der nächsten Flut.
Durch bewegter Schatten Spiele
Zittert Lunas Zauberschein,
Und durchs Auge schleicht die Kühle
Sänftigend ins Herz hinein.

The order here is determined by the natural phenomena themselves.
First, the familiar plain statement: Dusk descended from above. Then
we follow the veiling of the present scene, the sudden appearance out
of nowhere of the evening star, the blurring of contours as mists creep
up, the deepening into blackness of the forms reflected in the lake. We
experience in the east that faint lightening of the sky which heralds the
moon; a breeze stirs just enough for the hair-like leaves of the willows
to tease the water and for the shadows to move into play so that the
light of the moon-goddess trembles through them. And with her coming
the evening coolness steals through the eye and, soothingly, into the
heart. The last two lines are wholly characteristic of Goethe's relation
to the world outside. They might serve as a poetic illustration to his
statement that the objects of his perception entered into his thought and
were permeated by it, so that his perceiving was itself thinking and his
thinking perceiving.[7] He does not begin with his own feeling, or idea,
and project it on to nature. He just looks; he contemplates the evening,
his eyes wide open, until at the end its essence enters through the eye
and permeates the mind. His is the submissive role, actively submissive,
but submissive all the same. His heart and mind submit themselves to
the objects of the outer world, to know them as they are and to be
transmuted by them. And here, again, his mysterious, almost magical,
power to transpose the processes of nature into analogous processes of
language. By the swift sequence of tenses in the first four lines—
preterite, present, no tense at all (omission of any finite verb with
'emporgehoben')—he has created a linguistic semblance of the passage
of time being suddenly halted in the timelessness of a significant moment.

Critics have often noted the quality of objectivity in Goethe's poetry.
I would prefer to speak of its subject-object-ivity. For only thus can
we do justice to the personal element which is never absent from it.
Here, for instance, he can permit himself the first person singular, the
reference to his own feelings, without losing anything in what he himself
called 'Gegenständlichkeit'.[8] For when the object is truly contemplated

for its own sake, then the subject can come into its own in a relation which brings complete and ever-renewed fulfilment. When Heine makes his roses whisper fairy-tales to each other, or his violets 'kichern und kosen', he is imposing his fantasy on nature. When Goethe, in his poem, 'An vollen Büschelzweigen', speaks of the ripening fruit swelling within its shell and trying to reach the air, or here, in this poem, of the willows teasing the water, he is using human terms, but he is not thereby violating natural process and fact. The nature of the fruit and of the willow is respected. And this after all is the essence of 'Gegenständlichkeit': not that the observer, the subject, should be ruled out, but that he should not project on to the object. Hence the personal nature of Goethe's poetry, together with a complete absence of all urgent striving to impose himself upon the world. And hence, too, a certain quality of objectivity in poems where there is no mention of the objects and processes of nature, but only of the most intimate states of heart and mind.

Consider the other *Wanderers Nachtlied*:

> Der du von dem Himmel bist,
> Alles Leid und Schmerzen stillest,
> Den, der doppelt elend ist,
> Doppelt mit Erquickung füllest,
> Ach! ich bin des Treibens müde!
> Was soll all der Schmerz und Lust?
> Süsser Friede,
> Komm, ach komm in meine Brust!

In this prayer for peace the unbearable tension of the soul is neither described, nor yet evoked by image or analogy. It is transmuted into the syntactical structure of the verse. Goethe once spoke of the German language as the worst possible material for a poet to work in—'den schlechtesten Stoff'.[9] But here in this poem he has turned its very recalcitrance to poetical account, exploited that grammatical peculiarity which we foreigners find so difficult, and at which we sometimes even poke fun—the verb at the end in subordinate clauses. By piling up adjectival clauses, three of them, one on another, by placing inside the last of them yet another adjectival clause, qualifying the object of the third of these,

> Den, der doppelt elend ist
> Doppelt mit Erquickung füllest,

thus making the construction more tortuous than ever, Goethe has rendered an utter knottedness of feeling *directly*, through the 'turnings

intricate of verse'. The piling up of initial dentals enhances the effect of
clenched frustration. Language so pent and strained can only find outlet
in sheer exclamation:

> Ach! ich bin des Treibens müde!
> Was soll all der Schmerz und Lust?

And only then is the being, so long invoked, finally called by name, and
the brief main clause at last pronounced:

> Süsser Friede,
> Komm, ach komm in meine Brust!

This is a master's use of the very genius of his language. He can put even
its awkwardness to poetic use. And it provides an excellent example of
the way poetry achieves meaning through sheer form. For grammatically
speaking it is immaterial whether 'Süsser Friede' stands at the beginning
of the poem, as it would do in normal prose order, or is withheld as
here until the seventh line. Nothing is altered in the logical meaning
either way. But by withholding it Goethe has communicated tension
as surely as by syntactical tortuosity he has created clenched frustration.

Poetry like this turns us not inwards, but outwards into the poem.
Not, of course, in the sense that we leave ourselves behind and become
impersonal. But it does not make us 'dissolve and dissipate'. It does not
work its effects by sounding a few notes which call up a world of private
associations, and set fancy and fantasy roaming at their own sweet will.
It focuses the whole of us to a fine point of concentration upon the
experience which is here wrought in language, objectified in form. It is
not the kind of poetry which excites and disturbs the mind. It is the
kind which deepens and organizes it. We, the perceiving subjects, do
not have to contribute part of the richness and meaning, as we do with
more evocative poetry. The richness and meaning is all there in the
object. Nothing short of the whole meaning we can find in the words
and their arrangement is adequate to account for their effect. For this
reason Goethe's poetry demands a kind of agreeably flat, plain, reading,
in which the personal interpretation of the reader does not get between
us and the poem.[10] Its so-called objective quality is, indeed, intimately
connected with that plainness to which I referred earlier, with its un-
decorated simplicity, its lack of rich imagery and metaphor. At first sight
it seems unoriginal, unexciting and extraordinarily ordinary. The effect
is rather like looking into a deep well; the surface is smooth and flat,
two-dimensional, reflecting at first nothing but our own image. But as
we gaze down into it, undreamed-of depths are revealed. Only we have

B

to gaze long, to gaze intently and lovingly. There is no short cut to Goethe's greatest poetry. Every fine nuance has immeasurable significance. We have to be alive to each syntactical relation, to each formal relation of grouping or contrast, to the modification of a prefix, the modulation of a letter. To read it otherwise is to miss its quintessential meaning, for often that meaning is not expressed at all save through the form. And it can happen that in becoming aware of a detail in a poem we thought we knew, the meaning of the poem begins to grow in our mind until it is transformed almost out of recognition. Take, for instance, that line of *Wanderers Nachtlied*:

Was soll all der Schmerz und Lust?

'Schmerz' and 'Lust' are nouns of different gender and would normally require an article each. But here they are bound together by the single article *der*. The effect is to reveal pain and pleasure for what they are, opposite poles of one and the same thing, the ambivalent manifestation of that restless 'Treiben', from which the poet implores release. Once we become aware of this detail, we realize, as plainly as if we had been told in psychological concepts, that the tension within him has reached that degree of intensity, that temperature, at which the two states, pleasure and pain, are scarcely distinguishable.

I have dwelt at such length on this special quality of Goethe's poetry, because it crops up all over his work, not just in his lyrics and poetic dramas, but, disconcertingly enough, in his novels and essays, and, still more surprisingly, in his scientific writings. It has been described as lyricism; but the term has associations of feeling and subjectivity which are inadequate here. Goethe transcends such categories and makes them seem rigid and singularly inapt. What he often expresses by that untranslatable union of sound and sense which we are wont to call lyricism, is not just feeling, but extreme profundity of thought as well—we have only to think of the metamorphosis of 'Gipfel' into 'Wipfel'. For this reason I prefer to use the term *untranslatability*. We tend to accept without question that while pure poetry is untranslatable, prose is not. Goethe's use of language cuts across this distinction. Again and again in his prose we find that meaning, instead of being communicated explicitly by the disposition of logical concepts, has been so assimilated into the formal relations of language that there is no rendering it except by paraphrase. We find those 'dislocations', compressions, and extensions, of grammatical usage, which are essential to the predominantly affective intention of poetry, but alien to the predominantly purposive intention of prose: syntactical circularities, adjectives which look backwards and forwards, qualifying a noun which precedes as well as one that follows; the omission of prepositions to point unusual, or unusually close, relationship; doubleness of case, nouns which are both dative and accusative, or both dative and genitive; the transitive use of intransitive verbs, the intransitive use of transitives. In the last chapter of *Elective Affinities* it is said of Mittler: 'He listened, he gave way, he gave to understand.' What an awkward rendering, we might think. But the German is no less peculiar. 'Er gab zu verstehen' requires an object as much as does its English equivalent. What did he give to understand, and to whom? The apparent lapse is, of course, charged with significance. By this single stroke we know for certain where the author stands with regard to this controversial character. His principles are impeccable, the maxims he propounds unassailable. But his efforts more often result in harmful meddling than in fruitful mediation because they take no account of the needs and requirements of the people around him. The unaccustomed nakedness of the verb, bereft of grammatical object or complement, isolates pure activity, shows it pursuing its own absolute course unrelated to any particular concrete situation. The awkwardness of style here is not simply a *reflection* of Mittler's clumsiness. It is a re-creation in language of that fateful unrelatedness to environment which is the cause of his inappropriate responses; even as the subsequent scene in which, oblivious of Ottilie's presence, he dilates upon the heinousness of transgressing the seventh commandment, is a re-creation in dramatic terms of the same maladjusted rigidity.

Years before in *Egmont* Goethe had isolated mental activity by a similar though not so startling, absolute use of the verb. 'Der König meint aber, hörst du.' (III, 1) The English translator instinctively supplies an object—'That, however, is what the king thinks'—thereby shifting the emphasis from the mental vacuum in which Philip pursues his political calculations, and missing a highly significant thread in the thought-weave of the play. For even in this prose-drama Goethe pursued the meaning inherent in his theme into every delicate fibre of the poetic organism, just as he did in *Iphigenie* and *Tasso*. And in the translation of these poetic dramas what we lose is not just the values of rhythm and assonance— that we may expect and allow for—but whole tracts of meaning which Goethe is able to compress into language by virtue of his power to make it do many things at once. In the opening monologue of *Iphigenie* he exploits the syntactical structure of the relative clause with similar, if not identical, effect as in *Wanderers Nachtlied*. If the dénouement of *Tasso* is to be rightly understood, the verb 'vergleichen' in Antonio's provocative admonition to Tasso, 'Vergleiche dich!' (3420) must bear no less than three meanings, whilst the translator is lucky if he can produce more than one. Two lines before, 'sie' refers with enriching ambiguity both to 'Kraft', the feminine noun which is its immediate antecedent, and to the Princess, thereby making manifest in language Tasso's identification of his creative power with the woman who is his inspiration. The English translator, with the best will in the world, must renounce this 'doppelt erfreulichen Sinn',[11] and plump for 'it' or 'she'. The latest French translator,[12] with the advantage of gender at his disposal, misses a fine opportunity by translating 'alle Kraft' as 'toutes les forces'.

It is this quality of untranslatability which makes it so difficult to put Goethe across to the English reader, makes him seem either trite or stuffily profound rather than urbanely complex and infinitely subtle. But it is this same quality which puts him in the first rank of the pure poets of the world and gives him a unique place there. In his superb mastery of his medium there are few to vie with him and none to surpass him.

But no great poet writes pure poetry all of the time. It is only poets of lesser stature who put forth at rare intervals small gems of distilled experience on an expanse of white page. The great ones of the past, at any rate, have been less parsimonious, and have spent a good deal of their time putting the more superficial levels of experience into verse, ordinary, mundane, everyday experience. They have not scorned to be craftsmen in the intervals of being artists, nor even bothered very much about the distinction between the two. And none more so than Goethe. The immensely wide range of his poetry is bewildering. We feel this acutely when someone asks us to say in a few words what kind of a poet he is. Whether we try to do it by description or by comparison, we are equally embarrassed. For he ranges from the Watteau-like perfection of his rococo trivialities to the profound mystery and symbolism of *Faust II;* from the subtlest heart-searchings of a love poem such as 'Warum gabst du uns die tiefen Blicke' to that urbane mystery of his *West-Eastern Divan,* where sensitivity and pain are so suffused with play and irony that the universality of experience implied in the title is completely realized; from *Mailied* where for sheer joy he just plays with his medium, with a language which, since the Middle Ages, had not been used for such pure purpose of song:

> O Erd, O Sonne!
> O Glück, O Lust!
> O Lieb, O Liebe!
> So golden schön.

He tosses the words out to see how lovely they sound—at a point in the eighteenth century when in our own English language it would scarcely have been possible because the continuity of our literature had not been broken. To a large extent Goethe had to fashion his own medium and to make his own tradition. From this *Mailied*, then, to the scientific intricacies of the *Metamorphose der Tiere*. According to an eminent scientist,[13] this deals with a subject entirely unsuited to poetry; Goethe's amateurish passion for science here led him astray as a poet. But Goethe himself knew nothing of such water-tight compartments in the business of living. For him poetry and science presented no essential opposition, and it is wholly characteristic that he should address a scientific poem to his beloved:

> Dich verwirret, Geliebte, die tausendfältige Mischung
> Dieses Blumengewühls über den Garten umher.

For him love, science, poetry run fluid one into the other, and he casts any and every kind of thought and experience into verse, trite or trivial, humorous or satirical, didactic or sententious—or just plain everyday, as in his early poem *Diner zu Koblenz*, where he describes how he sat between two of his more philosophically inclined friends, just enjoying life while they discoursed upon abstruse problems of theology:

> Zwischen Lavater und Basedow
> Sass ich bei Tisch des Lebens froh . . .
> Prophete rechts, Prophete links,
> Das Weltkind in der Mitten.

As Mr. C. Day Lewis had occasion to remind us recently,[14] the colloquial element has played a considerable role in our own poetry. Less so in German. But Goethe's easy familiarity with it is often put to effective use even in such unexpected places as the Kingdom of Heaven:

> Von Zeit zu Zeit seh' ich den Alten gern,
> Und hüte mich, mit ihm zu brechen.

Even within one literary form, the ballad, for example, what variety of mood and style Goethe can achieve! Think of *Der Zauberlehrling*. Its roots are deep in the daemonic, elemental world of *Der Fischer*, but its upper levels are on the wholly human plane, for it is a tale with a moral, and its charm lies in its superb blend of incantatory power and ironic urbanity. It is as if Voltaire would collaborate with Coleridge to write a morality.

Common sense, down-to-earthness, humour, didacticism, Goethe the

poet possessed them all. In the last few decades we have become accustomed to think of pure poetry as obscure, esoteric, narrow in range,
pursued by aesthetes in reaction against poetry that had become too
ordinary, too like prose, too topical, too didactic or tendentious. We
have almost accepted as inevitable alternatives pure poetry or poetry
that is in touch with life. But Goethe, like Shakespeare, can combine
imagination with common sense, can reconcile complete mastery of
all the poetic resources of his medium with the common clay of rich
warm humanity. It is in this, and in the organic, objective quality of his
mature work that he is really akin to Shakespeare—not in the outward
trappings of those plays in which he seems to vie with him. It is to *Tasso*,
not to *Götz*, that we need to bring the kind of reading that we would
accord to *Lear*. If that quality I tried to define earlier puts Goethe among
the pure poets of the world, it is the combination of that quality with
range, weight and humanity which puts him among the great. At the
beginning of this century the Irish dramatist, J. M. Synge, wrote:[15]

> It is the *timber* of poetry that wears most surely, and there is no timber
> that has not strong roots among the clay and the worms. Even if we
> grant that exalted poetry can be kept successful by itself, the strong
> things in life are needed in poetry also, to show that what is exalted
> or tender is not made by feeble blood.

That is Goethe: feet on the ground, roots in the ground, and head in
the air, reaching even to the stars. His poem *Paria* provides us with an
appropriate symbol both for him and for the dual nature of our common
humanity:

> Und so soll ich, die Bramane,
> Mit dem Haupt im Himmel weilend,
> Fühlen, Paria, dieser Erde
> Niederziehende Gewalt.

III. *Wandrers Sturmlied*

A Study in Poetic Vagrancy

THE Romantic conception of the German people as a nation of wanderers, while as manifestly one-sided as such national images are bound to be, contains enough truth to give the impression of a striking likeness. It derives no doubt from the historical fact of the migration of peoples of the fourth and fifth centuries, finding early mythological support in the cognomen of 'Wanderer' which was attached to the god Wodan, was confirmed by the constant surge of the German emperors over the Alps in the Middle Ages and by the 'Sehnsucht nach Italien' of the eighteenth and nineteenth centuries, to be clinched, it would seem, by the 'Drang nach Osten' of recent times. Nor has the German tendency to wandering been confined to the geographical or political sphere. Which nation has adventured further into the realm of the spirit, soared to more dizzying heights of metaphysical abstraction, or plunged deeper into abysses of cosmic despair? And this same spirit of vagrancy, physical and metaphysical, is everywhere present in German poetry. Like myth, poetry not only reflects a people's image of itself, it also helps to form it. And it would be hazardous indeed to try to disentangle cause and effect. But it remains true that the Germans have had no lack of poems and songs with which to stir their nomadic romanticism and keep alive that ideal of *Wanderlust* which in the European mind is so indissolubly connected with the German character.[1]

No German poet has written more about wandering than Goethe. The story of the Wandering Jew seized his youthful imagination; *Wilhelm Meisters Wanderjahre* contains the sum of his own journeying through life. The two loveliest of his shorter lyrics are both called *Wanderers Nachtlied*, while some half-dozen others have a wanderer in their title. Early and late this image is a symbol for expressing every conceivable manner and mode of his 'wandering', from the simple impulse to roam in space, through the urge to dalliance and philandering, or the limitless aspiration of individual striving, to every variation of self-fulfilment, including that soaring of the human mind which we call poetic vision. But with him the complementary image of 'Hütte' is never far away. The one impulse at once calls forth its corresponding opposite, its regulative counter-force. 'Hütte' represents the other pole of man's being, and symbolizes an equally wide range of experience: the comfort of home, the cramping ties of domesticity, the irksomeness, but also the fulfilment, of self-limitation. The tension between the two receives every kind of artistic expression from painful dissonance to the most delicately adjusted harmony. For no German, poet or thinker, has explored more sensitively or more completely the relation of these two fundamental human drives, or has achieved, both in his life and in his work, a balance which even in old age still vibrates with a most fruitful tension.

His earliest wanderer poem, *Wandrers Sturmlied*, has found its way into most anthologies of his poetry, though perhaps more from a feeling of piety than from any sense of its peculiar quality. His own example might well have encouraged editors to leave it out. For he did not include it in his own collected poems, nor indeed publish it at all until after it had appeared without his permission.[2] While in *Dichtung und Wahrheit*,[3] faced with the accomplished fact of its unauthorized publication, he referred to it as 'Halbunsinn'. This has been enough to make some critics rally at once to its defence, on the assumption that the older Goethe was so loftily insensible to works he had outgrown that his disparagement is the surest guarantee of their excellence. While others took 'Halbunsinn' to be a confirmation of the obscurity of this difficult poem, and for them obscurity spelt profundity. But there is a good, and quite precise, reason for including it in any anthology which aims at a complete picture of the range of Goethe's mind, even though it is a poem which cannot easily stand on its own feet, without benefit of commentary. For it is not just another example of his youthful exuberance, nor just another poem on the theme of the wanderer. It is a wanderer-poem with a difference. It treats this romantic subject of wandering with a humour that is rare in German poetry, rare enough in any young man. Here is a poet with a sense of humour about his own genius, about his poetic inspiration. Which does not mean that his poem lacks a core of profound and serious meaning, only that he can be serious without solemnity, profound without pomposity. The translation offered below tries to give an impression of poetry as Goethe wrote it in his early twenties, reflecting both the unusual word-order and the almost total absence of punctuation in the original. Reflecting, too, our own inquiry into the formal relations of the poem: we have, for instance, not hesitated to retain the alternation between 'Whom' and 'Him' in the opening line of the first four stanzas; while 'woolly wings' (instead of, say, the more 'poetic' downy) reflects our conviction that the inspiration of the Muses is here being treated with a rare lightness of touch.

Wandrers Sturmlied

Wen du nicht verlässest Genius
Nicht der Regen nicht der Sturm
Haucht ihm Schauer übers Herz
Wen du nicht verlässest Genius,
Wird der Regen Wolcke
Wird dem Schlossensturm
Entgegensingen wie die
Lerche du dadroben,
Wen du nicht verlässest Genius.

Den du nicht verlässest Genius,
Wirst ihn heben übern Schlammpfad
Mit den Feuerflügeln
Wandeln wird er
Wie mit Blumenfüssen
Über Deukalions fluthschlamm
Python tödtend leicht gros
Pythius Apollo
Den du nicht verlässest Genius.

Den du nicht verlässest Genius
Wirst die wollnen Flügel unterspreiten
Wenn er auf dem Felsen schläfft
Wirst mit Hüterfittigen ihn decken
In des Haines Mitternacht.

Wen du nicht verlässest Genius
Wirst im Schneegestöber Wärm umhüllen
Nach der Wärme ziehn sich Musen
Nach der Wärme Charitinnen,
Wen du nicht verlässest Genius.

Whom thou never leavest Genius/ Not the rain and not the storm/ Breathes a dread upon his heart/ Whom thou never leavest Genius,/ Meets the rain-cloud/ Meets the hailstorm/ With his song as does the/ Skylark thou up yonder,/ Whom thou never leavest Genius.
Him thou never leavest Genius,/ Thou wilt bear above the mud-path/ With thy wings of fire/ He will wander/ As with flower-feet/ O'er Deucalion's sea of mud/ Python slaying light great/ Pythian Apollo/ Him thou never leavest Genius.
Him thou never leavest Genius/ Thou wilt spread thy woolly wings beneath him/

Umschwebt mich ihr Musen!
Ihr Charitinnen!
Das ist Wasser das ist Erde
Und der Sohn des Wassers und der Erde
Über den ich wandle Göttergleich.

Ihr seyd rein wie das Herz der Wasser
Ihr seyd rein wie das Marck der Erde
Ihr umschwebt mich und ich schwebe
Über Wasser über Erde
Göttergleich.

Soll der zurückkehren
Der kleine, schwarze feurige Bauer
Soll der zurückkehren, erwartend
Nur deine Gaben Vater Bromius
Und hellleuchtend umwärmend Feuer
Soll der zurückkehren mutig,
Und ich den ihr begleitet
Musen und Charitinnen all
Den Alls erwartet was ihr
Musen und Charitinnen
Umkränzende Seeligkeit
Rings ums Leben verherrlicht habt,
Soll muthlos kehren?

Vater Bromius
Du bist Genius
Jahrhunderts Genius
Bist was innre Glut
Pindarn war
Was der Welt
Phöb Apoll ist.

When he sleeps upon the cliff/ Thou wilt cover with thy guardian pinions/ In the
midnight of the grove.
Whom thou never leavest Genius/ In the whirling snow wilt wrap with warmth/
Towards the warmth the Muses wander/ Towards the warmth there wander Graces,/
Whom thou never leavest Genius.
Hover round me ye Muses!/ And ye Graces!/ That is water that is earth/ And the
son of water and of earth/ Over whom I wander like the gods.
Ye are pure as the heart of the waters/ Ye are pure as the marrow of earth/ Ye hover
round me and I hover/ Over water over earth/ Like the gods.
Shall he reach home/ The little, black fiery peasant/ Shall he reach home, awaiting/
But thy gifts Father Bromius/ And bright-gleaming warm-wrapping fire/ Shall he

Weh weh innre Wärme
Seelen Wärme
Mittelpunckt
Glüh ihm entgegen
Phöb Apollen
Kalt wird sonst
Sein Fürstenblick
Über dich vorüber gleiten
Neidgetroffen
Auf der Ceder Grün verweilen
Die zu grünen
Sein nicht harrt.

Warum nennt mein Lied dich zulezt?
Dich von dem es begann
Dich in dem es endet
Dich aus dem es quoll
Jupiter Pluvius.
Dich dich strömt mein Lied
Jupiter Pluvius.
Und Castalischer Quell
Quillt ein Nebenbach,
Quillet müsigen
Sterblich Glücklichen
Abseits von dir
Jupiter Pluvius
Der du mich fassend deckst
Jupiter Pluvius

Nicht am Ulmen Baum
Hast du ihn besucht
Mit dem Tauben Paar
In dem zärtlichen Arm

reach home courageous,/ And I whom ye accompany/ Muses and Graces all/ Whom
all awaits that ye/ Muses and Graces/ Have cast about life/ An encircling garland of
glorious bliss,/ Reach home discouraged?
Father Bromius/ Thou art Genius/ Genius of the age/ Art what inner glow/ Was to
Pindar/ What to the world/ Is Phoebus Apollo.
Woe woe inner warmth/ Spirit warmth/ Centre/ Glow in response to/ Phoebus
Apollo/ Or cold/ His princely gaze/ Will pass thee over/ Envy-stricken/ Linger on
the green of the cedar/ Which to flourish/ Awaits him not.
Why does my song name thee the last?/ Thee from whom it began/ Thee in whom
it endeth/ Thee out of whom it flowed/ Jupiter Pluvius./ Thee thee my song is
streaming/ Jupiter Pluvius/ And Castalian Spring/ Springs a rivulet/ Springs for

Mit der freundlichen Ros umkränzt
Tändelnden ihn blumenglücklichen
Anakreon,
Sturmathmende Gottheit.

Nicht im Pappelwald
An des Sibaris Strand
In dem hohen Gebürg nicht
Dessen Stirn die
Allmächtige Sonne beglänzt
Fasstest du ihn
Den Bienensingenden
Honiglallenden
Freundlichwinckenden
Theokrit.

Wenn die Räder rasselten Rad an Rad
Rasch ums Ziel weg
Hoch flog siegdurchglühter Jünglinge Peitschenknall
Und sich Staub wälzt
Wie vom Gebürg herab sich
Kieselwetter ins Thal wälzt
Glühte deine Seel Gefahren Pindar
Muth Pindar—Glühte—
Armes Herz—
Dort auf dem Hügel—
Himmlische Macht—
Nur soviel Glut—
Dort ist meine Hütte—
Zu waten bis dort hin.

idle ones/ Mortal happy ones/ To the side of thee/ Jupiter Pluvius/ Who dost
seize me and cover/ Jupiter Pluvius.
Not by the elm tree/ Didst thou visit him/ With the pair of doves/ In his tender arm/
With a garland of roses entwined/ Him the dallying flower-happy/ Anacreon,/
Storm-breathing godhead.
Not in the poplar grove/ Near the Sybarite strand/ Not in the high mountain/
Whose brow the/ Almighty sun illumines/ Didst thou seize him/ The bee-singing/
The honey-babbling/ The friendly-beckoning/ Theocritus.
When the wheels rattled wheel on wheel/ Swift away round the post/ High rose
the whip crack of youths glowed through with victory/ And dust rolled/ As from
the mountain down there rolls/ Hail of pebbles into the vale/ Then thy soul glowed
dangers Pindar/ Courage Pindar—Glowed—/ Poor heart—/ There on the hill—/
Heavenly power—/ Just so much glow—/ There is my cot—/ To wade just so far.

Either this poem was conceived with humour or it inclines to the ridiculous. No one can help seeing the twist in its tail. In the intoxication of genius this wanderer had defied storm and wind, surging onwards, soaring upwards. In the end, however, the physical situation has got the upper hand. Rain and mud have triumphed, and the inspired poet sees himself as a somewhat sorry figure wading to his hut. But is this the first time in the poem that he sees himself thus? The usual reading of the poem as an ode in the manner of the 'egotistical sublime',[4] a straight-forwardly rhapsodic 'Hohelied des Geniuskultus',[5] assumes that it is. In that case it is not always easy to maintain an appropriately sublime response. To hear, amid the solemn strains of an ode, of a tutelary genius with woolly wings, or to tumble to the fact that the poet is singing a hymn of praise to mud, is to drop from the sublime to the ridiculous. For let us call 'der Sohn des Wassers und der Erde' by name: his name is mud. Once this impinges upon the reader, he is lost to the solemnity of the occasion and laughs in the wrong place; or he keeps his counte-nance by letting the words wash over him, leaving vague impressions but not biting into the imagination. And what are we to make of a poet who, for all his soaring confidence in the power of genius to render him impervious to the rigours of the weather, expresses this confidence in images which betray a marked hankering after lulling warmth and being tucked up cosily against the fury of the storm? Do what he will to keep his mind fixed on higher things, his choice of words reveals unmistakably whither his desires are tending. The wish-phantasies of this bedraggled poet, wading through slush and mud, revolve around lightness and warmth as inevitably as those of a hungry man around food. 'Schlamm' insinuates itself into the poem from the second verse. The longing to be rid of the discomfort evokes visions of himself borne aloft above the muddy path on wings of fire, or tripping over it flower-footed, light as a god; and, in a final attempt to lighten the dead weight clogging his steps, his phantasy resolves it into its pure components of earth and water. Again, from the whole mythological store at his disposal he selects precisely those attributes of genius which will allow him to indulge his obsession with warmth. At first they are disguised by his conviction that, as a poet, he is proof against the trials and stresses of physical existence. But the disguise soon wears thin. Transcendent wings of fire give place to plain woollen wings, their function not to bear him aloft but to be spread beneath him and to cover him over; until finally the word 'Wärme' comes through in all its physical force, three times in three successive lines. There is no mistaking its insistence; and in a later version 'Wärmumhüllen' gets a line all to itself.

Such a reading finds us from time to time in the superior position, catching the poet out unawares, divining the drift of his imagery where it runs counter to the dithyrambic sublimity he would ostensibly have us hear. For in denying his challenge to smile *with* him we run the risk of laughing *at* him. Either we jib at some verbal inaptness, at a certain disparity of style and content, or we must recognize a playful humour which is aware of exploiting to the full every possibility of doubleness and contrast.

The physical situation is not simply a jumping-off ground for a visionary flight on the subject of genius and poetic inspiration. It is present throughout. Its symbolic implications are fully explored; but the humorous implications of the contrast between real and ideal no less. And by 'physical situation' we understand not only the mud and the rain but the physical aspect of the wanderer's compensatory phantasies. The myth of Apollo moving light-footed over the primeval slime to slay the python grips the poet's imagination because it can symbolize the power of poetry to overcome all ills. But what makes him fix upon this myth rather than another is its appropriateness to the immediate muddy situation. Again it is with a true poet's reverence that he hymns the purity of earth and water. But this breaking down of the heavy substance into its lighter elements is none the less a wish-fulfilment of his very human need. The characteristic unity of this poem resides in the poet's perception of this double perspective, in the complete fusion of sublimity and humour. They do not alternate. They co-exist. To interpret it as the fitful breaking through of exultant high spirits amid 'feierliche, ernste, tiefe Akkorde'[6] does violence to its fundamental form. The humour is there all the time; and whimsical rather than exultant, for it is provoked not only by the contrast between inner and outer world, but also by that more significant contrast within the imaginative world itself. Without destroying his own rapture the poet can smile at it, playing upon the incongruity between the uplifting and the down-to-earth aspects of his phantasy. Even a statement of such profound poetic importance as

> Weh weh innre Wärme
> SeelenWärme
> Mittelpunckt
> Glüh ihm entgegen
> Phöb Apollen
> Kalt wird sonst
> Sein Fürstenblick

Über dich vorüber gleiten
Neidgetroffen
Auf der Ceder grün verweilen
Die zu grünen
Sein nicht harrt

is refracted as it enters the imagination. For Apollo is not only the god of poetry, he is also the sun-god, the words 'Wärme' and 'Kalt' resound with physical implications, and the mind glances off and, without losing sight of the symbolic meaning, smiles at the thought of this cold poet trying by his own warmth to woo back the sun which is so markedly absent. On the other hand the line which most amusingly expresses the poet's consciousness of his drenched condition,

Dich dich strömt mein Lied,

at the same time embodies, as we shall see, the supreme discovery of his spiritual adventure. For this reason interpretation cannot be pressed too hard. This does not imply that the meaning is uncertain or ambiguous. But the imagination must be left free to play between the symbolic and the physical perspective as lightly as does the poet's own humour.

That Goethe himself attached more than allegorical importance to the physical situation is suggested by an early emendation of the last lines to

Dort meine Hütte
Dorthin zu waten!

where the emphasis is shifted from his goal, the 'Hütte', with its romantic associations, to his manner of getting there, and it is 'waten', with its ludicrous implications, which goes on echoing in the reader's mind. And the letter he wrote when he sent the poem to his friend, Jacobi, leaves no doubt of his own sense of the poem's double perspective. Jacobi was at the time wandering about the Bergische Land, living in the open, sheltering from a 'gewaltiger Platzregen in einem gewölbten Brunnen', a wanderer in the literal sense of the word: 'Ziehe aus mit weiter nichts als einer Jägertasche auf dem Rücken und einem Stab in der Hand, jede Bauerhütte gibt mir Obdach und Kost'.[7] Goethe expresses his joy at this expedition 'in freier Gotteswelt' in terms which point its symbolical significance without reducing it to a mere allegory of life, and his oracular postscript is as charged with double meaning as is his poem: 'Hier eine Ode, zu der Melodie und Commentar nur der Wandrer in der Not erfindet'.[8]

This seems to put the ordinary reader into a quandary. Must he be drenched and weary to be able to enter into the spirit of this poem and appreciate it to the full? Is Goethe suggesting that its significance is limited to the particular situation in which Jacobi happens to find himself and that it has no existence apart from such a chance context? On further reflection it becomes clear that he is not. To expect that the effort of physical movement can provide the key to melody and meaning, in fact implies that what might seem to be but a chance union of these three elements, is in truth an organic unity, each element of which reflects the whole and inevitably calls up the other two. How persistent was Goethe's belief that in a *Wanderlied* melody, meaning and movement are intimately related, is shown by an incident in *Wilhelm Meisters Wanderjahre*[9] which reveals, more clearly than his letter to Jacobi, that a *Gelegenheitsgedicht*, no less than any other, possesses an inalienable meaning of its own, which is neither limited to the occasion of its origin nor dependent upon some arbitrary fancy of the reader. Wilhelm tells his fellow-guests how, on his wanderings, the words of a song would come to him unbidden, allying themselves to 'leise Töne' which had been induced by the rhythmic tread of his feet. In response to their request he hands them the words of one of these songs, and after but brief reflection they voice their 'Commentar' in the language of music: they begin to sing a duet so perfectly suited to the rhythm of wandering that to Wilhelm it comes as a revelation of his own intention, and any other musical form of his song is now unthinkable. Through being received and interpreted his own conception has acquired objective validity, and he has the feeling, as other voices join in, of a whole *Wandergesellschaft* tramping over hill and dale.

The passage is transparently symbolic. Here we see how an apparently 'chance' creation is spontaneously re-created in its entirety by those who, though in a different situation, are fully alive to the one element in their possession, the words. Far from being arbitrarily subjective, the meaning of this 'occasional' poem is such that it can compel the imagination of different individuals to an identical response. The use of the word *erfindet* to Jacobi is surely significant. To Goethe, being receptive means: to discover by creative effort. The occasion created the poem; but once in being the poem can re-create the occasion, so completely have movement and melody been absorbed into the very texture of the words.

Hence to ask the reader to chant this *Sturmlied* is not to stimulate appreciation by artificially working up a mood. Nowhere is the incantatory element more important. For the rhythm draws us into the physical experience of the wanderer as surely as does the imagery. What could more directly induce the sense of flagging effort than the early cessation of the vigorous refrain? As the poet stumped along, his teeth set against the wind, the line which must have come to him unbidden was 'Wen du nicht verlässest Genius' with its trochaic tread. Down comes his foot on the 'Wen'; and down again on the 'Den'. The sense-rhythm would require the chief emphasis to be on 'verlässest'; but the pull here is all towards metrical stress. How else account for the alternation of 'Wen' and 'Den'? Admittedly there is some difference in meaning. But then why the change back again to 'Wen'?—if not for the sheer delight of playing upon these consonantal variations, as if by such device of rhythmic alternation and repetitive physical movement the wanderer would exclude the foul weather without, and be free to dwell on the life of his own inner world? In this tension between the free cadences associated with the ode and the restriction of a metrical scheme we have yet another key to the essential doubleness of the poem. For by this slight suggestion of a regular marching measure which helps the wanderer along, the poet imparts to his own soaring pathos a playfulness which smiles through the very rhythm of his verse.

It is no accident that the refrain stops just as the poet's phantasies are revealing themselves for what they are, as Genius temporarily drops out of the picture, and even Muses and Graces openly join in the search for warmth. All the stylistic elements point to an impending break in the poem. At this same point the sentence-structure changes: the future of confident assertion, repeated some half-dozen times or more, makes way for the supplicatory imperative, 'Umschwebt mich ihr Musen!' And the tension which has been gathering between the physical and the figurative implications of the imagery sharpens to an incongruity of style and content in 'Sohn des Wassers und der Erde'. With the use of this classical figure for common or garden mud, rhetoric trembles on the border of bathos. The sublimation of mud has reached its limits, and as his phantasy breaks it down into its elements there comes a break in the poem—a break which Goethe later indicated by a dash after the sixth verse.

There are now two figures instead of one. Whether the 'Bauer' has objective existence or is a figure on the landscape of the wanderer's mind, whether he derives from some mythological personage (he has been identified with Noah[10]) or from a passage in Fielding's *Amelia*,[11] is irrelevant to our present purpose, though by no means without interest of its own.[12] What is relevant is that he has not sprung from nowhere. He has his origins within the poem itself. The tell-tale adjectives 'feurig' and 'schwarz' betray his kinship with the dominant images of the first

part, warmth and mud. And if he is 'klein', it is by contrast with the
overlifesize, godlike figure the wanderer imagined himself to be. The
underlying physical significance of the poet's phantasies has separated
out and become embodied in an independent figure. We can see the
process of separation at work in the words. Each of the two levels of
meaning inherent in the single 'Wärm umhüllen' now receives unambiguously literal or figurative expression as it is resolved into 'umwärmend Feuer' and 'umkränzende Seligkeit'. The gifts of the gods are
here fittingly apportioned between the two figures: creature comforts
to the peasant, to the poet those insubstantial gifts appropriate to Muses
and Graces. What was single with twofold implication has become
openly two. And of the two it is not the peasant who is the figure of
fun. The word 'mutig' precludes this. It is at himself that the poet smiles
as the boundless sweep of his imagination is brought up short against
the limits of concrete reality, and he is forced to reflect that he, the
darling of the Muses, is yet impotent to reach the goal which the sturdy
peasant takes in his stride.

But this opposition between life and poetry does not last. A synthesis
is achieved, and achieved by identifying genius with the peasant's god.
They are both called Bromius.

This means that 'Vater Bromius' cannot be taken—as he usually is
taken[13]—simply as the god of wine, a sorry substitute for the inner glow
of inspiration that was Pindar's. But why should he be? The verse itself
tells us nothing directly about his value. It simply sets up a twofold
relation of analogy: 'Vater Bromius' is what inner glow *was* to Pindar,
what Phoebus Apollo *is* to the world. But indirectly, from the content
of these analogies, we learn that he has the highest value, since Pindar
without his inner glow was nothing, and the sun is indispensable to the
world.

Nor is there any note of disparagement lingering on from his association with the peasant. The peasant may be small and black, his horizon
may be bounded by the elemental things of life. But the warmth he
seeks outside him he also bears within him. It is with the word 'feurig'
that the central notion of inner warmth enters the poem for the first
time, and it is as a direct result of this encounter that the poet realizes
that he too must have inner warmth with which to respond to his god.
If the apostrophe to Bromius is to be read as an invective against an age
which finds its inspiration in material joys,[14] then it means that the poet's
realization that he has something to learn from the peasant is now
interrupted by a mood of revulsion, in which the peasant's god is invoked
only to be rejected at once as a deity unworthy of poets. This would

mean that the two worlds, of poet and of peasant, remain separate, that physical vitality is simply translated into terms of another level of experience, as in allegory. But we move here in a world of symbols, of identities not just analogous but, mysteriously, of the same substance. The peasant, as we saw, is no alien being, but another aspect of the poet, which he now re-integrates into himself. And it is in his dual aspect of man-poet that the wanderer is urged to glow towards Apollo in *his* dual aspect of sun-god and god of poetry. If the other gods here are inexhaustible symbols, it is unlikely that Bromius can be pinned down to one meaning. He too must stand under the poem's double sign of sublimity and humour. And it is because he is the god of wine and far more, that he plays such an important part in the wanderer's gradual discovery of the nature of his own genius. The Muses and Graces, for all that they attend him with glory and bliss, have left him in the lurch in his struggle with the elements. In a flash of recognition he perceives in Bromius possibilities not exhausted by the good gifts of the earth. He is the link between the most earthy and the most spiritual, and by defining him in terms of Pindar's inner glow and the life-giving sun Goethe presents him as a symbol of all vitalizing forces.

His source for 'Vater Bromius', the commentators tell us,[15] was Wieland's latest work, *Der Neue Amadis*, where he appeared as the purveyor of the best French Burgundy.[16] But in Pindar, whom Goethe had been studying in the spring of 1772, he could also have read of

the god with ivy bound whom we mortals call Bromius ... Clearly seen are the bright symbols of his sacred rites, whensoever, at the opening of the chamber of the purple-robed Hours, nectarious flowers lead in the fragrant Spring.

In this Dithyramb for the Athenians Pindar calls upon all the gods of Olympus to help him celebrate in song the festival of Dionysos, under his title Bromius, 'him of the loud cry'. Zeus is his father, his mother, Semele. At his coming lovely tresses of violets are flung on the immortal earth and the voices of songs ring to the sound of flutes. Wieland's jovial spender of wine is here the source of all vitality, god of the life-bringing spring, inspirer of sacred song and dance.

It was Herder in his *Fragmente* who recovered for German poetry the conception of divine intoxication symbolized by wine, and it is unthinkable that after meeting him Goethe should have used Bromius in his old anacreontic way. Had Herder not written in the section on Pindar and Greek dithyrambs:

The gentle Graces were not yet born; the forces of Nature were revered . . . and among the oldest gods there was always a god of wine; call him what you will. And now therefore drunken poetry was led to the altars to be purified. Here religion enjoined upon them drunkenness in wine and love, and their drunkenness in its turn conformed therefore to religion: their song was full of the animal-sensual speech of the wine and wine in its turn was exalted into a mystical-sensual language of the gods: a holy song in the twofold meaning of the word.[17]

Whether Goethe had read this before writing his poem or not, he was certainly familiar with the gist of it from those crucial conversations in Strassburg, which had taught him that poetry has its roots in the primitive, is no mere pleasant adornment of life, but its most vital manifestation. When he came to know Pindar at first hand this knowledge was more than confirmed. New regions of his being, he wrote to Herder,[18] had been opened up within him through the realization that for the Greeks the seat of thought and feeling was one, and located not in the head, but in the breast and belly. It is not by dabbling at this or that, not by pecking at other folk's achievement, but by concentrating all his innate powers of body and mind into a single unity that a man may achieve mastery. If what he found in Pindar was so swiftly assimilated, it was because his need of it was so urgent. His need of concentration, his longing for a task that would focus all his energies, had been the intermittent burden of his letters for a year or more. But it is in *Wandrers Sturmlied* that we first find the word *Mittelpunkt*, a word which was to occur again and again in his lifelong struggle to discover and strengthen the organic centre of his being.[19]

What he expressed to Herder in the language of concepts, *Sturmlied* tells us in the language of symbols. Here, in the brief progression

innre Wärme
Seelen Wärme
Mittelpunckt,

is the concentration of energy to a burning centre of effective activity. Here too the oneness of physical and spiritual powers. For this is the significance of 'innre Wärme' here rather than 'innre Glut'. Through being used of Pindar 'Glut' has been appropriated to the poetic sphere, while 'Wärme' is more neutral, having had physical associations playing about it from the first, and 'Seelenwärme' thus stands clearly revealed as an intensification, a more concentrated form, of vitality in general.

Thus neither internal nor external evidence permits a reading of the poem which separates life and poetry, body and mind, wine and inspiration. The liberating effect upon Goethe of this new knowledge is reflected in

Vater Bromius
Du bist Genius,

which has all the breath of a joyful discovery. It is difficult for the critic to do justice to this crucial verse. If he paraphrases, he has to utter in succession meanings which in the poem resound simultaneously. Like the inexhaustible Apollo, the phrase, 'was der Welt', eludes confinement within any paraphrase. It can mean both 'What the sun is to the world' and 'What the world knows as Apollo'. The basic simplicity of the construction makes it capable of all meanings consistent with the spirit of the poem. It may even carry an echo of Pindar's 'whom we mortals call'—that phrase by which the Greeks voiced their recognition that human knowledge of the gods is not exhaustive. A source of poetry known to Pindar is here recovered for an age wont to think of poetry only as form given by the Muses. Bromius, whom Pindar knew as inner inspiration, is what the world knows as Apollo. The two gods have been identified.

But though they may be one in essence, their manifestations are different. And in the next verse inner and outer glow are opposed. The poet has learnt that he must find the source of inspiration within himself. But it is not enough just to glow it forth. It must be concentrated to a focal point and directed towards Apollo. Or the poet will suffer for it. Even as life, drawing its strength from the earth, yet needs the fructifying force of the sun, so the poet's inspiration will remain only a potential unless submitted to the formative influence of the leader of the Muses. The cedar may flourish by its own efforts; but neither man nor poet can do without Apollo. 'Neidgetroffen' is a reminder of the disastrous consequences which may follow upon the hybris of self-sufficiency. But for this word, we might imagine the cedar to be wholly exemplary. By its power it excites the interest and envy of Apollo—but the envy of the gods involves the striking down of the beloved object.[20] The fitting relation between men and gods is exemplified, not by the cedar, but by the peasant, actively dependent upon their gifts. The fine balance between human effort and divine grace is reflected in equally fine nuances of style. 'Erwartend', by its meaning, presents the peasant waiting upon the bounty of Bromius. But its mood is active, and the activity enhanced by being set against 'den alles erwartet', which assigns a grammatically passive role to the poet. Through this formal relation of contrast fulness of meaning is restored to 'erwartend': reaching by looking towards, by watching. An equally delicate balance between his own effort and the grace of form is enjoined upon the poet. For the syntactical relation of 'Weh, weh!' is so indeterminate that it would be difficult to say which is the more to be deplored: the absence of fine frenzy, or a fine frenzy that remains diffuse and inchoate.[21] Here is no Promethean defiance of the god of form, but a recognition that inspiration and form are mutually indispensable. Thus inconspicuously there enters into German poetry that conception of which Nietzsche was to make so much, of Dionysiac ecstasy and Apolline form, and that it does so is due to Goethe's imaginative grasp of Pindar and Greek symbols.

The essential unity of these two aspects of poetry is symbolized by Jupiter, father of both these gods, and the source of all things—even of storms and dangers. The presiding deity of this hour is, after all, not the sun, conspicuous by its absence, but the omnipresent rain, Jupiter Pluvius. This wanderer's genius, nameless at first, has at last been identified. At the beginning it was the power invoked to cover him from the storm, storm and genius were separate entities, and both were outside his song—'Dem Schlossensturm entgegensingen'. Now, through the physical implications of 'strömen', genius and storm are completely one. It is the stormy element itself which covers him, and both have been assimilated into his song—'Dich strömt mein Lied'. This transitive use of *strömen* is not just grammatical waywardness. No other construction would give the same sense of god and rain being immanent within the song. The wanderer's own realization of the change comes out in

> Dich *von* dem es begann
> Dich *in* dem es endet
> Dich *aus* dem es quoll.

Whereas 'Dich' remains constant, the prepositions reflect a progression of inwardness. 'Beginnen von' defines a point of departure in space or time, a purely external relation. With 'enden in', the song already partakes of the nature of rain. With 'quellen aus', it has its source deep within the element.

The situation in which the poet happens to find himself is thus both the inspiration and the content of his song. He has found that the stormy elements, too, have fructifying power: inspiration has come from being drenched by them. And since Jupiter holds within himself not only Bromius but Apollo, form too is inherent within the situation. It is there within the stuff of life for him who has the courage to discover it. The power of poetry to say everything at once here reaches its limit. Nothing short of the whole meaning we can find in the words is adequate to account for their effect. Rain, genius, inspiration, form, they are all there in Jupiter Pluvius, and 'Dich strömt mein Lied' is the poetic articulation of all that Goethe meant by 'innere Form'.

The lines

> Glühte deine Seel Gefahren Pindar
> Muth Pindar—

are equally pregnant with meaning. The memory of the transitive use of *strömen* inclines us to read 'Gefahren' and 'Mut' as accusative: Pindar's soul glows dangers and courage as the song streams rain. But other echoes are at work here too. 'Glühte' inevitably calls up 'Glüh entgegen' and 'Mut' the 'mutige Bauer', so that we can scarcely escape the sense of a glowing response *to* dangers. But these impressions do not conflict. All the main threads of the poem are gathered up here, and Goethe has presented Pindar as so open and responsive to experience that experience enters into his soul to glow there as poetry. This is why the poet-wanderer dares to feel kinship with him rather than with those others, to whom Jove appears only in his gentler Apolline form, as guardian of the Castalian Spring, sacred to the Muses and Graces. Theocritus and Anacreon stand in the pleasant by-waters of life; but this wanderer, like great Pindar, has been singled out for more tempestuous visitation.

And yet how incongruous! No sooner does he realize the grace that has befallen him, than doubts as to his powers assail him. He will be lucky if he has enough glow to wade to his hut, let alone any to spare for poetry! The broken sentences reflect not only his breathless exhaustion, but the collapse of his sublime vision of the perfect unity of poetry and life. Yet he is not back where he started. The illusion that life with its storms can be ignored, and poetry wrought out of the fancies of his mind, has given place to a recognition of his real needs and powers. Humour has brought him to a more satisfactory point after all, and by a discontinuous and illogical process, not inappropriate to the image-world of dream and poetry.

But if illogical, not arbitrary. When critics speak of the arbitrariness in this wild ode, they might be referred to Coleridge:

> Poetry, even that of the ... wildest odes, has a logic of its own, as severe as that of Science; and more difficult, because more subtle, more complex, and dependent upon more, and more fugitive, causes.[22]

The 'causes', however fugitive, must be pursued, through all the formal relations of grouping, contrast, modification of words and symbols, until the obscurities yield their secrets and the order of the imagination is revealed. True, Goethe has not worked here in any traditional mould of external regularity; the form of this ode is not Pindaric form. But unless we are to lay ourselves open to the criticism he once levelled at the Germans—that their conception of form did not extend beyond metre[23]—we must recognize that it has an inner form of its own. Goethe may have sung it without conscious plan, but he did not sing it without shape. We may note, for instance, how the two main notions, warmth and response, at first shifting and undefined, so work upon each other that they coalesce, at the centre of the poem, in the quite precise conception of a mutual response of inner and outer glow, coalesce at the word 'Mittelpunckt'—a nice identity of form and content! The whole movement of the poem's form grows inevitably out of the mood and theme: a serious subject treated with a sense of humour.

Humour springs from a profound impulse to self-protection. It is a means of preserving inner security. But it is also a sign of it. For although a sense of humour implies as much susceptibility to the contrasts, contrarieties and conflicts of existence as the tragic view, it implies too a centre, however deep and unconscious, which remains immovable, a *Mittelpunkt* from which the disturbed balance may be recovered. In this poem the wanderer is exposed to the harsh incongruity between the ideal world of beauty and the actual world of storm and stress. But he is not annihilated by it. He neither succumbs to its tragic dissonance, nor takes refuge from it in self-pity or self-irony. Harmony is constantly being resolved into contrasts and tension; but some innate sturdiness always enables him to find a fresh synthesis. And the final perception of incongruity has none of Heine's brittleness. It is not a twist of irony which destroys what has just been established.[24] Pindar's lofty conception of the poet, as one who stands in the centre of life, setting the seal of eternity upon people and events, remains valid. But how should a young poet express his sense of affinity with this, except through the veil of humour? If Goethe laughs at genius here, it is not with intent to destroy but to preserve, to protect his secret aspirations from derision. Perhaps from Herder's derision. Humour often stood him in good stead in that relation, enabling him to get the best out of Herder's criticism without being withered by its blast. Some resource of native tenacity would press the spring and his defence mechanism go into action: 'I patted my genius in motherly fashion to comfort and encourage it', he writes to him on one occasion,[25] anticipating the mood of *Sturmlied*. And it is not impossible that the poem itself is a humorous answer—the only possible kind of answer—to Herder's challenge that no modern poet could write a dithyramb.

It was fortunate that Goethe could laugh at himself now and then when the tensions within him grew intolerable, and he wondered how he could go on living. It was one way of preserving the precarious balance of his delicately adjusted organism—a saving grace his Werther lacked. The oscillation between the two poles of self-realization and self-limitation is no less violent in *Sturmlied* than in his tragic novel. Whether in the cosy images of the opening verses, the warmth of the peasant's hearth, or the wistful pictures of idyllic contentment presented by Anacreon and Theocritus, the *Hütte* is constantly tugging at the soaring aspirations of the *Wanderer* and bringing him down to earth. But the tension here is held nicely in balance by the humour which plays with the two images. The harmony achieved by the older Goethe was not the cultivation of some alien way of life he happened to admire, but the bringing to consciousness of a dominant mode of his own being. This early ode reveals that at the irrational level where thought is image, a level more vital for the development of a way of life than any conscious system of thought, there is a tendency to balance, a balance often upset, but there all the same. Beneath its troubled surface the waters here are clearer in their depths than in perhaps any other poem of his *Sturm und Drang*. They reflect a proper awareness of man's dependence upon a higher power and the need to confess it. Nor does the thrill of assimilating Pindar lead him to deny a place to poets he has outgrown. Even his excitement about the momentous discovery of the Dionysiac nature of genius does not really throw him off his balance. For no more than his teacher Herder does he jettison Apollo. And even as he invokes the god of ecstasy, presiding deity of a new era, he can still hail him, fellow-well-met fashion, as Wieland's 'Vater Bromius'.

Humour, he once told Schiller,[26] is in itself a kind of poetry and lifts us above the raw material of the subject-matter. The Germans, he thought, were apt to let a subject weigh them down, and to become ponderous about it.[27] *Wandrers Sturmlied* is evidence of his own power to dispose of the weightiest matters with a playfulness which never deviates into nonsense. A modern German poet, Christian Morgenstern, protests against the description of his 'Grotesques' as 'höherer Blödsinn' because, he says, 'es kann von Unsinn nirgends die Rede sein; jedes Gedicht hat Hand und Fuss . . . man muss sich nur die Mühe nehmen, sich in die Grundsituation zu versetzen'.[28] When we take this trouble we find that *Wandrers Sturmlied* is 'im ganzen sehr vernünftig, im einzelnen ein bisschen unvernünftig', as Goethe declared all lyric poetry must be.[29] Perhaps after all 'Halbunsinn' is not just an old man's apology for the nonsense of his youth, but a plain description of the irrational nature of this very good sense.

IV. The Relation of Form and Meaning in Goethe's *Egmont*

I forget who it was who used to go about urging his friends to hang their pictures upside down now and again. It may well have been that fine art critic, R.A.M. Stevenson, the cousin of R.L.S. It was certainly he, so the legend persists, who as professor in Liverpool scandalized its worthy citizens by exhorting the old ladies who attended his lectures to turn themselves upside down—to tuck up their skirts, bend, and have a look at the world backwards through their legs for a change. It is perhaps not surprising that his stay there was of short duration. But the results of acting on his advice are so rewarding that one could wish it were possible to apply it to the world of literature too, and effect some such simple reversal with a novel or a play. It would be unnecessary if the remedy for staled vision were simply a little *more* attention to things grown familiar and for granted. But it is the quality rather than the quantity of our attention that needs the occasional jolt, and is affected so remarkably by even the briefest excursion into the world of upside-down. Relieved of the need to move and act, our routine-worn relation to things temporarily inhibited, we cease to select from the manifold objects displayed to our gaze only those which are relevant to our immediate interest or purpose; our vision is no longer dominated by the relation of cause and effect. And our stock reactions being thus cut off, a different kind of response can come into play. When we are right way up, that smoke trailing along the valley is cursorily registered by the practical set of our mind as an effect of a train in action, dismissed as a mere sign—there's the train coming in, it must be 12.45. But in the picture framed between our legs it is a line so intensely white and so straightly drawn that it may even defy recognition; and the relation which predominates is not its connection with that little black snaky line down there in the corner, but the boldness of its sweep against the rest of the picture. As may happen, too, in the reversed world seen through the looking-glass, a relation of cause and effect passes unnoticed, while a formal relation comes into its own.

A picture, one would think—unless we have got so used to looking at it that we no longer see it—challenges us to this kind of attention even when it hangs as it was meant to hang, just by virtue of being set apart in a frame as an object for contemplation. 'Looking at coloured dirt in a suitable frame', a painter said recently, 'ought to be a simple matter. The penny in the slot-machine of the mind drops and the mind reacts quite naturally to form and colour.' But if the critic suggests having a look at it the other way up, it is because he knows it is not quite so simple as that. The artist retains the 'innocent eye', the child's view undefiled; the rest of us have to make something of an effort to recover it. The story a picture tells, the message it seems to convey, the gestures of the figures, the expressions on their faces, all the familiar relations we have grown used to noting in the daily round, get in the way of a direct response to form and colour. Unless the painter forcibly inhibits our stock responses by turning the world topsy-turvy before putting it on to his canvas—as many modern artists do—most of us are inclined to see in a picture only what it represents, or to pursue the associative thoughts and feelings it may call up in us. We have in some measure to predispose ourselves to the unfamiliar if we are to appreciate the effect of colour and contour reacting upon one another, qualifying one another, intensifying, reducing.

And it is the same with literature. All too often the words with which it is made serve merely as an initial stimulus to set going in our mind some train of thought or feeling which then proceeds under its own momentum, gathering a mass of associations as it goes; or as rough cyphers to evoke in our imagination a three-dimensional world in which characters of flesh and blood begin to lead an independent life of their own. And while our imagination would be the poorer were it not peopled with these denizens of a fictitious world, there is a danger, once they become divorced from the words that give them substance, that they will acquire traits which in reality we have foisted upon them, act from motives which are none of the poet's making but of ours, swell out on this side and diminish on that according to our predilection or emotional need, receive a different emphasis and take on strange pro-portions, until the fabric of the world they inhabit is no longer that of the world the poet created—a danger, in short, of our falling victim to what Paul Valéry called 'literary superstitions'. 'J'appelle ainsi', he says in one of his aphorisms,[1] 'toutes croyances qui ont de commun l'oubli de la condition verbale de la littérature. Ainsi existence et *psychologie* des *personnages*, ces vivants *sans entrailles*'. To avoid this danger mostly re-quires some readjustment, though not necessarily of a physical kind. To see the world afresh we are fortunately not dependent upon gymnastic contortions, useful as the experiment may be. A new quality of vision may come upon us unawares when we are comfortably the right way up, startling the drabness of an ordinary day with poignant delight. Our practical interest snaps; the familiar table is no longer a cycle of the cares of domesticity, of laying and clearing and dusting and polishing, but a rhythm of gleaming surfaces catching the light and reflecting it into pattern. And we need not even wait upon the moment's grace. We can cultivate the salutary habit of disconnecting appearance from present circumstance; instead of the physical exertion of bending, we can make the mental effort of shaking off 'the lethargy of custom' and switching on a new current of response. And to see literature as the poet made it we can deliberately adopt a way of reading which is never unmindful of the 'verbal condition' of its existence, which refrains from speculating what the characters might have done or could possibly do, which, instead of skimming the pages as though the words were merely a shadowy notation designed to conjure up a real world behind or beyond, attends for a change to the words themselves, as to the painter's colours and shapes, apprehending them as a complex organization on a flat surface, noting their modifications and modulations, their relations of similarity and contrast and grouping.

All this is not to advocate struggling out of 'literary superstitions' only to fall into the heresy of 'pure form', that heresy which would have us believe that we are only making a truly aesthetic response when we abstract from the 'life' of a work of art, disregard its representational aptness and associative power and reduce it to a mere surface arrangement of pattern and design. That much misused word 'aesthetic' is too often narrowed down in this way to connote the delight, part sensory, part intellectual, afforded by the perception of such formal relations, as though these were in some sense separate from the *meaning* of the work. Whereas in its full and precise sense 'aesthetic' should connote our total experience of the work as a whole, with all that it may contain of thought, emotion, 'life', but with all these so transmuted through being presented as design and pattern, that they evoke a quality of experience of a completely different order from that which they would have evoked had they not been thus shaped and formed. For, in fact, our perception of its formal values directly affects our awareness of what a work *represents*, not only enriching, but modifying and adjusting, its meaning. Criticism which, in reaction against purely descriptive and appreciative interpretation, stops short when it has drawn attention to the balance of the masses, the arrangement of colour harmonies, the sequence of consonants and changes of rhythm, violates the wholeness of art no less than that which is content with a discussion of themes and ideas, characters and action. The central problem of criticism is to find a way of letting the total meaning of a work emerge out of formal analysis, instead of treating points of style and artistry as though they were a decorative charm super-added to its fundamental matter. Standing a work on its head to throw its formal qualities into relief is a useful device, but it is only a device. For if an artist has painted a scene involving human forms rather than cabbages and cubes, he assuredly wants us to appreciate the human significance of that scene—so long as we appreciate it in terms of his composition. Having observed the design made by the curve of the shawl round the Virgin's head and the folds of the king's robe as he kneels at her feet, the critic must go on to show how this design enhances the significance of the Christ Child which it frames; or having observed the recurrence of a word or a phrase at significant points in the structure of a play, he must seek to discover how this rhythm modifies the thought or affects the emphasis of character and motive.

I am well aware that in separating form and meaning at all I am using an abstraction. In a work of art they are one and indivisible. But it is an abstraction indispensable to the critic who—in contrast to the artist, at whose behest time stands still, and who can say everything at once— is forced to work in succession of time and through separation. Only by means of this abstraction can we describe the process whereby the meaning of a work of art grows in our mind as it is fed and transformed by our gradual perception of its formal qualities. And it is a useful abstraction, too, for throwing light on the varying importance of the formal element in the appreciation of works of widely different character. For the appreciation of a novel by Henry James, or by Proust, perception of its formal relations is patently paramount; for the appreciation of one by Dickens it is, by comparison, almost negligible. Goethe is so versatile in his manner that he seems to embrace the whole range. With him the emphasis in the ever-changing relation between form and meaning shifts, be it ever so slightly, from work to work. Our general impression of *Wilhelm Meister*, derived from attending simply to *what* is said, will be enriched and will be refined when we turn our attention to *how* it is said, but not, I think, fundamentally altered. For this reason it can be abridged, parts cut out here and there, without gravely endangering the whole organism. But this gives no clue to Goethe's manner as a novelist in general. The meaning of *Werther* grows quite differently in our mind. Whether at a first reading it takes us by storm, or merely makes us smile as at a sentimental story, once we begin to note the details of its formal structure, the incredible subtlety of its linguistic finesses, its meaning deepens until, looking back, it seems to have changed out of all recognition. With *Die Wahlverwandtschaften* it is different again. It is rare for this novel to capture anyone at a first reading. Its very 'life' is somehow dependent upon an appreciation of its formal values, and our original idea of its meaning may well have to be radically revised, even reversed, when, instead of simply following its narrative sequence, we explore its pattern of immense complexity, trying to discover the significant relation between one part and another, down to the smallest detail of style. Hence this work of prose fiction offers almost as much resistance to the translator as any poetry. More even than some. For such complex intercommunication of the parts[2] does not invariably coincide with regularity of outward form. *Hermann und Dorothea*, for all its classical hexameters and poetic diction, is a much sturdier, much less susceptible, organism than *Die Wahlverwandtschaften*. It will readily yield its meaning to a schoolboy frankly reading it for its story, a meaning which is only completed and confirmed by later attention to its form. *Faust* offers meaning and to spare to every kind of reading, casual or careful, philosophical or poetic. Thought, feeling, dramatic interest, myth, fantasy, symbol, it is all cast before us with such a lavish hand that it seems best to change our manner of reading from part to part; and it is only when we would define the general purport of this vast work that we realize the inadequacy of simply casting up the sum and substance of *what* has been said, and find ourselves embarked upon a long quest, through innumerable relations and interrelations, for the organic centre of what is surely the most complex poetic structure in world-literature. By comparison the form of *Iphigenie* or of *Tasso* seems simplicity itself. Yet despite their clear outlines, the smooth harmony of their proportions, their verbal fabric is of an intricacy unsurpassed in dramatic writing. Here thought is so completely assimilated into form that we can well believe Goethe when he says[3] that he pursued the meaning inherent in each of these themes into every delicate vessel and fibre of the poetic organism. But for all their stylistic similarity, the relation between form and meaning is not identical even here. The most cursory reading of *Iphigenie* cannot fail to discover profound thought, lofty ideas, noble sentiments. A cursory reading of *Tasso* will reveal only a period piece, whose chief charm is its unreality, and whose poignantly delicate verse seems wasted on a lot of pother about a poet who behaves like a wilful child. If we attend only to the gist of what is said in *Iphigenie*, to the general sense of each speech in its relation to that of the others, we may well fall wide of the play's intention, hover on the periphery of its meaning instead of landing dead in the centre. But that its intention is important and its meaning weighty we are never for a moment in doubt. But if we do the same with *Tasso* we not only get the meaning out of focus, we get the veriest trickle of meaning at all. Not that this poetry is obscure; but its urbanity is as deceptive as the grace of Mozart's music. Here is a most exquisite sense of the value of every word. And their roots strike deep. We read a line and think we have understood. Then a word catches us with some extra resonance; its dimensions increase—the line is not the same; the word occurs again and yet again—the play is not the same. There is a weightiness in this apparent lightness and simplicity which will never yield to an approach which interprets everything in terms of action and motive. The end has notoriously eluded interpretation;[4] it will continue to do so as long as we confine our attention to the substance of what Tasso seems to be saying at this single point of the play. For it tells its truth, as Browning says art may tell truth, obliquely. And understanding of this truth depends upon our awareness that every thought and every image of this final speech[5] has occurred before at other significant points, and upon the power of our imagination to embrace this whole pattern of relations. Here is no solution in the sphere of event, but a resolution in the sphere of form—a resolution which strikingly bears out the aesthetic axiom that all art aspires towards the condition of music.[6] Of all Goethe's works this is the most highly-organized and the most vulnerable, so vulnerable that not a part, scarcely a syllable, can be touched without impairing the meaning of the whole.

Egmont, by comparison, seems plain sailing. Its meaning lies wide open and unambiguous, its characters 'live', rounded and vivid as any of the great characters of literature, its action moves out freely into the bustle of political life. It seems to stand at the opposite pole of dramatic style. We only begin to love *Tasso* when we stop skating over the gleaming smoothness of its surface and become alert to every modulation of related word. Then we are stirred and challenged at the deepest levels of feeling and belief. And, paradoxically, its characters spring to life in the moment we stop expecting them to live as flesh and blood characters in a three-dimensional world. But we begin to love *Egmont* from that moment of our first reading when the hero roguishly deceives his love, and instead of sweeping her into his arms stands with them wrapped in his cloak, for all the world, as she says, like a babe in swaddling clothes, whilst she stamps and pouts until he throws back his cloak and reveals himself as she has always wanted to see him, arrayed in all the splendour of his Spanish finery. Or when Klärchen, with that movement of infinitely touching intimacy, kneels on a little stool, her elbows on his knees, looking up into her lover's face—Goethe, as always, has the master's touch in matters of love. How impossible it would have been if he had made Klärchen kneel to Egmont in any other way! These things move us independently of words—we know of them largely through stage-directions. And even scenes which are conjured up by words alone —the dramatic intensity of the moment when Alba looks down into the courtyard upon Egmont dismounting from his horse, all unsuspecting of the danger which awaits him—even these at once take on three-dimensional quality and become henceforth part of the structure of our visual imagination. Moreover, each of these incidents impresses us for itself alone; just as the meaning of Egmont's great speech, with its compelling image of the charioteer, seems exhausted by what it alone contains, and independent of its relation to what is said elsewhere in the play. The beauty, we feel, is in each of the parts rather than in the relation of the parts to each other.

And there is another way in which *Egmont* moves us differently from *Tasso*. Reading it in our generation, parts of it have come close to us with almost unbearable impact. The tramp of jackboots down the street —'*ein* Tritt, so viel ihrer sind'—soldiers of the occupation, stiff-backed and stiff-legged, with never so much as a glance to right or to left, so many robots each with a devil inside, the terror of them enhanced by that endearing contrast with the Flemish militia as they stand, their caps jauntily askew, at perpetual ease. Or this atmosphere of secret agents, of incitement to inform—even about members of one's own family; the wearing down of innocent victims by the unscrupulous ingenuity of the examining judges, against a background of rack and torture-chamber— these nowadays loom even larger than life in our total impression of the play, have the power to sound as though they had been written expressly for us, so immediate is their appeal. There is nothing in either *Tasso* or *Iphigenie* which is susceptible to this kind of response, which is dependent for its life upon the recurrence of a political situation.

Yet though we may love the characters of *Egmont*, though we are stirred by the dramatic power of its scenes, we have rarely been satisfied with the work as a whole. Since Schiller told us[7] that it is a play without a plot we have stopped looking for unity of action and meekly followed his injunction to treat it as a portrayal of Egmont's character presented in a sequence of dramatic scenes. And since Goethe hinted that it was a study of the daemonic,[8] we have only too gratefully followed this authoritative pointer, and taken the other characters and the portrayal of the Flemish people as mere background and foil to the dangerous career of a hero who, blind in his careless love of life, wilful in his reckless flaunting

C

of danger, rushes headlong to his doom. Even so, despite helps and hints, we have continued to jib at the end, as we jib at the end of so many of Goethe's works. *Tasso*, we complain, is inconclusive; *Iphigenie* is only made conclusive by idealizing the situation beyond all bounds of probability. It is all very well for Ottilie to be sanctified, but we baulk at Eduard lying there beside her, their illicit love hallowed by angelic forms who gaze down upon their tomb, not in compassion—that we could accept—but in serene kinship, if you please—'heitere verwandte Engelsbilder', a bold, and deliberate, allusion to the title of the novel. As for *Egmont*, it is not only the operatic turn it takes which disturbs us, but its apparent inconsequence. Why should a hero who has landed himself in gaol by careless mismanagement go to his death convinced that he is dying in the cause of freedom? The poet, we infer, must have changed his intention during the long interval before he revised and completed the play. What began as a study of the daemonic must have been fitted with an appendix on freedom and the seams still show. It has become, we say, a thing of shreds and patches.

But perhaps in looking for the meaning we think ought to be there, we miss much of what is there, and mistake the real intention. And it might be worth trying as an experiment with *Egmont* a way of reading which for *Tasso* is a necessity: 'turning it upside down' and directing our eye to its verbal texture for a change.

Egmont, we are in the habit of thinking, is a man blinded. Both his enemy and his friend say this of him; it has been a recurrent theme of most criticism of the play. And just as we find our way about the world in which we live by the convenient habit of noting just enough characteristics of objects to be able to recognize them, so we tend to move through this play guided by this one salient feature. But if we stop reading with a selective eye, and let each detail make its full impact upon us, this central figure begins to fill out in an unexpected way. For one blinded, his vision often seems extraordinarily clear. He *sees* not only the nature and needs of those near and akin to him, but the aims and motives of those set over against him. The fine balance of his judgment, both in large public issues as in his private assessment of individual behaviour, is matched by that of only one other person in the play, Machiavell. And of him we are significantly told that he 'sees' with the historian's eye, that we may know the value we are to attach to his utterances. It is Machiavell's opinion that Egmont sees *truly;* his own view of the political situation, of the wisest way to handle a people bred in freedom and independence, endorses Egmont's precisely; and it is this same Machiavell who confirms Egmont's own feeling about himself, that he had always acted in accordance with his conscience: 'Er scheint mir in allem nach seinem Gewissen zu handeln'.

This again is something of a paradox. Are we, then, not to think of him as carefree and careless, discharging his duties of state as perfunctorily as may be in order to be away on his horse by day, or stealing to his love by night? True, his scene with Klärchen, for all its carefree intimacy of a love fulfilled, does not exactly give the impression of a man free from care. Here, in this freedom of perfect knowledge and perfect trust, he reveals himself as he really is. The Egmont whom they all, court and people alike, take to be glad and gay, is in reality, we learn, an Egmont who must keep a tight hold on himself and change his face to suit the occasion, an Egmont whose eye, free of illusion and strangely prescient, *sees* sharply through the wiles of those out to ensnare him, as he *sees* sadly into the confused, ineffectual, devotion of his beloved countrymen, an Egmont weary with work and fruitless effort and dissimulation.

If we let ourselves be pulled up short by such apparent contradictions, it may begin to dawn on us that a great deal of this play is concerned, either directly or by implication, with different ways of *seeing*. It turns, broadly speaking, on a contrast between eyes wide open to the fulness of what is here and now, and eyes dimmed to the present scene while thought ranges into the distance of past or future. This is not argued out as an abstract problem; nor is it presented as a bald opposition between two modes of being upon whose relative merits we are invited to judge. That is not Goethe's way. It is spread out over the play as a problem of living which engages different people in different situations in a variety of ways, cutting across nationalities and opposing groups of characters. The two obvious poles are Egmont and Alba. Egmont, with his sense of living in the moment, makes a full and complete response to the totality of the person or situation before him—whether it is to recognize a face and remember the name and trade of a man he has once talked to, or to see that his secretary is chafing at being late for an appointment with his love; whether it is to handle a threatening riot with the sure touch of direct intuition, or to be aware of all sides of the case when meting out justice. Alba, on the other hand, is so closed to the world that he is likened to a bronze tower without a door, or to a spider of the thin-bellied variety which derive no visible benefit from the prey they assimilate. But even his shut-in-ness is not presented to us as wholly without value. Alba may be blind to the world around him, but his eye is fixed on a distant point. He never loses sight of his object, and it is by virtue of his inaccessibility that he was able to lead an army through hostile territory without a single incident.

Between these two extremes there is a finely-shaded gradation of vision. Nearest to Alba's elaborate scheming is Orange with his fore*sight* and far*sight*edness. Life for him is reduced to a chess-board over which he is perpetually brooding, watching his opponent's every move, scanning each change of tactics on this surface of schematic figures. Then there is Brackenburg, blindly indifferent to everything around him because his life is suspended between the memory of one kiss and the hope of another. Or Klärchen's mother, who would ruin the present certainty of her daughter's love by harping on the uncertainty of the future.

Nearest to Egmont is Klärchen herself, with her complete response to the presence of a person—she is so sensible to the call of the moment that, though fully aware of the ambiguity of her behaviour, she cannot forbear to return the pressure of Brackenburg's hand—her way of relying on direct perception rather than on thought to give her understanding. When she thinks about it in his absence, her relation to Egmont is a mystery to her. But he has only to appear, and she understands that and much more besides: 'Wenn ich so *nachdenke*, wie es gegangen ist, weiss ich's wohl und weiss es nicht. Und dann darf ich Egmonten nur wieder *ansehn*, wird mir alles sehr begreiflich, wäre mir weit mehr begreiflich'. But there are others, too, who rely on direct perception to give them understanding. For the simple Flemish shopkeeper, seeking to explain the people's love for Egmont, the touchstone is the immediate impact of his personality—'Weil man ihm *ansieht*, dass er uns wohl will'. As so often in this play, the contrast is between thought, as the self-propagating activity of the mind, turning over its few fragments of data, inferring, elaborating, combining, speculating; and knowledge derived from intuitive contemplation and dependent on ever-renewed contact with the objects of the outer world.

Just how complex is the presentation of this problem, how it cuts across the tension of the dramatic action, is best understood if we compare Egmont's way of seeing with that of Margarete von Parma. Poles apart in temperament, these two are at one in their impatience with those who impose grandiose plans from a distance, who evolve elaborate projects without an eye for the peculiar conditions of the situation on the spot; they are at one in their belief that it is more important to *see* the next thing at hand to be done, rather than adhere to a course of action conceived in the *mind*; and they are at one in their clear-sighted knowledge that, plan as he may, man is subject to powers beyond his control. But the image each uses to express this same awareness clearly reveals their temperamental difference. For Margarete man is borne helpless on a wave he thinks to command; for Egmont he stands erect, swept along in his chariot, but with some measure of guidance through the reins in his own hands. She feels herself a victim; he feels himself a master within limits. And it is this which makes for the difference in their way of seeing, despite much similarity. For Egmont has power over his thoughts, while she is a prey to hers. Hence his vision remains clear and true when hers becomes dimmed by care. She would, it is said of her, 'see deeply' were she not beset by suspicions.

If we read such comments merely as a means of revealing character, we miss the poetic intention. They are also evidence of the urgency with which the problem of vision has engaged the poet's mind so that it pervades the language of his play down to the smallest detail. He seems to take every opportunity to express some different aspect of it, some new contrast, some fine nuance; and the full value of each of these nuances can only be appreciated when it is seen in relation to the others and to the problem as a whole. One example must suffice. When we read Egmont's invocation to sleep, we hear an echo of words spoken by Margarete in the first act. Her *thoughts*, she says, will give her no peace; dreadful *images* so haunt her sight that nothing can delight or distract her. By contrast Egmont can find utter release from the rigid knotting of his *thoughts* in sleep, which merges all *images*, painful and pleasant, into a harmonious flow and thus restores the balance of his being. The contrast here is not between careless escapism and conscientious adherence to duty. Margarete cancels the day's hunting, not because there is business to be done, but in order to give herself up completely to the thoughts which have her in thrall. Egmont, knowing he is impotent to act, will not expend himself in vain worrying. He has the power to be free of care when care can find no outlet in action.

It is only in the light of this echo—and many others—that we can understand aright the words with which Egmont turns from his disturbing interview with Orange to seek release with Klärchen: 'Und von meiner Stirne die sinnenden Runzeln wegzubaden, gibt es ja wohl noch ein freundlich Mittel'. These words do not only reveal character, they do not only fulfil the dramatic function of engineering an effective scene between Egmont and Klärchen. They are also to be valued as part of the thematic texture of the play. They offer yet one more facet in this complex portrayal of how strangely thought and vision are related in the pattern of living; how taking thought inevitably means some loss of sensuous contact with the present, how preparing for the distant contingency conflicts with living the moment to the full, how foresight, of its very nature, impairs wholeness of sight.

This problem of sight is interwoven with the wider problem of free-

dom. There is in this play from first to last far more talk about freedom
than there is about the daemonic. The opening scene of the shooting-
match, with the opportunity it gives for toasting and discussing the
various political leaders, is usually recognized as a brilliant device for
setting the political scene and introducing the protagonists. But it is far
more than a colourful setting with expositionary value. Within its brief
compass it anticipates the whole idea of the play by sounding all the
themes, touching swiftly on all the elements which go to make up the
complex conception of freedom. Among these soldiers and citizens there
are those who see that freedom must be fought for, those who see that
fighting for it is in itself an infringement of freedom; there are those who
would live freedom fully and boldly, and those who would shelter behind it in comfort and security. This problem too cuts across nationalities and groups. There is no question here of neat contrasts: rulers versus
people, fair Flemish freedom versus black Spanish oppression. The toast
brought to the great Emperor, Charles V, evokes a personality as free
and open, as easy in his contacts with the ordinary folk, as Egmont himself; his son, Philip, is disliked for his stiffness and reserve, but the Regent,
Margarete, valued for her defence of their privileges; and in her prudence
and moderation she comes close to Orange, the solid bulwark which
guarantees them security. Nor is freedom parcelled out between these
citizens in the sense that each typifies an aspect of it. Soest, with his appreciation of Egmont's joyous love of live, of his over-flowing generosity
which does not calculate the need, clearly inclines to its more positive
side—freedom *for* not freedom *from*. Yet it is he who defends Margarete
against Jetter's attack, while Jetter himself, in his worrying anxiety akin
to Margarete and far removed from Egmont, is yet the one to reflect
something of Egmont's own awareness of the horrors of war. These are
living people encountering a living problem and coming to terms with it
each in his own way. And as if to symbolise this criss-cross of tensions
within the single idea of freedom the scene closes with 'a kind of canon'
in which various components of freedom are uttered by voices 'singing'
against each other and yet making a harmony. 'Security and peace' is the
burden of the one part; 'Order and liberty' that of the other. One seems
the negative, the other the positive pole of freedom. But there is tension,
too, at each of the poles. For the claims of security may conflict with
those of living in peace, even as the claims of order may conflict with
those of liberty. Far from being reconciled in philosophical abstraction,
these conflicting claims are here, as in the living practice of freedom, held
together in a vibrant unity of opposites.

This playing-off of the different aspects of freedom continues throughout the play. Brackenburg understands freedom as an abstract ideal—he could write an essay on Brutus and get top marks. But to understand it is not necessarily to possess it, and he has no freedom of action or being. He is a man bound, not by passion, but by a habit and a hope. Vansen, the political agitator, *uses* freedom as a bait to lure peace-loving citizens to overthrow the existing order. And yet much of what he advocates is a necessary condition for the preservation of liberty. The precarious balance between the negative and positive aspects of one and the same thing is beautifully rendered here. At each moment of this scene we face the challenge of where to draw the line, at what precise point to stop putting up with restrictions on liberty and begin to insist on traditional rights.

For Goethe none of these aspects of freedom or qualities of life is to be labelled good or bad in itself. It is a question of whether they form the appropriate response in a given situation. This for him is the key to the wisdom of living. There are two formal points in the play which make us realize it very clearly. There is a certain way of life which we associate both with Egmont, and with the Netherlanders in general, through phrases which are repeated several times: 'fresh and free', 'glad and gay', 'live and let live', 'let each go his own way'. In the first part of the play such qualities come over with positive value. This, we feel, and rightly feel, is the way to live: freely and fully. But the situation changes; and as Act IV opens, in an atmosphere of curfew and silence, we hear the familiar phrase 'Go thy way'—'Geh deines Pfads'—and against this new background of oppression it has a different ring. What in normal circumstances was a wholly appropriate response of admirable tolerance, betokens, in this state of emergency, an almost craven desire to steer clear of dangerous contacts, a passive acquiescence in oppression for the sake of security. Or again, Klärchen in her anguished efforts to save Egmont begs for a plan: 'Gib mir einen Anschlag'. *Anschlag*, this is a word we have hitherto associated with craftiness and mole-like scheming; it carries negative associations. But now as it echoes hollowly in the silence of these bewildered Netherlanders, who have yet loved their Egmont so well, we feel that a plan would be the one appropriate response in this particular situation. If only they knew how to plan as well as they know how to live!

It is only against this complexity of detail about different ways of seeing, different aspects of freedom, different responses to different situations, that we can see the character and fate of Egmont in its proper perspective. This intricate weave is not there simply to throw his peculiar problem into relief. It is there as an end in itself. And he is a part of the weave, not a solitary figure standing out against it. He represents the Netherlanders' way of life in heightened form. What in them—and in Klärchen—is naive and instinctive, is in him fully conscious and articulate. What he is by nature, he confirms by choice, giving the assent of his mind to the way he must go. The perfect freedom he possesses, freedom from fear, freedom from care, freedom from all possessiveness—this is the whole point of his committing Klärchen to Ferdinand before he dies—this freedom he also pursues by conviction. He believes in it, both in the political sphere and in the sphere of personality. We can go very wrong in our view of Egmont if we read the speech to his secretary, in which he demands the right to live in accordance with his own nature, without considering it in relation to that later speech, where he claims from Alba a respect for the inmost core of a people's individuality. What he asks for himself, he asks also for others. It is no headstrong egoism, but a steady belief.

How, then, is he blind, and in what sense is he bound? If we read his crucial scene with Orange, not just as a move in the dramatic action, but with the whole weight of the larger problems of the play converging in upon our mind, we find that what we witness here is the point at which a positive value inclines to the negative, not because its quality is in any way impaired, but because it constitutes an inappropriate response to a particular situation. To speak of Egmont's carefreeness degenerating into carelessness here, is to skim over his imaginative awareness of the horrors of war, the conscientious responsibility which makes him loathe to take any step which may bring that war the nearer, the earnestness with which he implores Orange not to be seduced by too much shrewdness, not to bring about a state he fears by forcing the issue, not to put himself in the wrong by closing every avenue of negotiation. To suggest that he lacks reason is to miss the function of this scene, which is to present reason on both sides. The formal arrangement itself forbids our taking sides. For there comes a point in the argument of these two men when they leave the specific and the concrete, and rap out at each other in the sharp hammer-strokes of stichomythia those generalities which embody universal truths: 'Wer sich schont, muss sich selbst verdächtig werden' / 'Wer sich kennt, kann sicher vor- und rückwärts gehen'.—'Das Übel, das du fürchtest, wird gewiss durch deine Tat' / 'Es ist klug und kühn, dem unvermeidlichen Übel entgegenzugehn'. Neither of these points of view represents the truth of the matter. Nor does it lie between them. They are its two poles, even as Egmont and Orange are the two poles of freedom. The whole view embraces both. If we take sides here, it is as if we would take sides in a battle of proverbs: Too many cooks spoil the broth / Many hands make light work.—Look before you leap / He who hesitates is lost. Such conflicting statements may be logically irreconcilable, but common wisdom has known that in the reality of living it takes both to make the truth. What Egmont and Orange are arguing about here is after all the crucial problem of political freedom: in the words of Burke, it is no inconsiderable part of statesmanship to know how much of an evil ought to be tolerated. And Orange might well have proved wrong. We are not intended to see prudence and foresight as invariably right or as invariably successful. Margarete pursuing a not dissimilar course fails utterly, and Alba with even craftier calculation only half succeeds.

It is not because his vision is false or blurred that Egmont is *blind*; but because his way of seeing, clear and whole as it may be, is not appropriate to every situation. And not to this one. Craftiness and cunning often need to be met by a narrowing down of vision until it becomes focused as cleverness and shrewdness. This does not make Egmont's openness and trust into a fault as such. It simply shows that even the most perfect virtue can appear as a fault if adhered to out of season. To be consistent with *life* we have sometimes to be inconsistent with *ourselves*. And it is in his unswerving adherence to his own way of seeing and to his own way of living that Egmont is bound. The daemonic, that in his nature which is inaccessible to reason, here, right at the end of the scene, gets the upper hand. And at the risk of sounding paradoxical, we may say that Egmont here becomes rigid in his adherence to flexibility, blind through his adherence to wholeness of vision. Nowhere in Goethe's works do we feel more clearly that his conception of wise living is essentially that of Ecclesiastes—'To every thing there is a season, and a time to every purpose under the heaven'.

Egmont, then, for all its theatrical effectiveness, for all its appearance of a character-drama built with broad, bold sweeps, is far more dependent for its full appreciation upon a perception of the formal relations in its verbal organization than we might think. And the close weave of this verbal organization should indicate to us the nature of the dramatic unity. It is a unity which not only resists those major cuts of character and scene which had such disastrous results in Schiller's adaptation for the stage.[9] It will scarcely bear any cutting at all. For we have to reckon with something more than the onward surge of a dramatic action. The threads of the language run backwards as well as forwards, cross and intersect in such a way that even the most respectful pruning[10] inevitably entails some false emphasis in the relation of the parts and a consequent distortion in the meaning of the whole. Every detail counts here, even such a slight touch as the brief reference to Ferdinand's mother, whose 'Leicht-

C*

sinn', as Alba chooses to call her spontaneous openness and trust, reflects the poet's constant preoccupation with his main problem—the tension between the ease and lightness which are the mark of freedom and the care and foresight which are necessary to preserve it.

In the light of such a reading we find that we have to revise, though not to reverse, our idea of the play's meaning. It is a question of adjusting the emphasis. This is certainly a play about the daemonic. But is it not simply a picture of a great daemonic character. And indeed Goethe never suggested that it was. The daemonic element is not confined to Egmont. How could it be when it is at work in all life, in all nature, even in inorganic nature?[11] What is it but the daemonic, that in us which is incalculable and beyond the control of reason, what is it but that, which makes Brackenburg come up to the surface when he was determinded to drown himself, makes him incapable of swallowing the poison he has asked for although his reason tells him that there is no point in going on living? Egmont is no more at the mercy of his own nature than Brackenburg, or Margarete, or Alba. And the difference is that Egmont knows and accepts this incalculability as the basis of all life. On this point he is by far the most clear-sighted person in the play. As indeed on many others. It is he who gets the lines containing the profoundest wisdom, not the far-sighted, clever, people. There is no call for surprise at this. For Egmont's spontaneity is not the blind unreflecting kind. He takes each moment as it comes and savours it to the full; but he also sees the shape and form of the experience it brings. His brimming enjoyment of life goes hand in hand with the liveliest awareness of its significance. Indeed, the basis of his wholeness of vision on the big ultimate issues of existence is precisely his habit of full response to the concrete situation and the individual case. Foresight and calculation, however succesful in the event, involve a narrowing of the eyes to fixed concentration on just those features of the situation which serve interest or purpose. They are conducive to shrewdness, but scarcely to wisdom. Hence it is Egmont, swift-moving, light of touch, gay in heart, who sees truly the nature of freedom and the governing of a free people, as he sees deeply into life and the nature of human existence. For if we give full value to each of the elements in the central image of the charioteer, we see that it does not merely reflect a *dangerous* way of living. It reflects life itself. The three main forces of human life are there—the dark drive of our own unalterable nature, the chance and circumstances we encounter, the freedom and reason which give some measure of control and guidance into our hands. What this play is really about is the relation of the daemonic to reason, of freedom to necessity, as they interweave to make the weft and woof of life.

The end, with its apotheosis of freedom, grows inevitably out of the rest of the play. It has been foreshadowed by the canon at the end of the opening scene, and prepared by the increasingly poetic quality of the language. This 'salto mortale in eine Opernwelt', as Schiller called it,[12] may indeed be compared to the sudden change from poetic prose to lyric poetry at the end of Goethe's Novelle. Goethe himself explained the necessity for this latter development by means of a botanical analogy:

But an unrealistic, indeed a lyrical, conclusion was essential and had to follow. For after the exalted speech of the father, which is itself poetic prose, there had to be some intensification (Steigerung): I had to go over into lyric poetry, indeed into song itself. If you want an analogy for the development of this novella, you might think of a green plant shooting up from the root, and for a long time putting forth nothing but sturdy green lateral shoots, until suddenly it ends up with a flower. The flower was wholly unexpected, utterly astonishing, but it had to come. [13]

In this process a difference of degree suddenly appears as a difference in kind, not by the introduction of something essentially opposed in character, but by the gradual intensification of what has been there from the beginning.[14] An examination of the verbal texture of Egmont demonstrates the organic necessity of its culmination by revealing the fine and complicated connections which run between the final scenes and earlier parts of the play. All the elements which constitute the positive, more active, pole of freedom are brought together here, those elements which Egmont shares with his people and for which they have loved him. Though temporarily in defeat, they are not destroyed. Nor ever can be, for they are rooted in natural impulse. Sleep, vital contact with the earth and its creatures, love and friendship, these have been to Egmont the gateways to perfect freedom, to the fulness of spontaneous living in the moment. It is right that, by one means or another, by evocation, recollection, or by actual presence, they should all be united now in this dungeon to herald in his vision of a people rising in defence of its freedom. For even our loftiest intellectual conceptions of freedom are born of just such natural and immediate experiences of it, and it is this fact which makes Egmont's last words neither empty idealism nor high-sounding self-delusion, but soundly-based conviction.

The apparent discrepancy between this conviction and the people's failure to respond to Klärchen's rousing appeal has not been left unmotivated. On the psychological plane it is motivated subjectively, in Egmont's consciousness, by his double view of the Netherlanders. They are, he confesses to Klärchen, uncertain and confused in their aims—'ein Volk, das nicht weiss, was es will'; but their core, as he assures Alba, is sound, for they know how to live freely and in tolerance; they may be pressed, but not oppressed. This double view is confirmed objectively, in the folk-scenes, not only by the choice of situation, but by each verbal stroke in a characterization designed to reveal not their weakness *and* their strength, as separate entities, but the weakness *of* their strength, the interdependence of defect and virtue. Their very aptitude for free living makes them slow to the disorder of violence and to those collective restrictions on freedom which are necessary to defend it against attack. But it is, on the other hand, this same aptitude which is the surest guarantee that they will eventually revolt against oppression, not perhaps from any very clear convictions of political thought or practice, but by a natural rhythm, as surely as any living thing will resist the force which seeks to crush its growth.

But the motivation is not exhausted by such analysis of character. As so often in Goethe's novels and plays, the poetic intention transcends the psychological without being in any way at odds with it. And Klärchen's appeal to the people remains without dramatic repercussions because the action is fast moving beyond the confines of time, place, and event. The aim here is not to knit together the threads of the plot, but to concentrate all the individual manifestations of spontaneous living into the very quintessence of freedom as a universal symbol. Everything points the same way: the blurring of the date as Egmont's sentence is read out; the recourse to music, the art most fitted by its nature to express the timeless and the universal; Egmont's remark to Ferdinand, 'Die Menschen sind nicht nur zusammen, wenn sie beisammen sind, auch der Entfernte, der Abgeschiedne lebt uns'. In its immediate context this refers to Ferdinand's assumption of Egmont's mode of living and its persistence through him into the future. But what gives double point to these words is the linguistic closeness of the Egmont and the Klärchen scenes in Act V. On the plane of event their ways may lie apart; but what they *say* in those final scenes, which alternate between his prison of walls and bars and her imprisonment within the bonds of impotence, is a duologue in which the voices are so perfectly attuned, so parallel in their movement, that their separation in space seems, and is meant to seem, of no account. Within the plot her death may indeed lend no support to his; but the manner of it is identical, in the ease and lightness with which the inevitable is finally faced and accepted, in the loving non-attachment which is the mark of complete inner freedom. And there is perhaps no clearer example of Goethe's method of heightening the realistic into the poetic by means of contrac-

tion than her appearance to him in sleep. All the elements of the vision
have appeared before at various points in the action: from the first she
has been associated in Egmont's mind with the restorative powers of nature; with her lullaby she has brought him the soothing release of sleep;
through her 'Soldatenliedchen' she has given expression to her longing
to fight side by side with him for freedom. Now, by a sudden contraction of the parts, all these are concentrated into the 'unexpected and
surprising' symbolism of the vision.

In this conception there is clearly no room for an Alba gloating in the
background over his victim as Schiller would have had him do. Not
only because, as Goethe told Eckermann,[15] such 'cruelty' was alien to his
own conception of Alba, but because the movement in Goethe's mature
works is through tragedy and beyond it.[16] Nor is the tragedy here confined to the clash between Egmont and Alba. We are aware of it at point
after point in the play, for, as in *Tasso* or in *Iphigenie*, what we witness is
not so much a tragedy of action as the tragedy of being. For Goethe
tragedy does not lie on the periphery of existence, in the exceptional case
and the resounding clash, but at its centre. It begins at the point where a
cell in order to grow must divide, and resides in the fact that it is the
characteristic of all life to tend away from symmetry. In the human
sphere it is at the heart of every silent choice in our daily living, in
every renunciation and every farewell, even in every achievement, for all
achievement is at the cost of infinite potentiality. There is a maxim in his
scientific writings[17] which would make the perfect motto for any of his
tragedies from *Egmont* onwards: 'Alles, was wir bös, unglücklich nennen,
kommt daher, dass sie [die Natur] nicht allem Entstehenden Raum geben,
noch weniger ihm Dauer verleihen kann'. It is because his tragedies have
their roots in the natural world that they stir us so deeply. True, they lay
before us the claims of civilized life and the cost at which it is maintained.
But the price paid in renunciation is not at odds with the most fundamental law of nature: the law of compensation, which decrees that
there is no gain without a corresponding loss, that one mode of response
inevitably excludes another because all behaviour, natural and human,
takes place in the dimension of time. In speaking to the moral man in us
Goethe's tragedies at the same time speak to the natural man, and hence,
in the end, compel our entire assent.

In *Egmont* Goethe is using a method which he will use several times
again in portraying tragedy, not only in his plays but in *Die Wahlverwandtschaften* too. What he does is to take some quality of life—freedom,
truth, humanity, poetic imagination, or that irresistible attraction which
we call an affinity—and shows it to us in its pure form, embodied in a

character, or characters, in whom it has become the dominant mode of response. He builds up an action which reveals and illuminates this quality of life from all sides—the impact it makes on the world and the reactions, negative and positive, it calls forth. And he shows us the sacrifice of its purity that life inevitably demands, the limitations which existence inevitably imposes upon its wholeness. Perfect freedom, as Egmont would live it, cannot be maintained in the face of life. In order to preserve it we have to let some of it go—or life will exact its toll. But at the end of *Egmont*, as at the end of his later works, Goethe offers us an apotheosis of the value which has had to suffer in the service of life. It is as if he would say:—Life must go on. Its value transcends that of any of the single values it contains, the claims of which are so often incompatible with its own over-riding claims. But let us not in giving our assent to life be unmindful of the cost. Let the mightiness that is slain, and the loveliness that is brought low, be remembered and cherished in our hearts.

v. Goethe's *Torquato Tasso*

The Tragedy of the Poet

The inexhaustible power of Goethe's *Tasso* derives from the richness and subtlety of its thematic texture. It moves on different levels of experience. Most obviously, and most superficially, it portrays the clash of genius with the conventions of society: the poet's impulsive, often childish temperament, with its sensitive irritability, its bewildering love of effect and admiration, in the face of well-meaning attemps to improve him and to ease the burden of his practical living. Less obviously, and more profoundly, it is concerned with an artist's inadequacy for life itself as distinct from the conventions of society; with his torturing doubts as to his own identity in the face of the undeniable existence and the inescapably tangible achievements of others. And on a still more obscure level Goethe shows the poet's imagination in relation to his craft, shows him fashioning his art out of the raw material of experience. Even then we have not exhausted this play. We have said nothing of the relentless but compassionate insight, the loving irony, with which each of these characters is presented, so that their duality is not inconsistency, but an enrichment of their personality: so that the Princess, for all her wish to keep the relationship on a Platonic basis, has a woman's wistful desire to be loved for her own person and is not a little put out at the suggestion that the poet's passion is in a certain way without content or significance; so that that other Leonore, for wanting a poet at her skirts as well as husband and children, is made complex but not condemned. While Antonio's character, that stumbling-block of the critics, is only unsatisfactory if we demand consistency of action or opinion instead of identity of personality.

As we see or read the play all these are come to meet in one single complexity of experience. But the critic, like the philosopher, is forced back into 'our sad dependence upon time', from which the artist in his work is so supremely immune, and must speak of the parts one after the other. Goethe himself consoles and encourages the critic in his function: 'Die wahre Vermittlerin ist die Kunst. Über Kunst sprechen heisst die Vermittlerin vermitteln wollen, und doch ist uns daher viel Köstliches

erfolgt.'[1] And in wise recognition of the limitations of the word outside
of poetry he indicates the critical method: 'Der Mensch, indem er spricht,
muss für den Augenblick einseitig werden; es gibt keine Mitteilung,
keine Lehre ohne Sonderung.'[2] If I now consider the play from one
aspect only, my intention is not to contract its import by putting it neatly
labelled into a pigeon-hole of the mind, but to follow this pointer and
take one thing at a time.

Many have spoken of the difficulty of venturing upon an artist as a
fictional character.[3] The significant struggles of creation take place in the
artist's workroom and cannot be shown on the stage. The stature of an
artist-hero is not therefore derived from any action we see, but is borrowed from an activity outside the scope of the play. His glory is a reflected
glory. Yet in *Tasso* Goethe has shown that the process of *poetic* creation at
least does not entirely resist dramatic treatment. And by that I do not only
mean that he lets Tasso talk about the process, or show the reflex of it in
his relation to other people. There is all that in the play too. But there is
more. Goethe actually makes us witness the poet creating. Not of course
the whole process. However elastic our idea of drama may be, it would
still be impossible to act the later stages of artistic creation. For no drama
can present the artist as he wrestles with the realization of his vision.
None can overhear his duologue with his medium. The portrayal of this
secret life demands the novelist's craft. Much of the process of artistic creation has nothing glorious or dramatic about it at all. The sharp ecstasy, the
moments of clenched despair, are only the high-lights. Embracing them
is the long patience, between them lie the periods of steady unspectacular
labour. The impossibility for others to share in this working-out process
is almost bound to make them impatient. Even the Duke, despite his injunctions to let Tasso dream his creative dreams undisturbed, chafes at an
activity which baffles him by its apparent lack of results, by its allegiance
to an ideal of perfection which is incommunicable:

> Er kann nicht enden, kann nicht fertig werden,
> Er ändert stets, ruckt langsam weiter vor,
> Steht wieder still, er hintergeht die Hoffnung;
> Unwillig sieht man den Genuss entfernt ...   *265-8*

It is the Princess who, with the eye of love, has understanding for this
fashioning impulse, for the care in the detail, the patient waiting on the
moment's grace, when the long prepared falls into place and assumes
inevitable shape. The circle must be completed as it was conceived in the
vision: 'Es soll sich sein Gedicht zum Ganzen ründen'; and with that rare

understanding for what Keats called the artist's 'readiness to measure time by what is done',[4] she adds:

> es ist die Zeit
> Von einem guten Werke nicht das Mass.   *279-80*

The gestation of a work of art, then, must necessarily take place off-stage; we have to assume it rather than witness it. But the moment of conception, elusive as it is, Goethe has succeeded in putting on the stage. This is assuredly the most difficult moment for an artist to communicate to others. For by contrast with the elaboration and execution which, as Goethe himself has told us,[5] is deliberate and conscious, this moment of inspiration is unconscious and fleeting:

> All unser redlichstes Bemühn
> Glückt nur im unbewussten Momente.[6]

Yet its very brevity makes it the only suitable moment of the creative process for the vehicle of drama which, unlike the novel, cannot render the long mute struggle of the artist to realize his vision in his chosen material.

I do not suggest that Goethe deliberately made poetic inspiration a theme of his play. But since he had chosen a poet for his hero, and the play was 'bone of his bone and flesh of his flesh',[7] what could be more natural than that he should show this poet not only as a temperamental, but as a *creative*, artist? Other men may have difficulty in adapting themselves to the forms of society, they may enjoy the ecstasies, and suffer the torments, of a great love. But just as through all vicissitudes and changing loves Goethe himself remained a poet, what makes Tasso Tasso, as distinct from some creature of wayward moods and fancies, is his creative power. And if Tasso was to become a convincing figure of a poet, if the storm at the end was to break not merely with violent but with tragic intensity, then he had to give evidence of this creative power to our eyes and ears. Hearsay would not be enough. To believe in him as a poet we must see the poet in him at work, so that when we come to the crucial lines,

> Und wenn der Mensch in seiner Qual verstummt,
> Gab mir ein Gott zu sagen, wie ich leide,   *3432-3*

we shall know of our own knowledge that he can do so, not just because he is the author of a world-famous epic, but because we have seen him do it on four occasions already.

On the first of these occasions he has just been crowned by the Princess with a laurel wreath. This symbol calls forth in him those inseparable yet conflicting emotions which are the inevitable response to a ceremony of such dual significance. For, as Goethe says elsewhere,[8] every initiation is both a consecration and a curse. The honour of recognition exalts him; it is entry into a fuller life. But an entry fraught with the pain of responsibility. The fear of being inadequate to its demands causes his strength to ebb, and he begs that the crown be taken from him. But even as he fears he has lost his power of poetry, it returns unannounced and makes its voice heard. He imagines himself hiding his shame and his joy in some remote grove and, thus withdrawn into himself away from the present scene, his attention is diverted to a scene which is taking shape in his mind. He sees himself Narcissus-like in a pool and begins to hold converse with this mirrored self. Rapidly he sketches in the details of a scenic background against which the heroes and poets of antiquity move in concord and mutual regard, rhythmically grouped into frozen life as on the pediment of some ancient temple. It might be the draft for a poem entitled 'The Coming of an Unknown Poet to the Elysian Fields'.

The second occasion is after he has been shaken out of his idyllic existence and brought up against the solid reality of the world of affairs by the arrival of Antonio. In the face of Antonio's substantial achievements, so tangible, so undeniably 'there', Tasso's own imaginings seem airy and ineffectual, and he has agonizing doubts as to his own existence. And yet it is in one of these fabrications of the mind that he takes refuge from his fear, not indeed as a mere escape into some private day-dream, but in evocation of a fantasy of universal import, in which every creature has its place and feels its own intrinsic worth. He draws a picture of the reality of the Golden Age, with a tender attention to detail which implies a conception already well advanced in the shaping.

Yet a third and a fourth time do we see Tasso forced back into poetic conception in order to escape from a reality which obtrudes itself harshly upon him. But unlike the first two these might well be mistaken for practical projects. For when Tasso tells the Princess of his plan for going home to his sister in the disguise of a pilgrim, or when, as the prospect of staying suddenly opens up before him, he begs to be sent as caretaker to some remote country-seat, his eyes are apparently turned to the immediate future, not to some past Golden Age or to some timeless Elysium. In these two dramatic scenes there is a busy activity which is in contrast to the chiselled movement of the Elysian Fields or the still life of the Golden Age. But this is only because the aggravation of the conflict and the impetus of the dramatic action have forced Tasso out of his mood of contemplation into the necessity of changing his condition. In both these later passages the initial impulse to take practical steps may be genuine enough; but before he knows where he is, he is off and away on a poetic flight, in which his intoxication with the images as they arise ousts all practical considerations from his mind.

In all these passages Goethe uncovers both the secret impulse of creation and something of its process. They all have certain characteristics in common, and if we could discover something of the mental processes involved we might be in a position to interpret the final passage of the play, which is of the same order of imaginative thought as these, yet has often been deemed unsatisfactory. And it might also help to throw more light on the poet's power, claimed by Tasso, and by Goethe, to ease his pain by ‘telling’ it.

The starting-point in each case is a personal feeling, even an emotion of great intensity. But at some moment it is no longer this personal emotion which guides Tasso's thought and governs the irruption of his images. For the abundance of the imagery, its elaboration, goes far beyond what is necessary for the communication of his personal emotion or intention. He relates details of Elysium which have no direct bearing on the situation in the garden at Belriguardo and are in strange contrast to his own feelings of unworthiness and impotence. He does this again when, reminded by the Princess of the ban which still forbids his return home, he tells her of his plan to steal back in disguise:

> Du warnest recht, ich hab' es schon bedacht.
> Verkleidet geh' ich hin, den armen Rock
> Des Pilgers oder Schäfers zieh' ich an.
> Ich schleiche durch die Stadt, wo die Bewegung
> Der Tausende den Einen leicht verbirgt.   3140-4

So far his remarks are in answer to her objections and on a purely practical plane. But then the images well up unsought in rapid succession. He finds a boat ‘mit willig guten Leuten’ to take him across the bay. That they are ‘willig und gut’ is relevant to *his* purpose. But there was no need to add that they are farmers come to market and now returning home, ‘Leute von Sorrent’. This reveals an interest in *their* purpose, in them and their doings for their own sake. And now the drama of this stealthy return has laid complete hold on his imagination. The images come crowding thick and fast, rich and precise:

> Im Schiffe bin ich still, und trete dann
> Auch schweigend an das Land . . .   3152-3

It is a ‘Spinnerin’ who shows him the way, the path climbs uphill, the children run alongside and stare at his wild hair, he comes at last to the threshold, the door stands open—without doubt the welcome was shaping in his mind, but the Princess breaks in upon it.

Another characteristic of these passages is a delight in recounting details of things observed with the impartial, loving, gaze of the artist, with what Rilke calls 'Bereitschaft zu unwählerischem Schauen'.[9] The ordinary man selects for observation only those things which are important for his own needs or ends. For the artist the whole world is grist to his mill:

> Was die Geschichte reicht, das Leben gibt,
> Sein Busen nimmt es gleich und willig auf.   *161-2*

The way the grass sprouts hardily through every chink in the stones and has to be as ruthlessly removed; the shining smoothness of marble floors; the effect of damp on pictures; the way the lemon trees are covered against the frost in autumn; the clean sand on the bed of a gently flowing river; the twist of a snake as it glides silently away into the grass: all these Tasso has lingered over and loved for themselves. He has 'looked upon the Sun, the Moon, the Stars, the Earth and its contents, as materials to form greater things'.[10]

These images are made up of details long since observed, perhaps even consciously elaborated, and then 'forgotten', suspended in the reservoir of memory. Tasso did not respond immediately to the stimulus of what he perceived. It was the gardener who was moved to action and covered the lemon trees. Tasso himself has the characteristic power of the artist to delay his response, to store away this impression along with countless others, as Goethe stocked his 'dramatische und epische Vorratskammer' with impressions of all kinds, good or bad, trivial or otherwise.[11] There they have remained latent until, activated by some chance stimulus, they emerge as coherent parts of a 'wondrous new whole'.[12] 'Das Ganze schoss von allen Seiten zusammen', as Goethe wrote of the conception of his *Werther*,[13] 'und ward eine solide Masse, wie das Wasser im Gefäss, das eben auf dem Punkte des Gefrierens steht, durch die geringste Erschütterung sogleich in ein festes Eis verwandelt wird.'

What, then, brings these images out of store if it is not the requirements of Tasso's immediate situation? For they do not arise at random and their arrangement is not chaotic. On the contrary their emergence is governed by the necessities of an artistic form, a vision which his mind has perceived. And it is this new unity which determines their selection. The actual moment of inspiration seems to depend on chance. The poet's imagination may be stirred by the magic of a phrase which, like a magnet, draws latent images into patterned activity. The mere mention of the Golden Age, a phrase evocative of so many associations for the poet, is enough to displace, or at least lift him beyond the range of, purely personal feelings. Once the process is set going, one image calls up another in rapid succession. A striking example is in his vision of the pilgrim, where it is clearly the word Sorrent—the farmers in the boat come from there—which gives further impetus and a new direction to the story he is making. The word Sorrent at once calls up his sister, and he adds with apparent inconsequence:

> Denn ich muss nach Sorrent hinüber eilen.
> Dort wohnet meine Schwester ... *3149-50*

We now realize what we may have suspected already: this is no carefully laid plan of action he is unfolding; he is making it up as he goes along.

The vision of Elysium seems to take shape in his mind from the moment he imagines himself mirrored in a pool. The dramatic action is held up while he elaborates what he sees reflected in this magic surface:

> Und zeigt mir ungefähr ein klarer Brunnen
> In seinem reinen Spiegel einen Mann,
> Der wunderbar bekränzt im Widerschein
> Des Himmels zwischen Bäumen, zwischen Felsen
> Nachdenkend ruht: so scheint es mir, ich sehe
> Elysium auf dieser Zauberfläche
> Gebildet. *532-8*

Tasso could scarcely have found a more appropriate image than this mirrored reflection of a strange, becrowned, self to symbolize the separation which now takes place within him between the man who suffers and rejoices and the creative mind which fashions. And a similar incentive to poetic creation is the thought of himself in disguise. Again, as in a mirror, he catches sight of himself as though he were someone else, and his attention is diverted from the pain of his own impending departure to the activities of this pilgrim—or shepherd—it does not matter which. This outcast wanderer, who is himself and not himself, begins to move and speak and live an independent life.

This tendency to see himself as well as to be himself accounts for the ease with which he falls into imagined dialogue, or rather into the form of the direct question which invites elaboration into dialogue if the conception is ever worked out:

> Still bedenk ich mich und frage,
> Wer mag der Abgeschiedne sein? Der Jüngling
> Aus der vergangnen Zeit? So schön bekränzt?
> Wer sagt mir seinen Namen? Sein Verdienst?   *538-41*

or again:

> und an dem Tore frag' ich:
> Wo wohnt Cornelia? Zeigt mir es an!
> Cornelia Sersale?   *3154-6*

All this implies a switch of attention from the practical situation to the fashioning of an imagined one, from the personal plane to the artistic plane. Or we may think of it as the gradual insinuation of another interest until it floods the mind and dominates the field of vision.

Now if we contrast these poetic visions of Tasso with apparently similar descriptions by other persons in the play we notice none of these characteristics. Listen to Leonore describing the gardens of Belriguardo:

> .. schwankend wiegen
> Im Morgenwinde sich die jungen Zweige.
> Die Blumen von den Beeten schauen uns
> Mit ihren Kinderaugen freundlich an.
> Der Gärtner deckt getrost das Winterhaus
> Schon der Citronen und Orangen ab,
> Der blaue Himmel ruhet über uns,
> Und an dem Horizonte löst der Schnee
> Der fernen Berge sich in leisen Duft.   *31-9*

The contrast with Tasso's imagined picture of a garden is the more marked because they mention the same things: the care of the lemon trees, the flowers in the beds. It is the technique that is different. Leonore's is a lively appreciation by a sensitive mind of things there and then present to the eye. The quality of delayed response to impressions is completely absent. As she sees, so she says it. Tasso, on the other hand, describes things which are not what he *now* sees. The fulness of *her* heart impels her 'sogleich zu sagen, was ich lebhaft fühle'. Tasso is not content to say what he is feeling immediately. He begins with that; but he fashions it into a whole wrought of old experiences and images, still charged with feeling, but developed and transformed and used in a new context. She describes the spring that is around her. Spring must be around him too since the action of the play lasts only one day. But his poetic conception demands the melancholy of autumn, and so remembered images leap up all ready

to drop into place. It is doubtless his own mood of imminent departure
which suggests the autumnal tone. But it has artistic value for his poetic
conception, for in this forlorn country-seat it must, we feel, be eternally
autumn.
The Princess, less swayed by immediate impressions than Leonore,
utters her most moving words when she looks into the long emptiness of
the future without Tasso:

> ... allein ich fühle schon
> Den langen ausgedehnten Schmerz der Tage, wenn
> Ich nun entbehren soll, was mich erfreute.
> Die Sonne hebt von meinen Augenlidern
> Nicht mehr sein schön verklärtes Traumbild auf;
> Die Hoffnung ihn zu sehen füllt nicht mehr
> Den kaum erwachten Geist mit froher Sehnsucht;
> Mein erster Blick hinab in unsre Gärten
> Sucht' ihn vergebens in dem Tau der Schatten.   *1854-62*

This is exquisite poetry, but it is Goethe's poetry, not hers. Despite her
poignant insight, despite her delicate imagery, this remains a personal
lament, a direct voicing of her fear, an unburdening of herself. She
chooses images which illuminate her own immediate emotion. There
is no switch of attention from the personal to the artistic plane. Tasso
may start with the personal, with the language of impulse and desire:

> Lass mich in Belriguardo hier, versetze
> Mich nach Consandoli, wohin du willst!
> Es hat der Fürst so manches schöne Schloss,
> So manchen Garten ...   *3188-91*

But then, perhaps with the rhetorical repetition of the indeterminate
'manch', the ear detects a different temper, a relaxation of the personal
tension, the rising of another excitement. The joy in repetition and symmetry, his sense of craftsmanship, is taking hold of him:

> ... so manches schöne Schloss,
> So manchen Garten, der das ganze Jahr
> Gewartet wird, und ihr betretet kaum
> Ihn Einen Tag, vielleicht nur Eine Stunde.   *3190-3*

And as the reality of this rarely visited residence presses in upon him,
unkempt, forlorn, needing care—'der vielleicht jetzt ohne Sorge liegt'
—there is a freer quality in the images, a leisurely spreading into detail.
They become not impersonal but more than personal; they widen from

the particular to the universal. Tasso manifests the poet's power of being other than himself and more than himself. Leonore's flowers 'schauen uns mit ihren Kinderaugen freundlich an'. In the manner of Heine, she endows them with human characteristics—a wonderfully subtle touch, in perfect keeping with her urban sophistication. Tasso does more than transfer his own life to the flowers. He feels his way into their life:

> Es sollen schöne Blumen in den Beeten
> Die breiten Wurzeln schlagen. *3201-2*

This is more than observation; it is participation in the plant-process. He has too the power of living in the soul of a character different from his own. And so he paints the unforgettable picture of the servant inside the palace, opening the windows at the right time, lightly flicking the dust from the stucco-work with his feather brush. This is not Tasso. He will never for very long devote himself to the care of gardens and pictures. When some new enthusiasm breaks he will forget like a child, not tired of the old, but captivated by the new. But he knows what it is like to make this devoted care the content of one's life; and this image of a faithful retainer, caring for garden and interior against the day when its owners will descend for a brief unexpected visit, is a universal, an eternal, image.

If these visions of Tasso are not yet poems, they are the drafts of poems. They reveal the characteristic qualities of the poetic mode of thought. Production may or may not follow, but this power to be impregnated is the essence of the artist: 'Der Meister stellt sein Werk mit wenigen Strichen als fertig dar: ausgeführt oder nicht, schon ist es vollendet.'[14] There is an authentic ring about Tasso's moments of inspiration, and it is not difficult to recognize in them Goethe's own manner of creation as he has described it in *Dichtung und Wahrheit*:[15] the almost unceasing flow of inspiration, the power to conceive under the full impact of experience, his recourse to his shaping power in moments of difficulty, his way of visualizing everything in dramatic scenes, the ease with which he converted 'Selbstgespräch' into 'Zwiegespräch'—he tells us that the composition of *Werther* was a development of his habit of calling up in imagination some person of his acquaintance, asking him to take a chair, walking up and down in front of him, and conducting an argument[16]—his frequent association of the aesthetic experience with a mirror,[17] his love of disguise, the dressing-up game, which was at once a symbol of the many characters in whom he lived and a device for entering into their personalities. Rarely has any poet permitted such insight into the act of creation as Goethe has done in these visions of Tasso. For in his letters or diaries, in his autobiography, he can only tell us *about* the act, but here, through his poetry, he lets us share it.

This is not true of Tasso's monologues. Neither there, nor in those painfully naked speeches after the carriage wheels have sounded the finality of parting, do we hear that more than personal, that universal, note. Tasso is still 'using his imagination'. There is a similar tendency to make much out of little, to work up slight material into fantastic fabrications, to 'create' in the popular, vulgar, sense. A word is enough to throw him into ecstasy or despair and 'any little vexation grows in five minutes into a theme for Sophocles'.[18] But there are profound differences. In his monologues the images do not derive from that latent poetic store on which he drew for his visions. The imperative which summons them to life is not a form he has glimpsed; they arise at the service of his own immediate ends and emotions. And they are not lingered over for their own sake. There is no entering into the life of other things, no doorway out of himself, but a turning inwards, whether in joy or in grief. Above all, these monologues depend for their understanding on a full knowledge of Tasso's present situation, whereas in the visions experience has been transformed into something which stands, or if completed could stand, in its own right, and be understood without reference to Tasso's life.

The monologues and the visions do in fact reveal similar mental processes, but at work on different material and at the service of a different impulse. In the monologues his phantasy works on the material of real life. He treats of real people—Antonio, Leonore, the Princess— and of his personal relation to them. And he assumes that he has the same sovereign control over them as over the creatures of his imagination, the gardener, the pilgrim:

> Dann soll geschehn was er sich denken mag.   *2128*

He arbitrarily assigns motives to their actions and sees connections between events where none exist. But outward reality refuses to be thus coerced into shape by phantasy. It has its own intractable independence which normally exercises a beneficial friction upon the mind of the individual. Tasso, to avoid this painful experience, sometimes withdraws into his own inner world, where there is none to gainsay him or to obtrude unwelcome facts upon him, where he can resolve all his doubts and arrange situations to his own liking. The danger is that he will withdraw too often and too far; that one day solitude will beckon with honeyed tones,

> ... komm, ich löse
> Die neu erregten Zweifel deiner Brust,   *754-5*

and that when he would turn again to the world of people and things the doors of his mind will have closed upon it for ever.

But it is not in his visions that he runs this danger. Here, where he is dealing with the figments of his imagination, he can legitimately dispose of his material as he will. Here he can fulfil his function as a poet by perceiving the hidden relations between things instead of spoiling his life as a man by establishing arbitrary connections between them. Here, as he points out to Leonore (558-61), he does not mistake the nature of outward reality, does not twist it to his own purpose. And there is a discipline, though it is not that of outward reality, a discipline imposed by the requirements of the form he has conceived, a discipline of craftsmanship. This is what makes these 'escapes' different from any other escape into the world of phantasy. Each of his visions begins with a phrase which implies flight. But it is flight to some kingdom of the mind which he then fashions in such a way that it is communicable and desirable to others. The Princess may say:

> . . . mehr
> Und mehr verwöhnt sich das Gemüt, und strebt
> Die goldne Zeit, die ihm von aussen mangelt,
> In seinem Innern wieder herzustellen.   *973-6*

Yet the vision of the Golden Age which follows immediately on these words is no private phantasy, but one 'nach der sich *jedes* Herz vergebens sehnt', a phantasy of universal appeal. So that however much the underlying impulse may be to escape to some inland territory, these visions hold the possibility of a return to outer reality from the moment he becomes absorbed in fashioning them.

In the monologues his phantasy runs riot, but is not fashioned. Imagination is there in plenty, but not the shaping spirit of it. Tasso is not making or conceiving poetry. For this reason they are on *the same plane of poetic expression* as the speeches of the other characters, however different their content. His monologues may be full of 'Gedanken ohne Mass und Ordnung', but in them Tasso is expressing himself as a character like any other, and what he says affects the dramatic action directly. He is the man, centred on his own joys, griefs, and grievances. In his visions he is the creative artist, and what he says is ineffectual as far as the impetus of the action is concerned. Like the rest of the characters, Tasso in his monologues expresses himself in fine poetry. But it is Goethe's poetry and not his. In the visions it is Tasso's poetry as well as Goethe's, poetry within the poetry, 'Poesie der Poesie'.

The difference is important because of the words, 'Gab mir ein Gott zu sagen, wie ich leide', and the implied release which comes from poetic utterance. Tasso's words at this point are immortal poetry; but they are also the dramatic crux of the play, the fulfilment of all that has gone before and, in their full meaning, the key to the final lines. It is essential to know what kind of utterance brings release. Certainly not the utterance of the monologues. However long he may go on unburdening himself in this way, giving voice to the chaotic fancies which teem in his overwrought brain, he will find no release. Freedom from an emotion comes when we put it outside ourselves, transform it into an object of our contemplation. It must be in some measure removed from us, so that although we still feel it we are not engulfed by it. But in the monologues the pain grows inside Tasso until the pain is Tasso and Tasso is the pain. He is the victim of his emotion; *it* manages him, *it* speaks out of him. In the visions it is *he* who speaks. He becomes master of his emotion by virtue of being able to shape it. There is in these passages a quality of freedom, an isolation of the spirit as it transmutes the passions which are its material. Here is the tranquillity which Wordsworth recognized as a condition of the creative mood, though the 'emotion' is still fresh and not 'recollected'. In thus letting Tasso conceive poetry under the full impact of emotion Goethe may be giving a faithful reflection of his own youthful urge to give immediate shape to experience:[19] these visions may, in other words, be a supreme naturalism, a unique case in which for a brief moment poetry is one with life. Or he may be taking advantage of the dramatic convention which allows events to be telescoped in time. But these are idle speculations. For what matters is the quality of the creative mood, not the lapse of time. The precise rôle of the time factor emerges clearly in the phrase of Schiller, which Wordsworth was echoing:[20] 'Aus der sanftern und *fernenden* Erinnerung mag er dichten'. Time lends distance. That is the advantage for the poet of remembered experience. But this distance can be obtained in other ways. For time in itself has no healing property. It may *take* time, but the 'tranquillizing' power is in *activity*, in the new interests which invade us, displacing old experience from the forefront of consciousness.

The poet is specially favoured among men in having an ever-present activity which does not exactly displace his manifold experiences, but incorporates them into a wider vision: the activity of his craft. This activity is in itself a source of emotion, of pain when words refuse to take the exact shape of his vision, when language seems 'unüberwindlich',[21] of rapture when the images flood him unsought, and he knows instinctively that the words are right. For to the poet words are not only an instrument of the intellect. They are a 'passion and a power'. He finds them

'sweet for their own sakes',[22] and 'looks upon fine phrases like a lover'.[23]
Of Tasso's delight in 'Melodie und Rede' we have evidence in plenty:

> Es soll das Estrich blank und reinlich glänzen;
> Es soll kein Stein, kein Ziegel sich verrücken;
> Es soll kein Gras aus einer Ritze keimen!   *3209-11*

What else is this but love of incantation, sheer delight in mouthing beautiful phrases and being carried away by the music of their sound? It is when this excitement of fashioning in words takes hold of him that his experience recedes from him as man and beckons to him as artist. The magic of words is the poet's means of distancing his human experience, allowing him to see it through a transparent veil.

It is not then *sagen* in the sense of confession that brings him release, not *sagen* as Leonore means it:

> Drängt mich doch das volle Herz
> Sogleich zu sagen was ich lebhaft fühle;   *86-7*

but *sagen* with all the incantatory associations of 'singen und sagen', *sagen* in the sense of *bilden*. 'Bilde, Künstler! rede nicht!'[24] *Bilden* and *sagen* are as implicitly synonymous for Goethe as they are explicitly synonymous for Rilke:

> O alter Fluch der Dichter,
> Die sich beklagen, wo sie sagen sollten,
> Die immer urteilen über ihr Gefühl
> Statt es zu bilden.[25]

Sich beklagen is what Tasso does in his monologues; *bilden* is what he does in his visions. To overlook the difference is not only to mistake the nature of poetic creation; it is to mistake the nature of the final lines of the play and to obscure the real source of his power to transmute his sufferings. For it is when he ceases to lament and begins the telling of the lament, ceases to pour out his feeling and begins to shape it, that the night of his tragedy lifts and Tasso approaches what Goethe calls his 'Verklärung'.[26]

It is this switch from one plane of poetic expression to another which makes for the very real difficulty of interpreting the end. Critics, from A.W. Schlegel and Platen onwards, have found it inconclusive.[27] Is it a tragedy or not? Is Tasso's clinging to Antonio a happy omen for the future? Or is it but a momentary lifting of the curtain before madness descends upon him for ever? Some have even wished the final lines away altogether and would have had Goethe stop with Tasso's recognition of his gift of song. But Goethe could not stop there, for his play was not finished. To complete it he shows this recognition issuing in action. No-where in the play have we been asked to take Tasso's poetic gift on trust, and Goethe does not ask us to do so now. He shows him in the very act of telling in poetry what he has suffered as a man.

Yet surprisingly enough this final vision does not develop simply out of the events of the catastrophe. Tasso is not working up into poetry his immediate experience of the fatal embrace and the tragedy of parting, bitter as that is. The mood is not, as we might perhaps expect, an elegiac mood of desolate abandonment. It is rather a stark mood of piercing recognition, and the tragedy is that of a man who, as the solid reality of familiar circumstance shakes beneath his feet, is forced to discover the reality of his own being. Self-knowledge, painfully and dangerously acquired—dangerously because Tasso has been to the brink of self-loss to discover it—that is the content of this vision. And for the personal experience which forms the stuff of it, we have to look not only to the speeches immediately preceding it, but back to the beginning of the play. For the fear of having no identity is a fear on which his thought has brooded at its deepest level since he first saw Antonio, set squarely upon the point of existence around which the poet hovers ineffectually:[28]

> Sein Wesen, seine Worte haben mich
> So wunderbar getroffen, dass ich mehr
> Als je mich doppelt fühle ...   763-5
> ... ich fürchtete
> Wie Echo an den Felsen zu verschwinden
> Ein Wiederhall, ein Nichts mich zu verlieren.   798-800

This fear of being nothing, of wondering, among all the identities he is capable of filling, which is his own, this is Tasso's most deep-seated problem. It becomes urgent whenever human experience presses close in upon him, forcing him to consider where his own centre lies. It is echoed in Act IV—'ich bin nicht mehr ich selbst'—'ich kenne mich nicht mehr'—and now most poignantly after the catastrophe. Note the agonized, be-wildered, groping for a sense of identity which alone can give signifi-cance to the thousand aspects of himself:

> Und bin ich denn so elend wie ich scheine?
> Bin ich so schwach wie ich vor dir mich zeige?
> Ist alles denn verloren? Hat der Schmerz,
> Als schütterte der Boden, das Gebäude
> In einen grausen Haufen Schutt verwandelt?
> Ist kein Talent mehr übrig, tausendfältig
> Mich zu zerstreun, zu unterstützen?

> Ist alle Kraft verloschen, die sich sonst
> In meinem Busen regte? Bin ich Nichts,
> Ganz Nichts geworden?
> Nein, es ist alles da und ich bin nichts!   *3407-17*

The heart of Tasso's tragedy is the dual consciousness revealed in this last line. When he thinks of himself as an object, all the attributes of himself are still there—in the third person: '*es ist alles da*'. But the continuous identity which gives them substantiality and weight, the sense of 'I', that is gone: '*es ist alles da und ich bin nichts*'. This crucial experience, here expressed directly in personal accents of pain and terror, is in the last lines of the play wrought into a poetic image. The poet's nature has the lability of the wave, its power of reflecting other identities:

> In dieser Woge spiegelte so schön
> Die Sonne sich, es ruhten die Gestirne
> An dieser Brust, die zärtlich sich bewegte.   *3442-4*

Tasso imagines that even when the storm sweeps up he can retain this wave-like nature, pliable, yielding, resilient, and change his shape and not be destroyed:

> Sie sendet ihren Sturm, die Welle flieht
> Und schwankt und schwillt und beugt sich schäumend über. *3440-1*

As long as he thinks of his poet's nature he can speak of himself as a wave in the remoteness of the third person. But then out of the depths comes the cry of self-loss, the immediacy of 'I':

> Ich kenne mich in der Gefahr nicht mehr.   *3446*

In a sudden veering of perspective he has seen the stormy scene from another, from a fixed, angle; from being a wave he has become a mariner in a foundering ship. His identity is not only limitless and ever-changing. However much as a poet he can reflect other identities, there is also this Tasso who says 'I', a creature of impulse, whose actions have repercussions in the outside world. Unlike the wave, this creature is of finite, unchanging, shape and can be destroyed by the storm; and as the ship of his existence shivers and splits, he clutches at the one reality which remains:

> So klammert sich der Schiffer endlich noch
> Am Felsen fest, an dem er scheitern sollte.   *3452-3*

These lines are spoken to Antonio and must, of course, refer to him.

But to say that the rock 'stands for' Antonio sets limits to the potency of the image, making it sound a single note instead of a chord of resonant meanings. As nothingness threatened to engulf him, Tasso heard the voice of Antonio bidding him recognize his own nature. The image of the mariner clinging to the rock is the concrete sensuous expression of his acceptance of that reminder. Yet it is surely more. In following Antonio's lead he discovers that, whatever else is stripped from him, the poet still remains—'Nur eines bleibt'; and so he comes to this ineradicable core of sensitivity, irritability, impulsiveness, and fertile imagination, to the identity which, for good or ill, he has been given, the naked irreducible minimum of himself when all else has gone; in fact to the rock of himself, to which he must cling if he is not to be lost, although it is on this rock as much as on Antonio that he has foundered. The actor's problem is to look at Antonio and to speak to Antonio, but to let his rapt and brooding gaze embrace much more:

> Er scheint uns anzusehn, und Geister mögen
> An unsrer Stelle seltsam ihm erscheinen.   *171-2*

How do we recognize this transition from one plane of poetic expression to another? By the same signs as before. Here is the same switch from the personal-practical plane—from the tone of 'allein bedenk, und überhebe nicht Dich deiner Kraft'—to absorption in the images for their poetic significance; the same quality of delayed response to an earlier stimulus; the same inner coherence which betokens unity of conception. The image of sea and rock and shipwrecked mariner which now 'comes' to Tasso is single, however complex. Its component parts have been in suspension in his mind ever since that first encounter with Antonio in Act II. Now the moment is ripe for these fragments to emerge in a new combination. The old image of constancy in the midst of instability, applied originally to Antonio only,

> Und auf des Lebens leicht bewegter Woge
> Bleibt dir ein stetes Herz,   *1255-6*

reappears, deepened and enriched, as a metaphor expressing the difference between himself and Antonio:

> Die mächtige Natur
> Die diesen Felsen gründete, hat auch
> Der Welle die Beweglichkeit gegeben;   *3437-9*

while the image of a ship in full sail with which Antonio had taunted him —'Du gehst mit vollen Segeln' (*1289*)—is modified by Tasso's present suffering and elaborated into the symbol of the shipwrecked mariner.[29] We may recognize the authentic voice of poetry in the intrepid leap from one image to another, from third person to first, in the to and fro between past and present. Here is that annulling of person and time which is common to dream and symbol, and is a mark of poetry when it is 'neat'[30] and undiluted by logical forms of thought.

Far from being an unconvincing poetic symbol appended by Goethe to the already finished action of the play, these last lines are an integral part of it. The inner and inevitable reason for their being there is to show Tasso doing what he had just said he could do: 'utter in song how he suffers'. Nevertheless they are the action of Tasso the poet, not of Tasso the man. The two levels of poetic expression on which he has moved throughout the play are merged into one in this last vision. For if the stuff of it is the whole experience through which he has passed, the form in which he utters it is the form of poetry. In this sense time stands still while he speaks. There is no further development on the plane of personal emotion and personal relationship. 'Verschwunden ist der Glanz, entflohn die Ruhe,' does not mark a revulsion of mood, a return of despair. It falls within the image he is creating and is the poetic expression of what did happen to him in the catastrophe. The same is true of 'Ich fasse dich mit beiden Armen an'. These words are not the accompaniment of a sudden gesture by which Tasso clutches at Antonio; nor are they a resolution for the future. Their tense, if any, is the historic present, for they refer to an experience already past: his acceptance of Antonio's support and injunction.

If we understand this orientation to the past, certain persistent problems of criticism do not arise. Whether Tasso and Antonio now become firm friends, whether Tasso is henceforth a reformed character, these questions are no affair of the play. It does not answer them; more important, it does not invite us to ask them. Because we know so much about Goethe himself, it is tempting to interpret the play out of that knowledge. But it can be more confusing than helpful, and in any case the poem must stand or fall by its own power to convince. Because it is the intention of the Duke to mould Tasso's character, this does not mean that it is the deeper intention of the play. And because Leonore observes that Tasso and Antonio are complementary opposites, this does not mean that we are to see them welded into one at the end. If, as critics have maintained, Goethe intended the last two lines to symbolize the fusion of the poet with the man of affairs, the 'assimilation' of the one by the other, then the image he chose was very inapt. An image may not be restricted to one meaning; but we are not therefore free to violate its nature. To let it speak to us is one thing; to put words into its mouth is another. It would be frivolous to comment on either the digestibility of rock or the digestive powers of sailors. But I have yet to hear of any mariner assimilating the rock on which his ship founders or, alternatively, being assimilated by it. All he does is to cling to it in his extremity. There is no hint in the play of Tasso assimilating any of Antonio's virtues. He remains Tasso to the end. True, he experiences a catharsis. But one catharsis does not make a 'Bildung'. It may well be that he will again be shaken to his foundations, that he will again touch these same or deeper depths, and in his need find only his power of song. Tasso's catharsis, unlike that of Orest, is essentially the catharsis of an artist. With his poet's eye he has penetrated to the inmost recesses of his being, and he is able to fashion this self-knowledge into poetry. In this sense there is an interpenetration of art and experience which may make him the greater artist. But whether it will make him a better man, whether it will affect his day to day living, is a question which is left entirely open.

Tasso experiences a catharsis; but the tragedy is not thereby mitigated. Its sting remains, for him and for us. Nothing is altered in the tragic facts. Whether the Princess returns or not, things can never be the same again. Something precious is irretrievably lost. Lost through his fault and, even more bitter knowledge, through his fate. His failure is and remains complete. Nor are Tasso's emotions changed in kind or lessened in degree. He has been close enough to annihilation to know its terrors, and the knowledge will remain with him. What *is* affected is the quality of his total experience. 'Vergleiche dich', Antonio says; and when Tasso follows this advice as Antonio means it, and looks in history for others who have suffered as he suffers, he can find no answer and no comfort. It is only when he interprets the 'Vergleiche dich' as a poet can, when his vision widens and he re-experiences his tragedy in images, that the tension is relaxed. It is through the mystery of words that the change is worked. Release comes—release, not comfort—when he puts his fate outside himself, making it permanent and immutable by fashioning it in a substance not himself, that is, in the medium of language. Through Tasso we understand

> ... wie Schicksal in die Verse eingeht
> Und nicht zurückkommt, wie es drinnen Bild wird.[31]

The tragic impression is immeasurably deepened if we recognize the extent to which Goethe has portrayed Tasso as a *creative* artist, shown the positive as well as the negative aspect of his imagination, its fruitful as well as its destructive power. Only then do we realise how inextricably linked

D

in him are *Schicksal* and *Schuld*. His fate is the nature that is given to him, his poet's nature. But within limits he commands the use of it, and herein lies the possibility of guilt. This was essentially Goethe's view of tragedy, of life itself, the interweaving of fate and fault; and Tasso, like Goethe's other heroes, is 'halbverschuldet', 'unschuldig-schuldig'. When he was finishing the play Goethe wrote to Herder[32] that he was now free of all desire to compose a work as 'konsequent' as Tasso. Whatever he himself may have meant by *konsequent*, it perfectly describes the relentless logic of the sequence of events, the remorseless necessity of the tragic circle. There is a stringent economy in the way Goethe has linked Tasso's gift of imagination with his guilt. The power by which he creates and which is his strength, this same power, used inappropriately, is his undoing; and again it is this same power which ultimately brings him illumination and release.

In a well-known letter[33] Keats spoke of the chameleon poet, an image which Goethe also used of himself: 'As to the poetical Character itself . . . it is not itself—it has no self—It is every thing and nothing . . . A Poet is the most unpoetical of anything in existence, because he has no Identity —he is continually informing and filling some other body. The Sun, the Moon, the Sea, and men and women, who are creatures of impulse, are poetical, and have about them an unchangeable attribute; the poet has none, no identity . . .' This unpoetical creature, with his varying identities, Goethe has succeeded in putting on the stage. But he has done more. He has shown him also as a creature of impulse, who at any moment may be challenged to find among all his varying identities a continuous identity which lends them coherence. In dramatic form he has presented the poet's dual consciousness: its delights, its dangers and its terrors, and—in a moment of intense singleness of vision—its power of illuminating release.

VI. Goethe's *Faust*

A Morphological Approach

WHEN in January 1825[1] Goethe received a duty-call from one of the many young Englishmen then living in Weimar, he enquired of him in the course of conversation what he had read of German literature. '*Egmont* and *Tasso* with much pleasure', came the answer, 'and just now I am reading *Faust*'. Then, with an understatement characteristically English, he continued: 'But I find it just a little difficult'. At this Goethe chuckled. 'Indeed', he said, 'I would scarcely have advised you to go on to *Faust*! It's crazy stuff, and transcends all ordinary forms of feeling. But since you've embarked on it of your own accord without first consulting me, it's for you to see how you get through it.'

'Wie Sie *durchkommen*'! The very word, with its sinister implications of getting through—or not getting through—examinations, is bound to leave on the reader's mind a sense of impending trials if not necessarily of disaster. And there are surely few works of literature which present the critic with such problems as does Goethe's *Faust*. Even its creator allowed that it was almost as 'incommensurable' as Nature herself.[2] There it stands, a mixture of tender lyricism and stark tragedy, of magic opera and realistic drama, of cosmic philosophy and unconscious symbolism, stubbornly resistant to traditional canons of literary criticism. Whether we come to it from Shakespeare or from the Greeks, from Racine or from Ibsen, measuring it by forms alien to its own, or whether we apply to it preconceived notions of what a drama or a tragedy ought to be, it remains equally intractable, defying every attempt to place it within accepted categories, one of the gigantic monuments of world-literature, refusing sphinx-like to disclose the secret of its 'law'.

Nor, at first sight, is Goethe himself very helpful in offering us a clue to its riddle. It is of no use at all, if we are to believe what he once said in the presence of Eckermann,[3] trying to find some central 'idea' which would explain everything and might serve the student as a thread to guide him through all the intricacies of its labyrinth. The words with which Goethe repudiates and ridicules attempts to either read out, or read in, any such 'idea' are unambiguous: 'And what a fine thing it would have turned out to be if I had tried to string a life as rich, motley, and as utterly diverse, as that I have displayed in *Faust*, on the thin and meagre thread of a single idea running through the whole.'

Must the reader, then, be content just to enjoy the various parts of this vast poem singly, each for itself and without reference to the whole? Not if we are to appeal to Goethe's own authority elsewhere. For in the second of his more important pronouncements on *Faust*, that long conversation with the historian, Luden, in 1806[4] which at first sight so blatantly contradicts, but in reality so perfectly supplements, the statements recorded by Eckermann, he expressly rejected the suggestion that the play might, perhaps, best be appreciated piecemeal. 'But that's a paltry, a fragmentary, sort of interest', he retorted. '*Faust* does after all possess interest of a higher kind—the idea, that is to say, which inspired the poet and binds all the individual parts of the poem into a whole, furnishing the law for each and every one, and apportioning to each its due and proper importance.'

The 'idea' of *Faust*! Is it not strange that, at a time when nothing of it had as yet appeared in print except the *Fragment* of 1790, he should have insisted to Luden that there resides in it an idea so dominant and so unifying that it ought to be apparent even from the as yet unfinished torso? And that then, almost twenty years after the publication of *Faust, Part I*, and with the *Second Part* nearing completion, he should have so categorically denied it any such idea at all? Is this just another of those many contradictions Goethe's critics are always ready to find in him? Or is it not rather one of those cases where—to quote from another conversation with Eckermann[5]—'the imperfections and inadequacy of language have caused the spread of errors and false opinions which at a later date are not so easy to overcome'? For the word 'idea' is in fact used in a different sense in each of the two contexts, and the exact shade of meaning can only be determined by attention to the verbal *milieu*. In the conversation with Eckermann the attenuated abstractions of philosophical interpretation are being contrasted with the living plenitude of poetry itself. The word 'idea' is there equated with 'abstraction', 'abstract thought', 'profound thought', and opposed to such words as 'perception' (*Anschauung*) and 'impression' (*Eindruck*). In the conversation with Luden, by contrast, the word 'idea' is roughly equivalent to 'centre': three times in succession *Idee* is placed in apposition to *Mittelpunkt*. And the words in its immediate vicinity which, so to speak, determine the climate of its meaning are not derived from the sphere of abstract thought at all, but from that of organic growth: Goethe speaks of 'organische Teile', makes use of the verb *erwachsen*, and is obviously preoccupied with his notion of *Gestalt*, or living form, with the reciprocal relation of the parts to the whole and the whole to the parts. The unifying principle he here has in mind is not a philosophical 'idea' at all, not one which can be abstracted from the poetic structure and formulated in other terms. It is rather the principle which is active in the living processes of the poem itself, the formative tendency, or *Bildungstrieb*, which organises all the parts, however diverse, into a meaningful whole. 'Idea' here signifies 'organic centre', 'nodal point', or 'focal point'—Goethe at various times employs all three words[6]—the point from which all the parts radiate and 'out of which, mutually replenishing and completing each other, they have all grown and could well go on growing'. 'The poetic tendency of the individual part', he insists, 'points at all times to a necessary connection, that is, to a common centre, to a primary idea.' Luden's fears that the 'fragments' he had learnt to love might get lost in the completed whole seemed to Goethe quite incomprehensible. To him the work was like a living, growing, thing whose green foliage would only appear in its true significance once the plant was ready to blossom and bring forth fruit. 'But how could the fragments', he protested, 'ever get lost in a whole from which they have themselves been taken? They will appear in that same whole as organic parts, and then, and only then, will they assume their true significance.'

It is not surprising that in his conversation with Luden Goethe should have made use of the language of morphology. For he was at the time intensively, if not exclusively, preoccupied with his scientific work. But long before he turned to natural science at all, long before he formulated those pregnant maxims concerning the relationship between art and nature—'What is beauty but a manifestation of hidden laws of nature'[7] or 'A work of art ought to be treated like a work of nature'[8]—long before this, in his early Strassburg days, he had, following Shaftesbury, spoken of works of art in terms of works of nature. The dithyrambic ardour of his song of praise to the great Gothic minster[9]—he likens it to a giant tree, in the innumerable branches and leaves of which the birds of the morning have their nest, the whole vast structure proclaiming the glory of God—should not blind us to the fact that there is embodied within it a concept to which he would much later give biological precision: the notion that in a living organism all the parts, down to the smallest of them—the tiniest little fibre, as he puts it here—are subordinated to the dominant principle governing the whole. 'Wie in Werken der ewigen Natur, bis aufs geringste Zäserchen, alles Gestalt, und alles zweckend zum Ganzen.'

Nor, even at this early stage, was he under any illusion that the language of plant-growth could afford more than an illuminating analogy. True, he did not, and probably could not, transpose these biological notions into terms of architecture.[10] He was after all not an architect. But he *was* a dramatist. And he could and did transpose them into terms of the theatre, exhorting his fellow *Stürmer und Dränger*[11] to concentrate on scenography, on pasteboard and canvas, boards and battens, grease-paint, lights and tinsel, and leave Nature where she belongs. And into terms of language too, defying even the severest critic 'to separate the merely translated passages [in his *Clavigo*] from the whole without tearing it to pieces, without inflicting, and not just on the plot alone, but on the very structure, the *Lebensorganisation*, of the play itself, a deadly wound'.[12]

If *Clavigo*, a work based on the *Memoirs* of Beaumarchais and exhibiting a surface regularity of form, a conventional structure in the French dramatic style—if such an obvious 'Komposition',[13] as it seems to us, was nevertheless thought by him to have a 'Lebensorganisation' too vulnerable to tamper with, how much more must this hold of *Faust*, which 'grew' out of the Gothic germ of the *Ur-Faust* until it finally unfolded into the Baroque exuberance of the *Second Part*. The critic—if not the reader or spectator, who may well feel it intuitively— is faced with a formidable task if he would try to articulate its formative principle, or follow Goethe's hint when he remarked to Luden that 'great scholars and gifted individuals had not considered it beneath them to search for its *Mittelpunkt*, or nodal point'.[14] How is he to communicate the 'law' of its growth without abstracting it from the living material of which the play is made, without himself forgetting, or leading his readers to forget, that this living material is the poet's words; words not just thought of as black marks on a page, nor as sounds without sense, but words having meaning —and yet at the same time nothing but words. For what we are looking for is, as Goethe says,[15] not 'some mystic something which lies behind or beyond' them, but a significance inherent within them. And not just the significance inherent in any one quotable statement, such as

> Wer immer strebend sich bemüht,
> Den können wir erlösen,   *11936-7*

or

> Das ist der Weisheit letzter Schluss:
> Nur der verdient sich Freiheit wie das Leben,
> Der täglich sie erobern muss,   *11574-6*

or even in a selection of such statements, but a significance inherent in the whole complex of words that go to make up the 12,111 lines of the play. In order to avoid equating the import of *Faust* with that of any lines snatched out of context, or—worse still—reducing its mystery to philosophy by 'atomising it into everyday prose', as Goethe puts it,[16] it may be salutary to remind ourselves, and especially with a work of such obvious and multifarious depths, that a true artist hides these depths on the surface.[17] Provided that soundings are taken at the right points, we should eventually encounter the mythical, religious or philosophical import, and in a way which keeps us more closely in touch with the *poetic* world of the play than if we had started our investigations from a point outside it altogether, from the theological premises of Faust's salvation, for instance, or from the occult sources on which Goethe drew. For, to revert to Goethe's own organic metaphor: If it is true that art, like nature, 'hat weder Kern / Noch Schale, / Alles ist sie mit einem Male',[18] then to explore the relations between words on the outer 'covering' must lead us to the most inward systems of the whole organism. Nor should we be unduly perturbed if the first stages of our search into the intercommunication between the parts—into the 'anastomosis' of the organism, as Goethe calls it[19]—should seem almost mechanical. He himself was quite content to do likewise, whether in his study of Lucretius[20] or of Dante.[21] 'There is no surer way', he wrote, 'of becoming intimate with the essentially *poetic* spirit of the poet than by a comparison of parallel passages.' And for a start we may well extend his comparative method to occurrences of individual words. *160603*

The path has been made easy for us by the *Wortindex zu Goethes Faust* compiled in 1940 at the University of Wisconsin. Let us select from it the word *Welt*. Not indeed at random, but because our general impression of the play tells us that it may well be a key-word. It would clearly be impracticable—even undesirable, an excess of critical zeal—to pursue all the ramifications of its 109 occurrences. But what a sense of interconnection and interweaving we get by following up just a few! From the cosmic panorama of the Prologue in Heaven, the 'Sonn und Welten' hymned by the Archangels, through Mephisto's scornful gibes at man, 'the little god of this world', on to Faust's ardent longing to discover 'what holds the world together at its inmost centre' and his bitter rejection of the narrow 'world' he has made for himself within the four walls of his study: 'Das ist deine Welt! das heisst eine Welt!' Or there is the fine frenzy of his impulse to venture forth from this into the 'real' world, the world of warm humanity, his unrealistic readiness to take upon himself the burden of all its 'weal and woe'; and, in pointed and ironic contrast to such a superhuman ideal, his egotistical urge 'durch die Welt mit allen Sinnen zu schweifen'. If we were to cut our enquiry short at this point, we might be tempted to think that the play turns on a tension between two worlds only: between the world of sense, to which Faust clings 'mit klammernden Organen', and the ideal world he is constantly building up within his soul, and which is the butt of so much of Mephisto's deflating irony. But this would be to confuse the work as a whole with the experience of one of its characters, and to string its 'so reiches, buntes und so höchst mannigfaltiges Leben ... auf die magere Schnur einer einzigen durchgehenden Idee'.[22] For it is Faust who feels this tension between the 'two souls warring within his breast'—and feels it chiefly in the *First Part*. The picture of 'worlds' offered us by his creator is much more varied and complex than this. There is Mephisto's mocking disdain of a 'clumsy world', 'diese plumpe Welt' of solid ordered reality, to which he opposes the—from his point of view—desirable state of chaos from which he himself derives, and which it is his whole aim to restore. There is the 'schöne Welt' of the Invisible Choir of Spirits, the fair world of illusions —but necessary illusions—which the mind of man is capable of building, and which is as vulnerable to the 'clearsightedness' of human despair and dis-illusion as to Mephistophelian negation. There is the tom-cat's satiric denunciation of worldly institutions in the Witch's Kitchen, a 'world' as hollow and brittle as a sphere of glass:

> Das ist die Welt:
> Sie steigt und fällt
> Und rollt beständig;
> Sie klingt wie Glas—
> Wie bald bricht das!
> Ist hohl inwendig.   2402-7

In the mouth of a Frau Marthe this 'common' world becomes as trivial as she is herself; when a pedant such as Wagner speaks of it, there is something pathetic about the distance it assumes, a 'world' seen, if at all, only on high days and holidays, and then only as it were through a spy-glass— 'Kaum durch ein Fernglas, nur von weiten'. This scholar's distrust of the 'world' of men and affairs is one of the things his famulus shares with Faust:

> Ich wusste nie mich in die Welt zu schicken.
> Vor andern fühl' ich mich so klein;
> Ich werde stets verlegen sein.   2058-60

In Gretchen's 'world', by contrast, Faust feels unexpectedly and reassuringly at home. It has all the closeness and cosiness of her warm domesticity. She is 'umfangen in der kleinen Welt', and he, 'the wanderer on the face of the earth', becomes its be-all and end-all, its boundaries co-extensive with his presence. Yet, small though it may be, it is through entry into this 'world' of hers that Faust embarks on the adventure of *experience*, and learns more about life than through all his learning in the 'world of learning'. It is here, as he destroys her little world, that he has his first taste of guilt and suffering, and realises that the tragedy of one single individual can symbolize the tragedy of all mankind: 'Mord und Tod *einer Welt* über dich, Ungeheuer' is his anguished answer to Mephisto's cynical 'She is not the first'. Now indeed he bears upon himself 'the weal and woe of all mankind'—not as before in the god-like presumption of his imagination, but through the concrete reality of a particular case. Whilst Gretchen, for her part, feels the 'little world' in which she so safely dwelt widen to embrace the whole world of suffering as she anticipates her execution and hears no answer to her cry of pain:

> Schon zuckt nach *jedem* Nacken
> Die Schärfe, die nach meinem zückt.
> Stumm liegt die Welt wie das Grab!   4593-5

Then from the 'kleine Welt' of the *First Part* we move into the 'grosse Welt' of the *Second*, into the world of the past and the future, into the medieval world and the world of antiquity, the world of nature and the world of science, the beginnings of natural creation and audacious attempts to short-circuit these in the laboratory—until we even catch a glimpse of the 'world' beyond the grave. A whole book might be written on the use of this word in *Faust*, and it would reflect not only the course of the action—'Vom Himmel durch die Welt zur Hölle'—not only the characteristic *Weltanschauung* of many of the minor as well as the major figures in the play, but the interplay of the different 'worlds', the different structures of reality, which may well exist within one and the same person at different times, or in different moods and situations. What we are offered here is not only a view of the intersection and interlocking of these many worlds but insight into the modifications and metamorphoses they undergo through their action and reaction upon each other—a realization, through the vehicle of poetry and dramatic action, of the truth that our 'worlds' are many and that we make them ourselves, and that those we make now are influenced by those that have been made in the past. Through exploration of the expansion and development of this one cell, the word *Welt*, we gain intimate know-

ledge of the movement and growth of the whole vast organism—so that
when we light again on Mephisto's words,

> Es ist doch lange hergebracht
> Dass in der grossen Welt man kleine Welten macht   *4044-5*

it strikes us with new resonance and is pregnant with our experience of
all the 'worlds' we have encountered whether in the poetry or the dramatic action.

At whatever significant point we strike this verbal surface—at *Brust,*
Fels, Feuer, Gefühl, Geist, Herz, Kraft, Kreis, Schlüssel, Weg—we are able
to follow up a similar pattern of meaning. Each makes its own pattern,
but interlocks with and supports the others, enriching and modifying
them. Take *Brust*, for instance, and its synonym *Busen*. It is a word which
falls naturally from Faust's lips as a symbol of the endless fertility of
nature:

> Wo fass' ich dich, unendliche Natur?
> Euch Brüste, wo? Ihr Quellen alles Lebens . . .   *455-6*

His own breast, on the other hand, his 'welke Brust', is symptom and
symbol of the sterile emptiness of his own study-world. In the mouth of
Mephisto the word takes colour from his habitual tinge of mockery, as
he admonishes the student to 'cling to the breasts of Wisdom' so that
each day he may experience a greater lust for it:

> So wird's Euch an der Weisheit Brüsten
> Mit jedem Tage mehr gelüsten.   *1892-3*

The erotic overtones are obvious here. And when, in order to excite, but
at the same time deride, Faust's lust for Gretchen, this Mephisto-Satan,
Hebrew devil that he is, quotes from the Song of Songs, *Brüste*—though
evoked only by the simile of the 'twin roes feeding among the lilies' (or
'roses', as Luther has it)—becomes offensively lascivious:

> . . . ich hab' Euch oft beneidet
> Ums Zwillingspaar, das unter Rosen weidet.   *3336-7*

All the finely calibrated nuances of sensuality and fertility, of eroticism
and spirituality, are made manifest in and through this image. And all of
them are united in one single occurrence when Faust, moved by the mysterious enchantment of love's first stirrings, imagines Gretchen lying in
her cot as a little child:

> Hier lag das Kind, mit warmem Leben
> Den zarten Busen angefüllt.   *2713-4*

But he has drunk deep of the witch's potion and, spurred on by Mephisto, he is soon all desire for complete union with his beloved:

> ... ach, kann ich nie
> Ein Stündchen ruhig dir am Busen hängen,
> Und Brust an Brust und Seel' in Seele drängen? *3502-4*

Yet, though Mephisto may think he has succeeded in severing divine from mundane love in Faust's heart, the sensual-erotic from the spiritual-tender, Faust's coupling of *Brust* and *Seele* in the same breath is in itself an indication of Mephisto's impending discomfiture. And from the way in which Gretchen herself uses this word we may follow the whole course of her overpowering love. More direct in the expression of her emotions, she had in the *Ur-Faust* voiced the intensity of her longing by fusing and confusing physical desire with the maternal urge to envelop the beloved in the security of the womb:

> Mein Schoss, Gott! drängt
> Sich nach ihm hin. *1098-9*

With the substitution of *Busen* for *Schoss* at this point in the completed play, Goethe weaves this single thread more firmly still into the texture of the whole, making Gretchen in prison echo, not only her own words, but Faust's 'Ein Stündchen dir am Busen hängen', and unite desire and trust in the completeness of her love:

> An seinen Hals will ich fliegen,
> An seinem Busen liegen! *4464-5*

The pattern made by *Brust / Busen* reaches its climax in the *First Part* with Gretchen's pathetic description of the churchyard where she will lie with her loved ones, her baby at her breast—but no lover at her side!

> Und das Kleine mir an die rechte Brust.
> Niemand wird sonst bei mir liegen! *4528-9*

Each of these verbal 'Zäserchen' is 'zweckend zum Ganzen'. Each has a definite function to perform in the aesthetic effect of the whole. Nor can the importance of its function be judged by the number of times it occurs. *Riegel*, for instance, only occurs nine times; but almost always at a strategic point, and each time with increasing weight of remembered or anticipatory significance. It first appears as a metaphor, to express Faust's despair that none of his instruments, neither of his learning nor of his craft, can 'raise the bolts' which bar the door to Absolute Truth and prevent him discovering 'was die Welt / Im Innersten zusammenhält'.

Truth cannot be compelled, he finds, neither by natural nor by super-
natural means. Yet it only needs a tiny human hand to 'leave the bolt
undone' on a door which admits him to love and guilt for him to be afforded a glimpse into life's deepest mysteries:

> Ich liess' dir gern heut' nacht den Riegel offen.   *3506*

The two poles, of uncommitted sensuality and tragic human relationship,
between which Faust is flung, back and forth, are exemplified through
this word *Riegel*. On the one hand, there is its appearance in the ribald
song of the student—

> Riegel auf! in stiller Nacht.
> Riegel auf! der Liebste wacht.
> Riegel zu! des Morgens früh—   *2105-7*

which anticipates, at the stock level of Mephistophelian comprehension,
Gretchen's impending surrender. But, at the other pole, it can be expressive—and even on such devilish lips— of human helplessness in the face of
deeds irrevocable, and crimes committed:

> Ich kann die Bande des Rächers nicht lösen, seine Riegel
> nicht öffnen. ('Trüber Tag')

It is often said that the connection between the two Parts of *Faust* is
extremely tenuous—hardly more, in fact, than the persistence of the two
protagonists and the sporadic reappearance of some of the other characters. The deliberate counterpointing of scene against scene—and not just
of the obvious ones, such as Classical versus Northern 'Walpurgisnacht',
or the 'un-bolting' of Faust's long abandoned 'Hochgewölbtes, enges go-
tisches Zimmer', this time to reveal a 'Laboratorium' beyond; the double
academic promotion—of student to famulus, and famulus to professor;
Faust's second restoration to life—this time by a chorus of nature-spirits
instead of Easter bells and angel-choirs; the return at the end to regions
approximating to those heavenly regions from which we started out—
all this would be enough to refute such a charge even as regards outer
structure alone. But if we keep close to the linguistic surface, we find that
the 'intercommunication' between the two Parts is more subtle still, more
intricate—and more 'inward' than this. When, for instance, on the second
stage of Faust's search for 'das Ewig-Weibliche', he and his Northern
companion set foot on Classical soil, Mephisto—true to type—'sniffs
around' (*umherspürend* is the stage-direction here) in Helena's habitat
exactly as he had done in Gretchen's bedroom (*herumspürend* was the
stage-direction there). Already disconcerted by the unashamed nakedness,

sensing his powerlessness over these serene figures of antiquity, casting a
nostalgic glance back at the obscene antics of those Northern witches
whom he could command at will, he lets an apprehensive eye linger
upon the Sphinxes, symbols of fertility and the repository of esoteric
wisdom,[23] and—half-attracted, half-repelled—evokes, without actually
using the word, all the accumulated connotations of *Brust*:

> Du bist recht appetitlich oben anzuschauen,
> Doch unten hin die Bestie macht mir Grauen.   *7146-7*

It is clear from this single example that a morphological investigation,
though it may start mechanically, cannot for long proceed mechanically:
the word *Brust* itself did not occur, but the notion was present. It may indeed be a salutary corrective to over-zealous probings after philosophical
significance to sit back and just let eye or ear register recurrences of the
same word. In this way hidden connections may well be uncovered, and
meanings poetic and dramatic, as distinct from merely discursive, thus
brought to light. But words are related, not by outer form and appearance
alone, but by their meanings as well. And it is the mind that must be on
the alert for these. Suppose, for instance, that we would look in *Part One*
for some antecedent of that Wanderer who appears so casually, and to no
apparent dramatic purpose, in Act V of *Part Two*. This figure appears so
completely out of the blue that we have even been told he can only be
accounted for by going outside the world of the play altogether and seeking his origins in Goethe's own early life. But surely there is an antecedent in Faust's life too. And a close one at that. Yet it is not really to be
found in any of the three early occurrences of the word *Wanderer* itself,
though each one of them is in its own way a poetic anticipation of this
figure and his fate. In the first of these, Faust feels himself no more than a
worm trodden under foot by the casual step of a wanderer. In the second,
the wanderer himself is threatened on every side by the exuberant and in-
imical forces of nature. In the third, moral evil—in the shape of Mephisto's
casual and callous dismissal of Gretchen's suffering—rears its head so alarm-
ingly that Faust prays for a return of the time when he was 'a wanderer
without grief or guilt' and the devil just a dog playing round his feet. But
closer than any of these—and a dramatic as well as a poetic anticipation of
the whole scene in which the innocent old couple, and their no less innocent guest, are destroyed when Mephisto exceeds his master's injunctions
—are those lines in 'Wald und Höhle' in which Faust describes himself as
'der Flüchtling ... der Unbehauste, / der Unmensch ohne Zweck und
Ruh'. He is indeed a 'wanderer' upon the face of the earth, though only
synonyms of the word occur, and a wanderer who, with all the frenzy of

a natural force, will destroy Gretchen's 'Ruh', her peace of mind and her whole little world, symbolized here by the 'Hüttchen auf dem kleinen Alpenfeld'. In the old couple, Philemon and Baucis, the aged Faust sees the Darby and Joan he and Gretchen might have become. He hates their 'Hütte', not just because it is a hindrance to his engineering plans, but because it is a reminder of his first great guilt. And so the cottage must go; and though, like Ahab, he is but half-responsible for the death of its inhabitants, what *we* witness through the brief appearance of these three figures, and their rapid destruction, is a symbolic re-enactment of aspects of Faust he had long ago destroyed in himself, aspects relating to innocent wandering and the haven of domesticity.

Here we see a word, image, metaphor, from the *First Part* turning into a full-blown dramatic personage in the *Second*. It is by no means the only time this happens in Goethe's works.[24] And it is not the only time it happens here. There is, for instance, Homunculus, the synthetic man produced in his retort by a Wagner turned scientist. He is a dramatic illustration of Goethe's conviction that a living whole is more than the sum of its parts. Though very much 'all there', he still feels the need to 'originate', to come into being by going back to the origins of life and passing through all the forms of living creatures; and it is he who exhorts his maker to remember, when trying to put living elements together, that the 'how' is more important than the 'what', the form than the substance:

> Das Was bedenke, mehr bedenke Wie   *6992*

If now we turn back to *Part One*, we can easily discover the origins of this engaging little creature in those lines in which Mephisto entertains the student by gibing at the scientist's claim to have discovered the essence of a thing by dissecting it:

> Wer will was Lebendigs erkennen und beschreiben,
> Sucht erst den Geist heraus zu treiben.
> Dann hat er die Teile in seiner Hand,
> Fehlt leider! nur das geistige Band.   *1936-9*

And then there is Frau Sorge, the only one of those four weird women who at the end of *Part Two* is able to penetrate into Faust's consciousness —and his conscience. She too is an old acquaintance. We have known her since Faust, in his first extremity of despair, vividly evoked her power to gnaw and nag at a man's peace of mind. No sooner does she take up her abode in his heart than she works in myriad guises to destroy him with needless fears:

Die Sorge nistet gleich im tiefen Herzen,
Dort wirket sie geheime Schmerzen,
Unruhig wiegt sie sich und störet Lust und Ruh.   *644-6*

Here already is the germ of a later personification. And it is already clear
that it will be a woman—for she is constantly putting on a new face!

Sie deckt sich stets mit neuen Masken zu.

And is not the image of womanly beauty which Faust glimpses in the
mirror of the Witch's Kitchen already half-way to being transformed
into the Helen of the *Second Part* when Mephisto whispers lasciviously
into his ear,

Du siehst, mit diesem Trank im Leibe,
Bald Helenen in jedem Weibe?   *2603-4*

Whatever Shaftesbury and the Neoplatonists may have meant by 'inward form', what Goethe meant by it was not some 'mysterious something' lodged within, but the growing awareness by eye, ear and mind of
the significance of such connections and cross-connections. He knew this
as certainly when he was twenty-five and writing about works of art,[25]
as when at seventy he rebuked those 'physicists' and natural philosophers
who, with Haller, postulated an inner essence in nature which is inaccessible to the human mind:

"*Ins Innre der Natur*"—
O du Philister!—
"*Dringt kein erschaffener Geist.*"

'I've been hearing that for these past sixty years', cries Goethe in his play-
fully serious little poem, *Allerdings*, 'and calling down curses upon it
—though surreptitiously of course.' And to such philistine heresy he
opposes his own belief that at point after point on the surface of nature
we have already penetrated to what is within:

Wir denken: Ort für Ort
Sind wir im Innern.

So far we have been taking as *our* points of departure on the surface of
Faust small verbal units—even though some of them may eventually have
been bodied forth as symbolic figures. Let us now consider larger units;
not indeed as large as a whole character or a move in the action, but size-
able enough to mediate between such dramatic and theatrical elements and
the fine-structure of the poetry. Gretchen's four songs serve this purpose

very well indeed. In the meagre verbal texture of the *Ur-Faust* they had stood out as pillars of an action which comprised little more than a love-tragedy, and in that narrower context it is illuminating to consider them from an architectonic point of view.[26] They there provided those turning-points of high tension around which the dramatic action—often left to the imagination—revolved. And in them the action itself was distilled into poignant lyrical[27]—or, perhaps more accurately, ballad-like—expression. But once these same songs have taken their rightful place in the far wider action of the whole *Faust*, once they have grown into the dense and intricate poetic weave out of which this action is made, their ramifications multiply, and extend far beyond the little world bounded by Gretchen's love and passion. In the *Ur-Faust*, 'Der König in Thule', so fashioned by Goethe that it might well have been among the store of folk-songs Gretchen knew, springs unbidden to her lips—a good example of Goethe's knowledge of 'the psychopathology of everyday life'—perfectly expressing her as yet barely conscious desire for the handsome stranger and the ingrained longing of every woman for a fidelity which will last beyond the grave. Its repercussions here are limited to this psychological moment and its dramatic implications. But in the completed work it anticipates her own fidelity beyond the grave and her intercession with the *Mater Gloriosa* on behalf of her erring lover. The next song she sings is far from having the appearance of a ready-made *Volkslied*. She is now all too conscious of the nature of her desires, and there is no question of 'Meine Ruh ist hin' springing inadvertently to her lips. Love has made her creative in her own small way, and what she now sings is a unique utterance of personal experience, of the profound disturbance of newly awakened desire. And in the *Ur-Faust* it is no more than this. If she feels that the world is like a grave when Faust is not there to fill it, this is no more than a metaphor:

> Wo ich ihn nicht hab,
> Ist mir das Grab,
> Die ganze Welt
> Ist mir vergällt.   *3378-81*

Only by implication does it point forward to her own tragic end, to the grave in which she will lie alone. But when Goethe came to complete *Part One* he made this connection explicit. As in her tortured imagination she feels the blade about to strike her neck, the dreadful silence of the whole world, the lack of answering resonance to her pain, is what appals her. And, in a different sense now, 'the world' is again like 'the grave':

Stumm liegt die Welt wie das Grab! 4595

Nor did he forget this 'Zäserchen' when he came to complete *Part Two*. The 'Ruh' she felt she had lost for ever with the invasion of her world by unsuspected forces, and in neither *Ur-Faust* nor *Part One* ever did recover, she does finally regain when, after Faust's own 'Grab-legung', she reappears transfigured as '*Una Poenitentium, sonst Gretchen genannt*', the double designation, in Latin and in the vernacular, perfectly exemplifying Goethe's abiding conviction that the universal is only to be found, and can only be shown forth, in and through the particular. And in this transfigured form she can even bear to recall the anguished accents of her third 'song', the prayer which in extremity she had addressed to the *Mater Dolorosa*:

Ach neige,
Du Schmerzenreiche,
Dein Antlitz gnädig meiner Not! 3587-9

Nestling close to the *Mater Gloriosa*, she varies both words and rhythm, as she awaits in bliss and blessedness the return of her erring lover—who now, in this order of being, is no longer 'getrübt', no longer subject to the refraction of light by the solidity of earthly bodies, neither to the play of colour they produce nor to the shadows they cast, nor indeed to any of the polarities which are the condition of our mortal existence:

Neige, neige,
Du Ohnegleiche,
Du Strahlenreiche,
Dein Antlitz gnädig meinem Glück!
Der früh Geliebte,
Nicht mehr Getrübte,
Er kommt zurück. 12069-75

The fourth song she sang, when awaiting execution for the murder of her child,

Meine Mutter, die Hur',
Die mich umgebracht hat!
Mein Vater, der Schelm,
Der mich gessen hat! 4412-5

is an actual folk-song from a fairy-tale. In its bare juxtaposition of images, its absence of logical or causal relations, it expresses as directly as Ophelia's bawdy the sexual phantasies and projections of a mind unhinged. It is with such literary antecedents, or with Goethe's astonishing insight into the unconscious workings of the mind—the essential rightness of Gretchen's projection of her own 'whoring' on to her mother, her identification of herself with the child she has killed—that the critic will be concerned if he is treating of the *Ur-Faust* alone. But if he is treating of *Faust* as a whole he must go on to the intercession of the three 'Great Sinners', the three Marys, for the soul of Gretchen—and, indirectly, for the soul of Faust—and to ancient associations between sin and holiness. It was a theme to which Goethe had already given universal expression in his two Eastern ballads: *Der Gott und die Bajadere*, in which the god descends to the whore and raises her up to him in glory; and *Paria*, a trilogy in which there is enacted the creation of a god whose sole care will be for sinners and outcasts. And in the context of his last and greatest work, the song he had some sixty years before drawn from the fairy-tale world of magic and madness, is assimilated into the overall tone of compassion which encompasses this mystery-play —for all the satire and irony which pervades so much of its action and its style. No wonder Goethe told Luden he need have no fear that the 'fragments' he had learned to love in the *Fragment* of 1790 would be lost in the vastness of the completed whole!

There remains the question of the 'Mittelpunkt' with which we started. It is, I am well aware, an enterprise full of hazards to vie, not only with those 'great scholars and gifted individuals' who had, according to Goethe, been trying to discover it from the moment the 'torso' appeared, but with the many who have gone on doing so ever since. But it is a task not therefore to be shirked; and the critic may console himself as he tackles it with the thought that it is an occupational risk—is indeed the very nature of his calling—not to be right. And, fortunately, he may even succeed in illuminating something when he is wrong. I shall in any case cover my retreat by suggesting that the specific scene I have in mind is not necessarily *the* 'Mittelpunkt', but certainly one of those nodal points at which Goethe located the sudden 'contraction' of all the plant-processes, the intense concentration of the sap, the systole before, in a complementary rhythm of diastolic expansion, the plant proceeds to the next stage of its life-cycle. There may, perhaps, be a shade of contrariness in singling out for such function 'Wald und Höhle', a scene which one distinguished scholar[28] even went so far as to describe as superfluous—'disturbing, misleading and best left out on the stage'— partly on the grounds that Goethe himself did not seem to know exactly where it belonged, placing it in the *Fragment* after Gretchen's surrender, and shifting it back later to a position immediately before it. But my

apparent perversity has the double advantage of throwing into sharp
relief the kind of law which governs the form of this 'monstrous' and
unique dramatic structure, and of vindicating the usefulness of a morphological approach.

If we consider this scene simply as one of the 'Ruhepausen' in the
action—and there are many—it could indeed be left out in any kind of
theatre which is solely concerned with the onward march of dramatic
events. But there is a long tradition of poetic drama which makes use of
monologue, or of chorus, as the vehicle of essential aspects of meaning,
and in which these are therefore inherent elements of the dramatic form.
And 'Wald und Höhle' consists of far more than the contemplative monologue with which it opens, important as this is in itself. Whether here,
or in Faust's subsequent dialogue with his now hated companion, we
find all the threads of the earlier action gathered together, and the shuttle
poised for a moment, before it is thrown forward again with new, and
now tragic, impulse to complete the pattern. The very first line of the
scene,

> Erhabner Geist, du gabst mir, gabst mir alles,
> Warum ich bat . . .   *3217-8*

challenges the critic to test the validity of a morphological approach to
the verbal fabric of this play. For the identity of this 'Erhabener Geist'
has been something of a crux. It can scarcely be the 'Erdgeist', some commentators have declared, since that spirit certainly did not grant Faust all
he asked for; on the contrary, it rejected him, reducing him to suicidal
despair with the words,

> Du gleichst dem Geist, den du begreifst,
> Nicht mir!   *512-3*

Against such an argument, there is of course the awkward fact that no
spirit other than the 'Erdgeist' had ever appeared to Faust as a 'Flammen-
bildung', and that Faust, when he now addresses the 'Erhabner Geist',
recalls that this spirit had in fact—and 'not in vain' either—turned his
face towards him 'im Feuer'. But scholars attached to the theory that the
two are not identical could of course counter this by saying that much in
this play happens off-stage; or else fall back on the stock 'argument from
the creative process', and warn us that anything which took a lifetime to
compose cannot possibly be free of contradictions. But if we reject un-
verifiable hypotheses about the operations of a mind long dead in favour
of close examination of the work we still have, we cannot fail to be struck
by the close verbal parallels between the two scenes. Faust's motive for
calling up the Earth-Spirit at all was profound discontent with what the

Spirit of the Macrocosm had to offer. It was a spectacle so grand that it made him feel 'like a god', the 'equal of spirits', and 'close to the mirror of eternal truth'. But sublime though it was, it was a spectacle and nothing more:

Welch Schauspiel! Aber ach! ein Schauspiel nur!   454

Recalling its cold remoteness now, he contrasts it with the rich insight into the processes of Nature which has been afforded him since, and tells the 'Erhabner Geist':

Nicht
Kalt staunenden Besuch erlaubst du nur,
Vergönnest mir, in ihre tiefe Brust,
Wie in den Busen eines Freunds, zu schauen.   3221-4

Instead of the cosmic play, at which he could never be more than a mere onlooker, he had longed for the closeness of participation, and therefore conjured a spirit closer to earth and, as he thought, more akin to himself:

Du, Geist der Erde, bist mir näher;   461

or again,

Geschäftiger Geist, wie nah fühl' ich mich dir!   511

only to find that it rejected his claims of equality by scornfully referring him to a spirit he might be capable of comprehending. Now, in 'Wald und Höhle', having dilated, in ecstatic terms strongly reminiscent of the 'Erdgeist' scene, on his power to enjoy and participate in the living processes of nature, he breaks off sharply. There is a turn in his monologue here—a turn, from the gifts which bring him ever nearer to the gods, to the thought of the now hated, if indispensable, companion who is apparently the inevitable concomitant of such gifts—a turn which parallels exactly his former deflation by the Earth-Spirit, and makes it clear beyond all doubt that the spirit to whom he was then contemptuously referred is in fact the Mephistopheles whom he now admits to having received from the Spirit he still feels inclined to address as Sublime:

Du gabst zu dieser Wonne,
Die mich den Göttern nah und näher bringt,
Mir den Gefährten, den ich schon nicht mehr
Entbehren kann . . .   3241-4

And when this companion, this Spirit of Negation, now enters the scene, he does not miss the opportunity of pricking the bubble of Faust's 'presumption' again, of deflating his recurrent impulse—which is indeed his saving grace—to remember that he is 'made in the image of God'. And he pricks it in terms not at all unlike those of the Earth-Spirit:

Erdgeist   Wo ist der Seele Ruf?
    Wo ist die Brust, die eine Welt in sich erschuf
    Und trug und hegte, die mit Freudebeben
    Erschwoll, sich uns, den Geistern, gleich zu heben?   *490-3*

Mephistopheles   Ein überirdisches Vergnügen!
    In Nacht und Tau auf den Gebirgen liegen,
    Und Erd' und Himmel wonniglich umfassen,
    Zu einer Gottheit sich aufschwellen lassen . . .   *3282-5*

One could almost believe he had been listening-in on that early discomfiture—as indeed he probably had!—and is now parodying that whole scene.

Such close linguistic parallels are the 'unveränderliches Factum' [29] from which the critic must start if he would broach the apparent contradiction between the Earth-Spirit's rejection of him and Faust's subsequent assertion that he has, notwithstanding, granted him all he asked. This is the world 'as the poet has made it', and its logic takes precedence over the logic of any of the 'worlds' in the occult sources on which he drew. It matters not a whit if in the hierarchy of spirits there an Earth-Spirit would have been precluded from sending Mephistopheles to Faust. [30] Here, in Goethe's play, that is what he does. And it is up to us to try to understand in what sense this 'Erhabner Erdgeist' may be said to have granted Faust's wishes. Surely in the sense that what he had longed for was participation in reality *as known under earthly conditions*, that is, in terms of polarity. The Spirit he summoned because the spectacle of the macrocosm left him unsatisfied was a spirit who was in the thick of life, 'weaving the living garment of God', and weaving it in terms of interdependent opposites:

        In Lebensfluten, im Tatensturm
        Wall' ich auf und ab,
        Webe hin und her!
        Geburt und Grab,
        Ein ewiges Meer,
        Ein wechselnd Weben,
        Ein glühend Leben . . .   *501-7*

Nor is there any question of Faust being unaware of the essentially 'polar' nature of the Spirit he summoned. It was precisely because he felt a rising courage to bear the woe as well as the weal of the world (*465*) that he summoned it at all. And it is precisely this polarity that he insists on again when he makes his wager with Mephisto. The devil's traditional temptations, of unlimited knowledge and unlimited pleasure, are rejected with contumely. What this 'servant of the Lord' demands are pleasures which will never satisfy, which will turn in the moment of satiety to new desire (*1675-87*). And when Mephisto still fails to grasp either the direction or the compass of his mind's intent, he rounds on him with 'I tell you it's not a question of *pleasure* at all'. In a speech compounded of oxymora and antitheses, he then announces that from now on he is dedicated to the reeling tumult of existence, to its pain no less than its pleasure:

> Dem Taumel weih' ich mich, dem schmerzlichsten Genuss,
> Verliebtem Hass, erquickendem Verdruss.
> Mein Busen, der vom Wissensdrang geheilt ist,
> Soll keinen Schmerzen künftig sich verschliessen,
> Und was der ganzen Menschheit zugeteilt ist,
> Will ich in meinem innern Selbst geniessen,
> Mit meinem Geist das Höchst' und Tiefste greifen,
> Ihr Wohl und Weh auf meinen Busen häufen,
> Und so mein eigen Selbst zu ihrem Selbst erweitern,
> Und, wie sie selbst, am End' auch ich zerscheitern.   *1766-75*

If now, in 'Wald und Höhle', he recalls with bitterness, and in the compression of a chiasmus, those terms on which he had so impatiently and impulsively insisted when making the pact—

> So tauml' ich von Begierde zu Genuss,
> Und im Genuss verschmacht' ich nach Begierde,   *3249-50*

this, at least, is not one of those 'contradictions' which critics have always been ready to find in the work and which Goethe so vehemently denied were there: 'In der Poesie gibt es keine Widersprüche. Diese sind nur in der wirklichen Welt, nicht in der Welt der Poesie.'[31] This change in Faust is one of the contradictions that are to be found in plenty in 'the real world' and form part of life itself. It is a change which has come about because he has now felt in his very flesh all that the generous presumption of his earlier demand implies when realized in a concrete situation. He now knows—and to the end of his days he will not cease to make discoveries of a similar kind—the difference between knowledge glimpsed through the imagination and knowledge bought through bitter experience. And it is out of a hard-won realization that man's finest endeavours of mind and will are inseparable from his power to do evil and

know pain that, in his monologue in 'Wald und Höhle', he can fall from
the sustained soaring of the first twenty odd lines to a heavy but realistic
acceptance of human imperfection:

> O dass dem Menschen nichts Vollkommnes wird,
> Empfind' ich nun. 3240-1

Rarely can the particle *nun* have had to bear such weight of experience as
it is here given by the caesura.

But the threads of this scene run further back still, beyond the pact
or the conjuring of the 'Erdgeist', to the Prologue in Heaven. It was
with a synonym of *Gefährte* that the Lord there announced why he
gave the Devil to man—

> Des Menschen Tätigkeit kann allzuleicht erschlaffen,
> Er liebt sich bald die unbedingte Ruh;
> Drum geb' ich gern ihm den Gesellen zu,
> Der reizt und wirkt und muss als Teufel schaffen— 340-3

and it was in words not unlike those of the Earth-Spirit that the Archangels
spoke of the polarities existing in the fair but turbulent life on earth:

> Und schnell und unbegreiflich schnelle
> Dreht sich umher der Erde Pracht;
> Es wechselt Paradieseshelle
> Mit tiefer, schauervoller Nacht. 251-4

The fact that this Prologue was written some ten years *after* 'Wald und
Höhle' is no objection to the view that the threads run *backwards*, any
more than it is relevant when considering the present function of the scene
to recall that Goethe had doubts and hesitations about where it ought to
go. He certainly often spoke of his works 'growing' in his mind; but he
was as aware of the limitations of the plant-analogy when he used it of the
creative process as he was when he used it of the finished products. The
last letter of his life, in which he talked about the completion of *Faust* in
the larger context of mental processes in general, makes it abundantly
clear that for him the 'growth' of the human mind, or the 'creation' of a
work of art, implied not only those unconscious and half-conscious activities which proceed under their own momentum, but 'taking thought'
and reflection too, the fully conscious acts of selection, adjustment and
revision. The time when he conceived and wrote 'Wald und Höhle'—
during his first and momentous visit to Italy— may certainly be regarded
as a 'nodal point' in his own growth, a moment of rejuvenation and
rebirth, as he repeatedly called it, a 'Mittelpunkt' from which he looked

backwards and forwards, taking stock of himself and making decisions for the future. It is not at all improbable that in the case of *Faust*, a work which accompanied him through so much of his life, this phase of contraction and intensification should have brought forth a scene which may likewise be regarded as a 'Mittelpunkt'. But however that may be, of one thing we can be certain in the light of Goethe's many utterances about the way he made his poetry: whenever he took up again a work he had left lying, he felt his way back into a new mood of conception which both embraced the old conception and modified it, and he let the activity of revision and completion proceed at both the conscious and the unconscious level. We cannot know by which of these two kinds of mental operation he produced for 'Wald und Höhle' lines reminiscent of either the 'Erdgeist' or the pact-scene, or for the Prologue in Heaven lines which would then seem to anticipate all three. Nor does it matter. And if we raise the question of the *place* of 'Wald und Höhle' at all, the appropriate way to frame it is not 'Why' but 'How'—even though within the context of Goethe's morphology the two would coincide. For in the study of forms, whether of nature or of art, he found the antithesis cause/effect, useful as it may be in other contexts, as inadequate as the antithesis inner/ outer. And it is important to ask the right kind of 'How'. To suggest that the scene was moved back to a position before Gretchen's surrender in order to ennoble Faust's character—by making it appear that he had not had repeated intercourse with her—is to proffer a moral explanation. But to see the tragic intensification which is achieved by letting the hero pause for a moment on his headlong course, and—however much he is driven by unconscious forces—deliberately take upon himself some measure of responsibility by assenting, with his eyes open, to the possible destruction of himself as well as her and her whole little world; or to observe how, through this change of position, the Gretchen tragedy can now run its stark inevitable course in a rapid succession of brief scenes, uninterrupted by anything but the dream sequences of 'Walpurgisnacht' and 'Walpurgisnachtstraum'—this is to offer an aesthetic reason.

The threads from 'Wald und Höhle' run forward at the level of poetic language as well as that of dramatic action. Nor are they cut short at the end of the *First Part*. One example from many must suffice. The obscene gesture with which Mephisto derides Faust's 'hohe Intuition' (*3291*) points forward to his gibe in the Garden-scene when he has been eavesdropping on Faust's ardent wooing of Gretchen with high-sounding phrases about the impotence of words to express the Ineffable, whether of Feeling or of God.[32] 'Du übersinnlicher sinnlicher Freier' (*3534*) is

Mephisto's taunt this time. And the clear note of erotic mysticism, or mystic eroticism, which it sounds, though temporarily muffled by the pagan and classical adventures of the *Second Part*, resounds again in the final Choruses, and reminds us of what we learnt from our investigation of the word *Welt*: that all our ways of thinking, all the structures of reality we build, all the deeds we perform—whether it is our attitude to nature or our way of wooing a girl—are influenced by all the ways of thinking, all the manifold cultural worlds, we have inherited from the past. If, bearing in mind that for Goethe the distinction between 'law' and 'phenomenon' is—like that between 'inner' and 'outer' or 'cause' and 'effect'—no more than a convenient way of talking about things—if, despite this, we are bold enough to try to enunciate the 'law' of *Faust*, we might venture a conclusion to which we are forced more firmly perhaps by such morphological study than by any other critical approach. It is this: What is being shown forth here, through an individual case at a particular time, is Western man himself, as he has become and as he now is, heir of all he has ever been. Through all the resources of language and the theatre we are presented with the very form of his being: its strengths, its weaknesses, its glories and its vices, its endangeredness and problematicness, and its possibilities of salvation. This, we might say, is the 'idea' of *Faust*—so long as we do not forget that when Goethe used this word, in some contexts at least, it still had for him all the force of its primary meaning, 'form'.

VII. On the Study of Goethe's Imagery

Images, however beautiful, though faithfully copied from nature, and as accurately represented in words, do not of themselves characterize the poet. They become proofs of original genius only as far as they are modified by a predominant passion; or by associated thoughts or images awakened by that passion ...

Coleridge, *Biographia Literaria*, Ch. XV.

IMAGE-HUNTING has become a favourite literary sport of recent years. We have only to recall the names of Ernest Jones, C. G. Jung, Hermann Pongs, Maud Bodkin, Caroline Spurgeon, Wolfgang Clemen and C. Day Lewis. But image-hunting as an academic pursuit is nothing new. Goethe tells us[1] how as a student in Leipzig he was sent out by his teachers to look in nature for images with which to embellish his poetry; and, fired by his example as much as by the modern fashion, I too have joined in the game, sent my own students out a-hunting, and a few years ago published an essay[2] tracing the images of the horse and the charioteer in Goethe's works, from their early appearance in *Götz* and *Egmont*, or in his well-known letter to Herder of July, 1772, through their 'Verbürgerlichung' in *Wilhelm Meisters Lehrjahre* and *Hermann und Dorothea*, or their use as symbols of the daemonic in his own life at the end of *Dichtung und Wahrheit*, to the transformation of symbol into allegory in the figures of 'Euphorion' and 'Knabe Lenker' in *Faust II*.[3] But as I re-read it I am not altogether satisfied with its method. The problems involved are more numerous and more complicated than they appeared at first sight, and I have felt the need to come to closer grips with them.

'We do not sufficiently bear in mind', says Goethe, 'that language itself is but a matter of symbols, of images, that it never expresses things directly, but only as in a mirror.'[4] The word 'image', the dictionary informs us, is derived from the Latin *imago*, itself cognate with *imitare* (just as the German *Bild* is the root of *bilden*), and denotes an imitation or representation of the external form of some object. Figuratively it implies a mental picture or impression aroused by bringing together two more or less distant realities: 'Sleep is the image of death'; the sea is for

Byron 'the image of eternity'. Obviously as a figure of speech the word 'image' embraces, or at least has close affinities with, simile, metaphor, parable, allegory, symbol, in all of which a picture takes the place of a thought, thereby giving it greater pregnancy and vividness. It is thus a move from the conceptual to the perceptual, an appeal from the mind to the senses and, as such, a retrogression to a more primitive way of thinking. For the earliest mode of thought both in the individual and the race is picture-thought. A child will assimilate the illustrations of a book long before he can understand the letter-press; his technically immature drawings often betray a complexity of thought far beyond what he can express in language. 'Previous ages', Goethe told Riemer,[5] 'conceived their ideas in imaginative form; ours turns them into concepts. They embodied the great truths of life in shapes and in the figures of gods; nowadays we turn these into concepts too'. The poet reverts to this earlier mode; or rather he preserves it. For he differs from both the child and the primitive in that he goes on speaking in images long after his power of conceptual thought is fully developed. And he differs from others of his fellow-creatures who still have recourse to images in that he uses them not merely as illustrations to his thought but for their own sake. Of others we might say that they sometimes think *with* images, of him that he frequently thinks *in* images. They are for him the high-lights of that material of words which it is his delight to handle. They are the means by which since Homer he gives life to lifeless things and 'bodies forth the forms of things unknown'.

New impetus has been given to the study of poetic imagery by the psychologists' delvings into the unconscious regions of the mind. The investigations of both Freud and Jung have revealed in those mysterious realms the prevalence of images and symbols. In the phrase of the latter, the language of the unconscious is essentially 'picture-language'. They have revealed, too, the significance of these images in the interpretation of man's thoughts and motives. A poet's dreams, it seems now to be established, are of the same stuff that ordinary dreams are made of. But all the same, not every dreamer is a poet. It is only when the images which come welling up from the unconscious are articulated by the poet in terms of his medium that they become poetry. He is a poet by virtue of the forming and the fashioning which make his dreams universally communicable. As Schiller told Goethe,[6] it is precisely the business of the poet to make the unconscious conscious : 'Das Bewusstlose mit dem Besonnenen vereinigt macht den poetischen Künstler aus'.

This is too often forgotten. Since its close connection with the unconscious was discovered, poetry has tended to become a happy hunting-ground for the psychologist in search of further illustrations for his case-book. This applies equally to those who, like Freud, reduce poetry to a mere manifestation of the personal unconscious of the poet, and to those who, like Jung, interpret it as the symbolical expression of intuitive perceptions deriving from the collective unconscious of the race. The whole potency of poetry, according to Jung, depends on the archetypal nature of its imagery, which can restore to modern man, rationalized, torn and disintegrated, something of the magic wholeness and fullness of the instinctual life. 'He who speaks in primordial images', he says,[7] 'speaks with a thousand tongues ... He transmutes personal destiny into the destiny of mankind, thereby evoking in us all those beneficent forces that have enabled mankind to find a release from every hazard and to outlive the longest night.'

There is obviously truth in this. An image of general human significance, deriving from some deep and ancient level of consciousness, is bound to evoke deeper and more powerful responses than one deriving from the shallower and more transient levels of experience. But what in general the psychologist ignores is the different effect these images have *in* poetry and *out* of poetry. The prevalence of primordial images cannot of itself distinguish poetry from what is not poetry, though it may provide a gauge by which great poetry is distinguishable from lesser poetry—if 'great' be taken here not as an indication of poetic excellence, but of magnitude or profundity of content, 'lesser' as an indication of slightness of theme or lightness of mood. It is only within the context of poetic composition that the *poetic* quality of images can be determined. Individual images in themselves have no poetic value—except that hovering about them from the memorable poetic contexts in which they have already been used.

This sharp divergence of the strictly aesthetic from the psychoanalytical approach to poetry is reflected in two distinct trends among the literary critics who have investigated poetic imagery. Middleton Murry and C. Day Lewis, for example, are concerned with the *organization* of the images in a poem rather than with their psychological significance, with the way they work upon each other to produce a certain effect, with the difference between simile, metaphor and symbol, with the distinctively poetic processes, whether in creation or appreciation. Miss Bodkin and Miss Spurgeon, on the other hand, are intent on discovering what the images can tell us of the poet as man. By their images Ye shall know them! 'The poet', Caroline Spurgeon writes,[8] 'unwittingly lays bare his own innermost likes and dislikes, observations and interests, associations of thought, attitudes of mind and beliefs, in and through the

images, the verbal pictures he draws to illuminate something quite different in the speech and thought of his characters. The imagery he instinctively uses is thus a revelation, largely unconscious, given at a moment of
heightened feeling, of the furniture of his mind'. Maud Bodkin, as an
adherent of Jung, goes beyond the personal idiosyncrasies of the poet, and
declares that 'all poetry, laying hold of the individual through the sensuous resources of language, communicates in some measure the experience of an emotional but supra-personal life'.[9] Her interest is thus more
than mere detective-work. She is concerned to discover in the poet's unconscious symbols the source of his poetry's potency and power. But,
while not unaware of the importance of the poet's use of his medium, she
makes no proper distinction between the psychological effect of the symbol as such and its aesthetic effect in a context of poetically organized relations. The German scholar, Hermann Pongs, on the other hand, has so
little regard for the aesthetic effect of images that he actually deprecates
as decadent that kind of poetry which works its effects through formal
values rather than through the quasi-mystical value of primordial
symbols. There is a constant danger, he insists,[10] that the poet, by seizing
on the individual rather than the racial significance of images, will put
them to his own egotistical, and consequently to spurious, use. For
Pongs the very term 'aesthetic effect' carries with it derogatory associations of illusion and deception. He goes so far as to speak of the 'trüge-
rische Hülle des aesthetischen Scheins'. This is not only a betrayal of
our belief in reason and individual consciousness, but a misunderstanding, or misuse, of the term 'aesthetischer Schein' as conceived by Goethe
and Schiller. Far from being 'trügerisch', a snare and a delusion, the
world of aesthetic form, of 'schöner Schein', was for them a manifestation of the highest mode of human consciousness.

To be complete, or even valid, the study of a poet's imagery must embrace both approaches, the psychological and the aesthetic. And it is not
enough for them simply to meet and combine, for the results of the one
study to be added to those of the other. They must not only combine,
they must fuse. The premises of each study in fact require it. For psychology cannot in the long run avoid coming to terms with that most subtly
complex form of human experience, aesthetic experience. Aesthetics, on
the other hand, with its insistence that form and content are one, cannot
in all honesty ignore any of those deeper levels of content which the discoveries of psychology may reveal to it. Ultimate union of the two approaches seems inevitable, and a time will surely come when C. Day
Lewis will no longer need to lament[11] that the psychologists may well be
right but that what they have to say about the effect of poetry seems all

the same to have very little to do with the specifically aesthetic emotion it affords *him*. Since the formal organization of images in an aesthetic context itself modifies their psychological implications, it is only by treating these two aspects as inseparable that the full poetic potency of the images can be revealed at all.

No poet so directly challenges the critic to explore his *poetic* imagery as does Goethe. For in him we are relieved of the temptation to seek in his poetry for clues to his life or to the skeletons in the cupboard of his mind. His life and mind, unlike Shakespeare's, stand revealed to us through the mass of evidence in his letters, diaries and conversations. We know what he was doing and thinking from day to day, almost from hour to hour. And from these same letters, diaries and conversations we know too what his favourite images were, and can easily infer what psychological significance they held for him. For he uses identical images inside his poetry and out. He can easily do this, for they are of a simple, unassuming, almost humdrum, nature. Indeed what first strikes the reader of Goethe's poetry, in contrast to that of other great poets, is its plain matter-of-factness and the apparent paucity of his invention. Goethe's poetry makes none of the bejewelled effect, the impression of a richly embroidered texture, that some of our own great poetry achieves. Like the Hebrew prophet, he often seems content just to call by name the elements of nature: the sun, the moon, the stars, the waves, the hills, the rocks and the trees. Yet the forms of beauty here named have symbolic value because Goethe possesses in supreme degree the faculty of 'elevating, as it were Words into Things and living things too'.[12] And just as he uses and re-uses the same situations and motifs in his novels and plays, so we find the same few images recurring with stubborn persistence in all his works, poetry and prose, from the beginning of his life to its end: the horse, the wanderer, the hut, the goblet, the mirror, the well, the ship, the loom. They recur so inevitably in certain typical situations that it is gradually borne in upon us that they must symbolize certain fundamental human urges or drives, and we scarcely need the psychologist's confirmation that they are in fact primordial images. But that they are comparatively few does not mean that their effect is monotonous. Their very plainness, and apparent neutrality, has the advantage that it makes them capable of constant metamorphosis. They take on variety of colour and shape from their immediate context and surroundings. And in this great economy which Goethe practises in the use of his images, he betrays the close affinity of his creative mind with the processes he had discovered in nature, which, as he says,[13] 'from the simplest beginnings produces the infinite variety of phenomena'.

There can be no doubt that Goethe knew very well what his images meant. In *his* case, at least, there can be no question of any unwitting betrayal of the furniture of his mind when he puts them into the mouth of his characters. He forces us to face the fact that a poet may very well be fully conscious of the symbolic import of his imagery, and be using it with a deliberate subtlety of intention, which, if missed, can wholly mislead us as to the true nature and tone of his poetry. From quite early on he was as aware of the uncounscious element in his creative process as it was possible for a poet to be in the pre-psychoanalytical era, and he set himself the task of bringing both the contents and processes of the irrational into the clear daylight of reason. He is, for instance, quite explicit about the constant symbolizing activity of his mind. 'Ich bin der ewige Gleichnismacher', he writes to Frau von Stein as early as 1781; [14] and a few years before his death he was still writing:

> Gleichnisse dürft' ihr mir nicht verwehren,
> Ich wüsste mich sonst nicht zu erklären, [15]

thereby confessing his complete dependence upon images for the communication of his thought. 'Whenever I look for words', he writes in the *Italian Journey*, [16] 'I see images'—'so stehen mir immer Bilder vor Augen'. And in his autobiography he tells us: [17] 'I had inherited from my father a certain didactic loquacity, from my mother the power of representing clearly and forcibly everything that imagination can produce or grasp ... Both these parental gifts accompanied me throughout my whole life, united with a third, the need to express myself in figures and symbols'. His constant endeavour from his early twenties onwards was to express his thought with direct immediacy, without the intervention of conceptualizing and discursive processes, to be able to think and express his thoughts in one operation. [18]

Again, with Goethe we are not driven back upon an analysis of his poetic imagery in order to establish through which of the senses he was wont to experience the world. He tells us himself quite frankly that he was essentially a visual type: 'Das Auge war vor allen anderen das Organ, womit ich die Welt fasste'. [19] But, as Herder had taught him, perception by sight involves close and complex interaction with perception by touch; [20] and it was no hyperbole that Goethe was using when in one of the *Roman Elegies* he wrote:

> Sehe mit fühlendem Aug', fühle mit sehender Hand,

thus expressing the co-ordination of sight and touch into one unitary sensation. His hearing on the other hand was less developed, and it was a source of great grief that the more technical aspects of music were a closed book to him:

> Was dem Auge dar sich stellet,
> Sicher glauben wir's zu schaun;
> Was dem Ohr sich zugesellet,
> Gibt uns nicht ein gleich Vertraun.[21]

Goethe, then, himself relieves us of many of the tasks which are wont to preoccupy the student of poetic imagery. But the very plenitude of the information he so freely provides brings its own peculiar problems. There is a constant temptation to let this fulness of biographical material take the place of a critical examination of his poetic writings as works of art existing in their own right. It has far too often side-tracked the critic from his proper function of concentrating on the aesthetic effect.

Goethe's confession that he was a visual type, for example, cannot serve as a ready-made key which automatically unlocks all the doors of his poetic imagery. The effect produced by an image within a complex of related thoughts and images may well not be predominantly visual or tactile at all, whatever he himself may have said. It is obvious, for instance, that the meaning of the central image in *Egmont*, the famous image of the charioteer, is not to be exhausted solely by dwelling on its visual and tactile aspects. Its very essence is the feeling of movement in the plunging horses—a kinetic image—and the effort of control in the charioteer as he reins them in—a muscular image. Only inasmuch as the visual recedes, and gives place to these much more intimate bodily sensations, do we appreciate that relation between unconscious drive and conscious direction which Egmont is here trying to communicate, and which is the main theme of the play. Only through a close examination of the immediate and the wider context can we determine the nature and significance of this image in this particular play. And we must be bold enough to let the context decide, and to acknowledge the autonomous existence of the poetic impression, independently of its relation to the poet's conscious intention.

Similarly the *psychological* meaning of any of his recurrent images, which may easily be deduced from his diaries and letters, can never exempt us from the critical task of discovering its *poetic* meaning in a particular context. The meaning of the two related images, wanderer and hut, is clearly stated in *Werther*:

> Ich habe allerlei nachgedacht, über die Begier im Menschen, sich auszubreiten, neue Entdeckungen zu machen, herumzuschweifen; und

dann wieder über den innern Trieb, sich der Einschränkung willig zu ergeben, in dem Gleise der Gewohnheit so hinzufahren, und sich weder um Rechts noch um Links zu bekümmern.[22]

Here, at a crucial point in the novel, when Werther has found the peace of Lotte after his wanderings, we find reduced to their simplest terms the two cardinal but conflicting tendencies in the life of man, the separate poles of his striving, which taken together make up the unity of his being: the impulse to wander, the longing to return home; the urge to philander, the need to settle down and found a family; the limitless aspiration of individual striving, the merging of the self within the community. And then, to illuminate these psychological concepts and to give body and shape to his own elusive feelings, Werther has recourse to images:

So sehnt sich der unruhigste Vagabund zuletzt wieder nach seinem Vaterlande, und findet in seiner Hütte, an der Brust seiner Gattin, in dem Kreise seiner Kinder, in den Geschäften zu ihrer Erhaltung die Wonne, die er in der weiten Welt vergebens suchte.[22]

From innumerable references in his early letters and poems we know that Goethe felt himself flung helplessly back and forth from one of these poles to the other. But we should go very wrong if we applied this knowledge mechanically to the poem *Wandrers Sturmlied*. Here the precise nature of the tension between wanderer and hut, between the young poet's excursion into soaring sublimity and the down-to-earth pull of domesticity and comfort, can only be grasped by an exhaustive study of the complex formal relations of this very difficult ode. The 'predominant passion', as Coleridge would say, which here modifies all the images and thoughts, is a kind of humour and lightness, a playful contemplation of the incongruous contrast between the ideal and the real. And it is this 'predominant passion' which must be taken into consideration whenever we are trying to discover the meaning and effect of any of these recurrent images in any particular poetic context.

To take yet another example. From an examination of Goethe's correspondence during his last years in Frankfurt and first years in Weimar we know quite well the symbolic significance which the image of the wave had for him at that time. He is constantly using it, in conjunction with the ship, to express his sense of being carried on the current of life, of the risks and dangers to which he is exposed: 'Still on the waves in my little open boat', he had written to Herder in July, 1772. But after his arrival in Weimar it seems to him that he is definitely launched on the voyage of life: 'I am now well and truly embarked on the wave of the world, fully determined to make discoveries, become successful, to fight, to founder, or to blow myself and my cargo sky-high'.[23] As fine, as appropriate, an image as may be to express his immediate state of mind, but isolated, one moment in a succession of time, having no relation to any larger unity. If it may be said to be 'composed' at all, it is as an allegory, easily translatable into terms of Goethe's own particular situation. But when the Princess in *Tasso* uses this identical image its effect is quite different:

> Und glücklich eingeschifft trug uns der Strom
> Auf leichter Woge ohne Ruder hin.   *1876–7*

This not only voices her distress over Tasso's imminent departure, as she imagines their sailing together down the stream of life, blissfully abandoned to the current of its waters; it is also a symbol of the life-stream on which we are all borne; and it includes our own life-flow and all its attendant circumstances. Clearly it bears for the Princess a similar meaning as for Margarethe von Parma in *Egmont* (I,2): 'For what are we, the great ones of the earth, on the wave of humanity?' But in *Tasso* the meaning has become even richer and more pregnant because the image of the wave has been organized by the poet into a larger unity. It bears close and intimate relation to the numerous images of ships, sea, storm and shipwreck in which the play abounds, until it finally coalesces with them all in that grandiose composite image of the last scene, where the 'predominant passion' which inspires the play, the relation of the poet to society and to his own art, is summed up in an inexhaustible symbol. And now we see how wrong it would have been to equate *Woge* or *Welle*, when used by Tasso of himself or of others, simply with the stream of life. For by its association with other images—with the mirror and its already established aesthetic connotation, with the rock which stands firm against the storm, with the ship to which Antonio has already likened Tasso— this whole cluster of images becomes so intertwined and interrelated that the significance of each is modified by all the others as well as by the predominant passion which has awakened them. The 'sturmbewegte Welle' no longer symbolizes man in general borne on the stream of life, but a particularized man, the poet. For him the image of the wave is especially apposite. It expresses all his lability, his power to be whipped up by the storms of life, without being destroyed:

> die Welle flieht
> Und schwankt und schwillt und beugt sich schäumend über.   *3440–1*

Here we may see not only how a cognate cluster of images is used with cumulative effect, but how the effect can be still further heightened as other images used in the play are drawn into the pattern. Thus the phrase 'und beugt sich schäumend über' is apposite to the wave which breaks against the rock without losing its identity; but it also recalls echoes of the many times this image of 'bubbling over' has already occurred in the play in other connections. 'Schäumend' depicts Tasso's rising anger against Antonio's denigration of his poetic genius; it is also the adjective with which Tasso likens his love for the Princess to the foaming wine which overflows the cup.

This linkage of images constitutes the finely woven texture of the play. It is nowhere more clearly visible than in the association of the *Becher* image with the seascape imagery at the end of the play. There is no need to labour the significance of the *Becher* as an erotic symbol. It is known to every psychologist. It has been connected with sensuality since Solomon wrote of his beloved that her 'navel was like a round goblet which wanteth not liquor'. When Goethe first used it in his early poem, *Der König in Thule*, it may perhaps have been without full consciousness of this sexual significance. But by 1775, when he translated the *Song of Songs*— 'the most glorious collection of love-songs that God ever made', he calls it[24]—he can be in no doubt as to its meaning. As so often with Goethe, what may well have been a primordial image of irrational origin, has received confirmation from literary sources; as the image of the horse and charioteer did from Pindar and Plato, or that of the wanderer from the *Odyssey*. From now on the *Becher* image is always used with full awareness of its erotic significance. Critics have even thought that its frequent use in his letters and poetry at the time when his relation to Frau von Stein was obviously reaching a climax, might afford some clue to the degree of their intimacy. The poem, *Der Becher*, composed towards the end of September 1781, symbolizing as it does the lips and body of the beloved through this admittedly erotic image, is often adduced as the poetic avowal of her physical surrender:

> Einen wohlgeschnitzten vollen Becher
> Hielt ich drückend in den beiden Händen,
> Sog begierig süssen Wein vom Rande,
> Gram und Sorg' auf einmal zu vertrinken.

In order to put the inquisitive reader off the scent this poem was printed in the *Tiefurter Journal* as 'a translation from the Greek'.

However this may be, in many a poetic context we should be obscuring or violating the meaning if we were to concentrate exclusively on the erotic implications of the *Becher*. For in addition to its erotic significance, it has an obvious use as a receptacle for wine 'which maketh glad the

heart of man', and from time immemorial wine has been celebrated by
the poets as provocative of love and as the parent of poetry. Goethe was
but following in the old tradition when in his ballad he makes the *Sänger*
require of his patron no more than 'den besten Becher Weins' in recom-
pense for his song. And so when Tasso, the poet, would give utterance to
his pent-up passion for the Princess, what is more natural than that he
should use the image of the brimming goblet, symbolic of both love
and poetry?

Prinzessin:
> Wenn ich dich, Tasso, länger hören soll,
> So mässige die Glut, die mich erschreckt.

To which Tasso protests:

> Beschränkt der Rand des Bechers einen Wein,
> Der schäumend wallt und brausend überschwillt?   *3265-8*

By taking the adjective *schäumend*, used here of love and wine, and making it in the final seascape an attribute of wave, itself symbolic of the
lability of the poet's nature, Goethe brings the lover and the poet into
most intimate connection. Here we see very clearly how we should be
missing most subtle implications and overtones of the *Becher* image, if we
were to adhere too closely to its psychoanalytical interpretation.

Nor can we interpret at all mechanically the significant variants of the
Becher. Sometimes it appears as *Kelch*, sometimes as *Schale*. Since H.
Schöffler[25] made us aware of the religious colouring of *Werthers Leiden* we
have been accustomed to see the hero's sufferings as a mundane counterpart
of Christ's passion. In the first exuberance of his pantheistic joy in nature
Werther had made ready to drink as deeply from the 'foaming goblet of
the infinite' as Faust does from the springs and breasts of mother nature.
But as the story progresses to its tragic close the *Becher* is gradually modified by the prevailing sacrificial mood into a *Kelch*, or chalice. In his final
preparation for death Werther writes to Lotte, with obvious allusion to
the words of Christ in the Garden of Gethsemane: 'Hier Lotte! ich schau-
dere nicht, den kalten schrecklichen Kelch zu fassen, aus dem ich den
Taumel des Todes trinken soll! Du reichtest mir ihn und ich zage nicht!'
Fifty years later Goethe was to use this identical image of his frustrated
love for Ulrike von Levetzow in a letter to his daughter-in-law:[26] 'So be-
greifst du das Bittersüsse des Kelchs, den ich bis auf die Neige getrunken
und ausgeschlürft habe'. And appropriately enough, the *Trilogie der Leidenschaft*, in which this love of the old poet of seventy-four for the young
girl of nineteen is enshrined, begins with an invocation to Werther.[27]

Werther himself had rung the changes on *Becher* and *Kelch* as his mood was gay or sad, and Lotte has but to smile, or give him her hand, for the *Kelch*, even though he knows that it is filled with poison, to revert to a *Becher* once more. In the first version of *Wilhelm Meister*, written not very long after *Werther*, the equation of *Becher* with joy and *Kelch* with pain might seem fixed when Aurelie contrasts Hamlet's first treatment of Ophelia to his last by saying: 'He offers her the bitter cup (*Kelch*) of sorrow in place of the sweet goblet (*Becher*) of love'.[28] But it would again be wrong to assume that this equation is absolute: the form of the image is each time determined by the mood of the immediate context. If, in an earlier chapter of the *Theatralische Sendung*,[29] Wilhelm refers to his very sensual passion for the pretty actress, Marianne, as a 'Rausch des Taumel-kelches', is it not because a love which begins in ecstasy and ends in sorrow can only be embraced by such an oxymoron? The hero of the contemporaneaous *Die Geschwister*,[30] on the other hand—another Wilhelm —is moved by the pain which is an inevitable concomitant of intense joy to respond to a love which has taken the reverse course (threatened to end badly and found an unexpectedly happy solution) with the barest, but nevertheless significant, variation on the same image: 'Ich muss den Freudenkelch austrinken'.

The study of Goethe's imagery, cautiously used, can assist the literary critic in many ways: it can, as we saw, provide the indispensable clue to the meaning of such a difficult play as *Tasso*; it can confirm the prevailing mood of a poem or a novel, as it did of *Wandrers Sturmlied* and of *Werther*. It can do this and more. It corroborates the underlying unity of Goethe's poetic and scientific thought. The *Kelch*, for instance, can at one and the same time, as in his poem, *Die Metamorphose der Pflanzen*, symbolize both erotic excitement and the culmination of a plant's reproductive development. Behind the images of *Wanderer* and *Hütte* one clearly senses, not only human drives, but that rhythm of systole and diastole he discerned everywhere in the phenomenal world. Sometimes a repeated image can help to establish the date of composition: the reference to the 'Ratte, die Gift gefressen hat' in his letter of 17 September, 1775 to Auguste von Stolberg is commonly accepted as evidence that the 'Rattenlied' in *Faust* was in existence at that time. Cautiously and scrupulously used, the prevalence of the *Becher* image in the letters of 1781 might eventually help to establish that the great love-scene between Tasso and the Princess was already part of the *Ur-Tasso*. Similarly the occurrence of this image in the *Fragment über die Natur* printed in the same year: 'Durch ein paar Züge aus dem Becher der Liebe hält sie [die Natur] für ein Leben

voll Mühe schadlos', might be used as evidence to strengthen Goethe's
own hazy recollection that he was perhaps the actual author, and not just
the spiritual begetter, of that orphaned essay.

It would be even more profitable to follow an image such as the *Becher*
through the modifications it undergoes in Goethe's works in order to
throw the changes of his developing style into greater relief. We should
see how the Gothic *Becher* of which Gretchen sings becomes, after the
Italian journey, a classical *Schale* from which Faust is about to drink the
poison on Easter eve, or the *Schale* which contains the rejuvenating potion
of the 'Hexenküche'. And it is of course in this same form that it appears
in the Helena tragedy. But its erotic potency is in no wise diminished by
the classical shape it takes, and the vampire bride of Corinth pledges
her doomed lover in most passionate terms:

> Und dem Jüngling reichte sie die Schale,
> Der, wie sie, nun hastig lüstern trank.

Whilst, then, the intrinsic quality of the image remains, its accidentals
are modified by the setting. In Italy Goethe had learned to value the
craftsmanship of antique vases. He records this appreciation poetically in
Die Braut von Korinth:

> Und er will ihr eine Schale reichen,
> Silbern, künstlich, wie nicht eine war.

Objects are now seen and valued for their own sake and often designated
in precise technical terms: the characteristic glasses in which Rhine wine
is served are described in *Hermann und Dorothea* with loving accuracy:

> Mit den grünlichen Römern, den echten Bechern des Rheinweins.
>
> *I, 168*

When we move on to Goethe's symbolic period, we find in *Elective
Affinities* the same *Becher* used again as the symbol of undying love and
fidelity beyond the grave, just as it had been in the early ballad *Der König
in Thule*. But now it is elaborated, and its symbolic significance pointed,
by the effect of its cumulative use in infinitely varied poetic contexts
during all the years that have gone between.

A few years before his death Goethe explained to Eckermann[31]—*à pro-
pos* Byron's characters—the significance of woman for the modern poet:
'That, after all, is the only vessel we moderns have left into which we can
pour our highest ideal of perfection. There is no doing it with male characters any more. For in Achilles and Odysseus . . . Homer has done it all
for us'. The sexual implications of the *Becher* are here expressly sublimat-

ed, and its dual function in poetry fully recognised. A year or so later he
expresses the same thought in such a way that no trace of the conceptual
remains. 'Today', Eckermann records, [32] 'Goethe expressed himself very
beautifully concerning women. They were, he said, silver vessels (*silberne
Schalen*) in which we lay apples of gold'. This is a happy illustration of
that complete fusion of image and thought which characterises Goethe's
latest period. That Goethe can do this so naturally, and almost casually, in
conversation, is because his remark contains the quintessence of sixty
years of making poetry about *Becher* and *Schalen*. And with this illustration we come back to our beginnings. It is a perfect example of that power
which great poets possess of being able to think thoughts and express
thoughts in one operation; of being able to do, consciously and deliberately, what primitive man had done intuitively: to express the deepest
thought by uttering the appropriate image.

But above all the study of Goethe's imagery forces us to come to terms
with the all-important problem of the poet's creativity, in its power to
modify and complicate the material at his disposal ,whether it be history,
thought, personal experience, or the images which rise from the depths of
his unconscious to the surface of his mind. That he 'composes' or organizes them at all means that he enters into some different relation to them,
perceives their dramatic, their poetic, potentialities, shifts them here,
adjusts them there, elaborates, reduces, lets one work upon the other. To
abstract them out of this setting, out of this living and subtly inter-
connected whole, and interpret their psychological significance for the
man, as opposed to the *poet*, without allowing for the free creative power
of his poet's mind, is inevitably to draw false conclusions too about his
nature as man. Over and over again we have evidence, in Goethe's use of
images in and out of poetry, that the confessional element—of which we
hear so much—must be taken with more than the proverbial pinch of
salt. For the confessional impulse was very definitely tempered by a strong
feeling for artistic effect, and this at a much earlier age than we might
suppose. The poetic phrases by which Werther confesses the awakening
of his passion for Lotte are—we might say —'lifted' from a letter written
three years earlier[33] where he confesses his passionate absorption in the
writing of his first play, *Götz von Berlichingen*. 'I am seized', he writes, 'by
a passion, a quite unexpected passion. You know how such a passion can
throw me in upon myself, so that I forget sun and moon and the dear stars
themselves over it'. As he writes *Werther* these seem equally suitable terms
for describing a passion for a woman, and he makes Werther write of his
first meeting with Lotte: 'And since that time, sun, moon and stars may
quietly go their daily round, and I do not know whether it is day or night,

and the whole world about me ceases to exist'. Clearly it was the power
and effectiveness of the image which had seized his imagination. The
womanizer might say 'the lesser Goethe he'. But did not Keats say of
Shakespeare's *Sonnets* that they 'seemed to be full of fine things said unin-
tentionally—in the intensity of working out a conceit', thereby showing
a truer awareness of the intimate relation of form and experience in the
mind of the creative artist? And it is at his peril that the critic attempts to
arrive at the significance of a poet's imagery by abstracting it from the
formal relations in which it lives and grows and has its being.

Das Was bedenke! mehr bedenke Wie![34]

VIII. The Poet as Thinker

On the Varying Modes of Goethe's Thought

'SINCE, however, neither matter without mind nor mind without matter, ever exists, or can ever be effective ...'[1] We may take this to be an accurate reflection of Goethe's attitude to a venerable and persistent problem of philosophy, partly because it was written, towards the end of his life, as part of a considered statement of his mature view of natural process, but chiefly because in such union of complementary opposites the student of Goethe comes to recognize the authentic stamp of his mind. The complete interdependence he postulates between the two aspects of what is in reality an undivided unity is reflected in the chiastic structure of his sentence.

Goethe did not always express himself with such balanced completeness on philosophical issues. The deeper cause of his more one-sided statements was undoubtedly the many-sidedness of his mind. His lability, from earliest youth, shewed itself not only in openness to experience in the more immediate sense, but in successive surrenders to an immense variety of cultural influences, and in a tendency, while still under the full impact of any one authority, to take on something of its colour. Add to this that no one has ever had perpetuated so much of what he said off the record and in his off-moments; that he had, too, his fair share of human contrariness, issuing at its lowest in sheer petulance, at its highest in a pedagogic propensity to redress the balance, in a conviction that paradox is a genuine means to truth—and it is easy to see why such varied and conflicting schools of thought can find in him whatever they want to make of him. Even in the letter just quoted, where he is after all solely intent on establishing the inseparability of mind and matter in their intimate interworkings, he might seem to give a handle to the dialectical materialists by assigning linguistic primacy to matter: 'the former [principle] appertaining to matter conceived of as material, the latter to matter conceived of as mind'. But it would be a partial critic who ventured therefore to impute to him a materialistic interpretation of the world-process—however

E*

dialectical it may be. The idealists could come along with any number of
aphorisms to prove the opposite, especially those in which he invokes
not just Ideas but *the* Idea: 'The Idea is everlasting and one; to use the
plural too is misplaced. All we apprehend, and are able to speak of, are
but manifestations of the one Idea'.[2] By a judicious selection of evidence
one can build up a convincing case for his being Platonist or Aristotelian,
Spinozist or Kantian—and refute them all.

Yet, despite this, Goethe is unmistakably Goethe and not a mere reflec-
tor of other people's thinking. What he has recorded is the growth of his
mind, not a formal and finished system of philosophy. But it is a highly
characteristic growth, and organic in the strict sense of the term; for it
proceeds not by simple accretion, but by the double action of assimilation and elimination. If his enduring capacity for change and transformation was due to the ease with which he appropriated to himself elements
of his cultural surroundings, the original stamp of his thought was due
to his firm instinct to eject those which proved incompatible with his own
nature. He retained only what he could and must, what could be absorbed into the life of his continuing identity without jeopardizing its inherent pattern. An honorific word for this process would be the fashionable 'integrative', which could, of course, be countered with the pejora-
tive 'eclectic'. But a distinction he makes himself will lead us away from
the heady but sterile ardours of such verbal warfare towards the realities
of thought and person in the situations of actual existence:

> There can be no such thing as an eclectic philosophy; but there are
> eclectic philosophers. An eclectic, however, is anyone who assimilates
> from his environment, and the activities that go on there, whatever is
> commensurate with his own nature; and this is the sense in which all
> that we call formation, development, whether theoretical or practical,
> has meaning ... And if we only look about us, we shall invariably
> find that each and every one of us proceeds in this manner, and hence
> can never understand why it is impossible to convert others to his own
> opinion.[3]

It is hard to say what is more striking here: the psychological realism
which recognizes that thought, of all kinds, is always deeply involved in
the personality of the thinker—or the complete absence of any reductive
implication that what we call objective thought is, therefore, 'in reality'
nothing more than a 'mere' reflection of the personality of the thinker;
the careful safeguarding of the rigorous self-consistency of systematic
thought by the uncompromising rejection of an eclectic philosophy—or
the subsequent largeness of vision which sees the static abstractions of

discursive reason against a background of thought in the wider sense, thought which is acted on and believed, which is involved with life at the same time as it contemplates it, which is, one might say, nothing less than experience aware of itself.

What Coleridge aptly called the 'notional understanding' is here, as elsewhere in Goethe's writings, made dependent on an irreducible—call it—temperament, and put at the service of living; but its function, though limited, is never despised. Nor is his own command of it to be despised. If we say that his 'nature', the native set of his mind, was predominantly practical, we mean predominantly, not exclusively. His famous dictum that only what is fruitful is true[4] was a criterion to be invoked *after* intellectual effort, not *before* it. It did not absolve him from the struggle for truth, but served as a standard of reference for the various kinds of truth discovered by the mind in its adventuring after knowledge. It was a reminder of what there still remains to do after all theorizing has been done: 'Men are annoyed to find that truth is so simple. They should remember that they have all their work cut out to put it to practical use'.[5] His preoccupation with metaphysics—there is evidence in plenty—was both genuine and lasting; as he once observed, there are problems in science which can never be adequately discussed without its help (though he qualified this statement by insisting that he did not mean mere logic-chopping, word-wisdom, as he called it, but 'what was, is, and ever shall be, before, with and after physics').[6] But the best energies of his mind were always intent, not on any theory of being or knowing, but on how to live in the world in which we are and know.

For this reason it is inept to want to press him for an answer as to which is primary, mind or matter. For him it is enough that, as things are in the world we know, we never find the one apart from the other. And in giving voice to the Spinozian view that they are the same reality conceived now under the attribute of thought, now under that of extension, he can afford to give linguistic precedence to matter since he does not have to believe in the primacy of mind in order to be convinced of its potency. Others may indulge our speculations about origins and causes. He is one of those whose virtue it is to make us aware, in innumerable contexts of existence, that there is no separating the activities of these two aspects of reality.

And it is no less misplaced to labour the point that he knew that reality is not just 'given' to the mind but (to use a phrase of Dewey's) 'taken' by it. Certainly he did. But so did Schiller and Wordsworth, so did Schelling and Coleridge and Keats—so, for that matter, does recent natural science,[7] and with all the enthusiasm of belated insight. That 'all knowledge rests on the coincidence of an object with a subject',[8] is a conviction shared, explicitly or implicitly, by divers, and most divergent, minds. The fascinating thing is to see the different kinds of reality they manage to evolve on the basis of this common epistemological assumption; how variously they conceive of the relating of the two factors, of the balance between the self and the world outside. The point about Goethe is not his recognition that both have a part to play in the production of knowledge. That he had always taken for granted. What Whitehead has called 'the bifurcation of nature', the Cartesian dichotomy of reality into subject and object, was for him, at most, an instrument for one kind of thinking, never an actual experience of severance. 'I had never separated them', he wrote in his account of how he came to terms with Kant;[9] and we can believe him, for there is proof of it in the smallest movement of his thought and in the detail of his style. It was, as he put it, a 'naïve' conviction, which he was pleased enough to have confirmed by the intricacies of Kant's discursive reasoning, but which derived its existence, and its strength, from levels below that of philosophical persuasion, from the deeper levels of insight and attitude and action.

No, his special interest lies—and it is there that critical emphasis should fall—not in his ready recognition that 'we only receive the reality we know according to the forms and faculties of our own mind',[10] but in his avoidance of the dangers attendant upon such recognition, dangers inherent alike in conventional idealism and in our modern scepticism about the possibility of any kind of 'objectivity' outside of what science has to tell us of the quantitative and the measurable: the danger of saying that the subject confers meaning rather than construes it, that the mind is constitutive of experience rather than interpretive of it, the danger of isolating mind from world, of elevating it to the sole arbiter of knowledge, thus making it the self-sufficient centre of its own existence, with the consequent frustration of the private world and the despair of real communication between man and man. For Goethe, communication with the not-self, whether objects or persons, is the task to which man is called and which—as the author of *Werther* knew only too well—he relinquishes at his peril. The very involvement of subject with world, which is the condition of our existence, he sees as a challenge to objectivity; not indeed as something out there, independent of us, waiting to be 'known', but as something ever to be created—yet only to be created in collaboration with objects. He used the analogy of a game[11] when arguing that, on the higher levels of his activity, even the rôle of the scientist is less that of an observer than of an active participant. And it is an analogy which illuminates his whole conception of man's relation to the outside world. For it is not what you know about a game that matters but whether you can play it; the other player has a dual rôle—you play both with him and against him; the rules are fixed and agreed on, but if it were not for the incalculability of the moves there would be no game. Goethe's interest starts, in fact, where the epistemological statement ends: reality is neither in the subject nor in the object but in the activity-between. His preoccupation is with the practical management of that activity. And it is not with the metaphysical subject, identical in all of us, endowed with the same abstraction, the faculty of reason, but with the concrete phenomenon, the empirical, psychological, subject: with the atrophied senses and the distorting emotions, the intellectual prejudices and preconceptions, with all the snares that beset the individual in his efforts to commune with world.[12]

To know, and to say boldly,[13] where one stands is, then, the first condition of objectivity in Goethe's sense, as it is the only guarantee of genuine exchange with like- or with alien-minded. As opposed to the seeming objectivity of leaving the personal position out of account, true objectivity must include not only knowledge of the object but knowledge of one's self in relation to the object. Neither can be achieved in isolation from the other. The complexity of the two-way movement is again reflected in a chiastic structure: 'Der Mensch kennt nur sich selbst, insofern er die Welt kennt, die er nur in sich und sich nur in ihr gewahr wird'.[14] The reciprocity is complete. And the next sentence goes on: 'Jeder neue Gegenstand, wohl beschaut, schliesst ein neues Organ in uns auf'. If the first condition of objectivity is self-knowledge, the second is to let objects speak to us instead of imposing ourselves upon them or ratiocinating about them in their absence. And in commenting on his own mode of thought he assigns initial activity to the 'Elemente der Gegenstände, die Anschauungen'.[15] These perceptual forms, the elementary abstractions made in that primary encounter between self and world which we call sense-experience, enter, he says, into his thinking and become intimately permeated by it. This is the most striking feature of the way his mind worked, repeatedly analysed by Schiller for whom it retained a provocative fascination: not the activity of mind at all levels, from the simplest sense-perception upwards—that takes place, involuntarily and unconsciously, in all of us—but the continuing presence of sense even in the highest generalizations of which mind is capable, the sensuousness of his ideas. Even when he abstracts the forms of forms, the archetypes, or, going further still, the formative process itself, he never arrives at a disembodied concept. Like the Greeks, he knew how to think with the mind's eye, and used the word 'idea' as though he were aware that it was cognate with the Greek for 'seeing' as well as 'knowing', and that its prime meaning was 'form'.[16]

His rôle as thinker is essentially that of mediator between doctrines which have often seemed mutually incompatible. This is the particular contribution he has to make. And it is the hard core of him, what he would call his inborn 'Vorstellungsart', his fundamental attitude of mind, which determined all his philosophical acceptances and rejections, and to which his more one-sided statements should always be referred. His inconsistency of intellectual position is in truth biological wisdom and yields, to the broad view, a remarkable consistency of its own. There was a point in most systems of philosophy beyond which he could not go—the point where things which he felt belonged together began to get separated. As he wrote to Schiller[17] after reading Schelling's early work (aspects of which appealed to him strongly), he saw no prospect of such transcendental idealists ever getting from mind to bodies any more than the naïve realists were ever likely to bridge the gap from bodies to mind; and until the philosophers should have agreed among themselves how to join together again that which they had put asunder, he himself proposed to remain 'in dem philosophischen Naturstande' and make the best possible use of his 'undivided existence'. It was a consistently held conviction, reiterated some twenty-five years later thus: 'All controversies, whether among the Ancients or the Moderns, right down to the present day, derive from putting asunder that which God when he created nature joined together.'[18] But this awareness of the interdependence of what, during the development of man's consciousness, have become differentiated as opposites—mind and matter, subject and object, inner and outer, ideal and real—had first dawned on him with all the warmth and immediacy of a need fulfilled in his early experience of making form.

It is in that crucial decade 1770-80 that we find him learning, through the practice of his art, certain fundamental truths by which he was to live —and think—for the rest of his life: that art is a fusion of the most earthy and the most spiritual; that the artist is one who sees the universal in the particular, the ideal in the real, who endows external objects with a life from within and tells of his inner world in terms of the outer, so that in seeming to speak only of himself he yet symbolizes the secret life of us all. The powerful movement of his mind towards unification first becomes clearly articulate in that emphatic *eins* of his well-known letter to Herder of July 1772: 'das ist alles, und doch muss das Alles eins sein', though his letters during the two preceding years offer evidence in plenty of the growing urgency of his need to bring coherence into the bewildering diversity of his activities, to reverse their wildly centrifugal tendency

THE POET AS THINKER

and find within himself a centre to which his manifold functions of mind and body could be related. This inward pressure was undoubtedly clarified, but it was also aggravated, by Herder's trenchant criticism of what he was and did. It did not find release until it encountered, in the Greek poets, and especially in Pindar, a view of man and nature which revealed to him the unity of things supposedly different. Only then, when, in the achievement of perfectly fashioned verse, he read truths which confirmed him as well as criticized him—confirmed him in his inmost nature—was a new world opened up within him; only then could his diffuse feeling for what was wrong in his own being and creating be focused into a burning-point of energy; only then could much that Herder had been telling him become fruitful as activity.

Hence this amazing document, occasioned by Herder's negative verdict on his *Götz*, is a young poet's testimony of how he begins to find himself through becoming conscious of what it means to be a poet. In it he confesses both his realization of the need to fuse into one unified activity mind and body, head and hand, vision and technique, and his determination to achieve this fusion. Here we find a complete reversal of the notion that mind is the *cause* of overt acts and utterances which are its bodily *results*, that hand simply carries out what head tells it to do, that his medium is merely the vehicle whereby an artist's vision gets communicated to other people. At every stage, we learn from this as from other letters of the period, there is constant intercourse between him and the world outside. Not only do thought and feeling permeate medium and technique; these in their turn permeate thought and feeling. Not even the minutest detail of his craft can an artist afford to ignore, not just because this might mean failure to ensure complete articulation of a conception already evolved by his mind—the Greek that Goethe quotes, and the way he quotes it, make it unmistakably clear that it was not the importance of craft as such that 'pierced his soul' and opened his eyes to the nature of mastery, but the importance of *oneness*, oneness of head, heart and hand. He must be able to tune his instrument or mend his quill, because craft influences conception, because the sense-perception and muscular activity involved in it are themselves a source of insight. Only when he shuts his eyes and sees with his hand—again the context makes it clear that, as analogy, this is intended to hold for all the arts—can he acquire such sureness that the work he creates is informed throughout, in every smallest part, by the unifying feeling which makes it a self-contained whole.

This letter leaves us in no doubt that from now on truths discovered about, and through, the making of art were at the same time to be truths for living. This was yet another important sanction that Goethe obtained

from Pindar.[19] The recasting of his *Götz* may be uppermost in his mind;
but it is evident in every turn of phrase that mastering poetry is his particular means to mastering himself. And at the end of the decade, in a
diary entry of 14 July, 1779, where the impulse to unification of vision
and craft is no less articulate, and cast in not dissimilar terms, mastery of
art is still synonymous with mastery of life:

> Die Materie woraus einer formt, die Werkzeuge die einer braucht,
> die Glieder die er dazu anstrengt, das alles zusammen gibt eine gewisse
> Häuslichkeit und Ehestand dem Künstler mit seinem Instrument. Diese
> Nähe zu allen Saiten der Harfe, die Gewissheit und Sicherheit womit er
> sie rührt mag den Meister anzeigen in jeder Art . . . Man beneidet jeden
> Menschen den man auf seine Töpferscheibe gebannt sieht, wenn vor
> einem unter seinen Händen bald ein Krug bald eine Schale, nach sei-
> nem Willen hervorkommt. Den Punkt der Vereinigung des Mannig-
> faltigen zu finden bleibt immer Geheimnis, weil die Individualität eines
> jeden darin besonders zu Rate gehen muss und niemanden anhören
> darf.

Wherever we look in these years, among his diaries and letters, in
essays or reviews, in poems about art and the artist or in poems where
that is not the ostensible subject at all, we find the same tale. Its burden is
unification. And it is the same whether he is talking of the process of
making form or of completed forms. His clear awareness that mind and
body are not an inner and an outer, that mental activity is therefore not
something which takes place in the hidden recesses of a 'mind', safely
tucked away from world, but that the traffic between the two is unceasing and entirely reciprocal, this awareness prevented him from ever
letting the fashionable new doctrine of 'inner form' dissipate into mere
inwardness or transcendentalism. His reaction against outer form never
went in the direction of reducing it to a mere vessel for the containing of
an inner essence. On the contrary. If anything here is to be thought of as a
container, it is—if we take his language as seriously as we should—inner
form itself. It is, as he puts it, 'diese innere Form, die alle Formen in sich
begreift'.[20] Inner form, then, may be inward in the sense that it does not
immediately hit you in the eye, in the sense of requiring considerable dis-
cernment of thought and feeling for its perception. But for Goethe it is
nevertheless the larger unit, the all-embracing concept. The immediately
palpable symmetry and proportions it sometimes exhibits are but aspects
of it, even as in a living thing the shape we see is not just shell or outer
covering for the 'real' being housed within, but an area of extreme
sensitivity comprising the terminal points of some of the most inward-

reaching systems of the organism, points at which they make contact
with the environment.

This analogy with natural organisms Goethe was not to draw with such
exactitude until much later on. But even at this early stage he is pretty
clear just where the analogy with works of nature breaks down. Some
brief notes on dramatic form of 1775,[21] in which the carelessness of the
manner belies the coherence of the matter, make it as clear as did his letter to Herder of 1772 that such organic unity as the notion of inner form
implies is only to be achieved in works of art by concentrating on medium
and on technique. In the last paragraph of these notes—strangely ignored
in discussions of Goethe's early conception of form, perhaps because the
casual 'übrigens' with which it opens seems to disavow its intimate connection with the rest—he urges the dramatist to leave nature where she
belongs and focus his energies on creating his own world of illusion with
all the props and properties, and within the limitations, that the theatre
affords him. With this he particularizes in terms of drama what in the
preceding paragraph he had said about artistic form in general. There,
in order to express the essential unity of the three aspects under which
form may be considered, he had recourse to alchemistic imagery. Form,
whether thought of as process or product, is, like the philosopher's stone,
at once the vessel, the material and the treatment; it is the whole mysterious operation whereby what is unorganized becomes organized into a
new creation.[22] True this new thing, the work of art, will have something
'unreal' about it—however much feeling has gone to its making. But
only by means of this 'unreality', only by accepting the conditions and
conventions of his medium, can an artist bring forth a symbol of the
universal instead of the pallid fragment which ensues when he tries to
emulate the freedom of nature.

Here, at twenty-five, Goethe's attitude to inner form is, in all essentials, the same as in the criticism he made of the doctrine when he was
much older.[23] In this latter he rejects what is, oddly enough, at bottom
a quantitative notion: the idea that spirit suffers an inevitable loss when it
descends into matter, that the intensity of the vision in the artist's mind is,
as it were, diluted, spread out thin, when it takes on sensuous shape. On
the contrary, says Goethe: if the marriage between mind and matter is a
true one, what is begotten may well surpass either of its begetters:

> Eine geistige Form wird aber keineswegs verkürzt, wenn sie in der
> Erscheinung hervortritt, vorausgesetzt, dass ihr Hervortreten eine
> wahre Zeugung, eine wahre Fortpflanzung sei. Das Gezeugte ist
> nicht geringer als das Zeugende; ja es ist der Vorteil lebendiger
> Zeugung, dass das Gezeugte vortrefflicher sein kann als das Zeugende.

These later notes on inner form differ, however, from the earlier ones
by being set in a wider context. The terms of reference make it clear that
his rejection embraces not only idealistic aesthetics but idealistic philosophy altogether. 'Die Idealisten alter und neuer Zeit' are, it is true, accord-
ed a measure of sympathy in their endeavour to rescue the creative principle of the universe which seems so obscured in the individual phenomenon, to safeguard the eternal changelessness which tends to be forgotten
in our preoccupation with the changes of this mortal life. But this tole-
rant appreciation of an alien viewpoint only serves to throw into greater
relief the radical difference of his own native position when, with a characteristic 'but on the other hand', he insists on the deprivation we suffer
if in our pursuit of the One we lose sight of the Many, and proclaims his
allegiance to the conditions of our phenomenal existence:

Wir Menschen sind auf Ausdehnung und Bewegung angewiesen;
diese beiden allgemeinen Formen sind es, in welchen sich alle übrigen
Formen, besonders die sinnlichen, offenbaren.

This is our human lot. But the style leaves us in no doubt that it is for
Goethe at the same time our challenge and our chance. As powerfully as
anything in the whole of his writings, these two short paragraphs, distilled out of the fulness of his experience of art and nature and living, communicate his conviction that fulfilment comes through exploring limitations to the limit, that the only way to transcend conditions is to accept
them, that our only means of access to the universal and the ideal is
through infinite devotion to the individual and the real. They show too,
especially when considered in the light of his earlier and so similar attitude to art, that the only kind of philosophy he was prepared to accept
was one which would endorse his own first-hand experience of form.

Not every artist feels this need to have his avowed philosophy in tune
with what he knows practically about art and the making of it. The one
kind of knowledge may be completely insulated from the other, as
it seems to have been in Shelley, whose explicit underestimation of the
significance of sense-experience is startlingly at odds with his obviously
sensuous exploration of his medium. Or they may keep uneasy company,
as in Coleridge, in whom the discords between transcendental belief and
his doctrine of the imagination are never wholly resolved. While the precarious peace between poet and philosopher negotiated by Schiller in his
Aesthetic Letters is the outcome of a bitter struggle to save himself as an
artist from the ravages of idealism by wresting from it (and with its own

weapons) an acknowledgement of the powers and prerogatives of nature and the senses.

Goethe never got himself involved in such an ambiguous and ambivalent relation with philosophy. Standing more securely on his own, poetic, ground, he is at once less enthralled by analytical thought and less aggressive towards it. Against Schiller's plaintive surrender, 'Alas! we only know that which we separate',[24] we may set his unruffled statement of fact, 'Man, whenever he speaks, outside of poetry, is bound for the moment to become one-sided. There is no communication, no theory, without separation'[25]—more accurate than Schiller's and less resentful because, in recognizing that the function of analysis is rooted in the nature of discursive language, he is able to concede its unique power to make experience logically explicit, and hence communicable in general terms, without ceding to it the whole realm of knowledge. Not overestimating what it can do, he is the more equably just to what it alone can do.

The independence of his attitude towards analysis derives, I would say, from his being so completely sure of the intuitive knowledge he wanted it to analyse. The practice of his art, the nature of form, was experience known with such intimacy of knowledge that for him it was valid beyond dispute. But he required discursive reason to do more than just make this experience explicit. He asked it to furnish him with an epistemology which should be adequate to account for it. And he also wanted to explore the forms of nature in accordance with the most fundamental truth of it: that man and the world outside him are inextricably involved with each other. In this very broad and general sense it might be said that his philosophic and scientific thought are elaborations of poetic intuitions.

But only in this sense. Without careful qualification such a statement is open to grave misunderstanding. For it might be held to mean that he did not really *think* at all. The underlying belief of this assumption is that there can be no real thinking except in discursive language (or in such refinements of language as mathematics). On this view, the knowledge embodied in art derives from 'intuitions' which, as a modern philosopher ironically puts it,[26] 'are supposed to be born in some crepuscular depth of the mind, without any midwifery of symbols, without due process of thought'. But while it is true that there can be no thinking (not even that which precedes, often at a half-conscious level, the sudden intuition) without symbols of some sort—'symbolization is an act essential to thought and prior to it'[27]—not all articulate symbolism is discursive. To say that a musician *thinks* in his medium of music is more than a manner of speaking. And language, in its function of poetic material, is like any other artistic medium, at once a means to, and a vehicle of, *thought*.

Or, alternatively, the statement might be held to mean that Goethe's thinking was entirely restricted to *poetic* thinking. This view assumes that poetry is made by a particular faculty which is naturally and inevitably at war with the faculties involved in the production of science or philosophy. But, as was brought home forcibly to Goethe through his early encounter with Pindar, poetry is made with nothing less than the whole man. Nor are imagination and intuition the monopoly of the artist. Inspiration, as Pushkin once wrote, is as necessary in geometry as in poetry. This is not to imply that there is no difference between the various modes of thought, but only to suggest that the difference is more likely to be understood by reference to the symbolisms used, and the results produced, than by the assumption of separate and conflicting faculties. To say that Goethe's *Urpflanze*, for instance, was a *poetic* intuition is to foster linguistic confusion.[28] Poetic intuitions are born through poetic symbols (a mode of language) and give rise to poetry. His *Urpflanze* undoubtedly was an intuition; but it was preceded by thought and practice of a kind quite different from that required for the making of poetry: by observation, classification and analysis of plant-phenomena. And it certainly was, as Schiller insisted, an idea. But this, too, can be confusing if not further defined. For it was not, on the one hand, a purely verbal abstraction of the kind some minds, including Schiller's own, seem able to entertain, and move about like counters through complicated processes of thought without reference to physical things or their images. Ideas, for Goethe, were symbolized by phenomena, and only became abstractions when uttered in the language of discourse. The aphorism quoted above[29] in which he says that all we apprehend are but manifestations of the one Idea, continues: 'What we utter in language are *concepts*, and *to this extent* the Idea itself is a concept'. If at first he balked at being told that his *Urpflanze* was an idea, it was because, as he once wrote to Schiller,[30] he himself could never dwell for long in this realm of verbal abstractions; the immediate impulse of his mind was to flee out into nature and seek a distinct and sensuous form, an *Anschauung*. But this is no resaon for dubbing his archetypes *poetic* ideas—though when conceived and uttered as poetry in, for instance, his elegy, *Die Metamorphose der Pflanzen*, they *become* poetic ideas. Such concrete, imagistic, thinking is not confined to artists. It is, as Agnes Arber points out,[31] indispensable to the morphologist, for example, and many of them, from Aristotle onwards—not just the poet Goethe—have in fact been strongly visual. Goethe's *Urpflanze* is an idea because it was conceived as the very principle of vegetative organization to which no actual plant of experience is entirely adequate. But it felt to *him* more like an experience because it was still, even at this stage

THE POET AS THINKER

of abstraction, saturated with innumerable visual and tactile images of plants he had known—and was, incidentally, capable of modification by further experience of plants as yet unknown.

Finally, it would be unfortunate if our recognition of the intimate connection between poet and thinker were held to imply that his thought was thereby, of necessity, somehow less 'pure' as thought, less fit, and less entitled, to be comprehended and judged in its own right; that his scientific work, for example, was in the nature of a pathetic attempt to bolster up, by paraphernalia and methods borrowed or adapted from science, knowledge arrived at initially by pure intuition. The validity of his findings must be left to the scientist—or, more accurately, to the historian of science. Our concern here is with the various modes of his thinking. And the exact nature of his scientific thinking, the precise difference between his approach and that of the physicist, was authoritatively analysed, almost thirty years ago now, by Ernst Cassirer.[32] It lies not, as is still often asserted, in his neglect of observation, experiment or analysis—he used all three; nor in his reliance on intuition for the establishment of hypotheses —the physicist relies on it too; nor yet in the way each of them orders his facts—Goethe knew as well as the physicist (and says so quite explicitly) that the isolated phenomenon proves nothing by itself, that facts have to be arranged in such a way that each develops out of the other, and that if such series are not given in experience they have to be produced under the artificial conditions of experiment. The difference lies not in their subsequent procedure, but in the initial step the physicist takes when he translates a qualitatively apprehended world into quantitative symbols; when, in order to generalize about natural phenomena and processes, he breaks down their complexity into elements which can be rendered in terms of mathematics and so projected into a new complexity of a quite different order. What Goethe feared from the development of physical science was not the loss of the phenomenal world—that is still there to be enjoyed through the senses, contemplated with the imagination, interpreted by poet and artist, however schematic a picture of it the physicist may evolve. What he resisted was the threatened decay of any systematic investigation of this world in all its qualitative concreteness, complexity and movement, the denial that a strict method for such investigation is even possible, the monopoly of 'science' by a science which, in leaving out the subject's relation to the world, offers us knowledge of only half a world, the loss, in short, of any unified conception of nature to which the findings of the various fields of research can be referred. Now whether we see in his own approach suggestive insights for widening the scope of science to include aspects of reality which have proved refractory to exploration by the concepts of quantity and causality; or whether we prefer to accept the attenuated meaning of the ancient and comprehensive term science, say that what Goethe was trying to do lies outside the sphere of science proper, and envisage the unification of knowledge taking place under the sign of a new philosophy: whichever side we take in this battle of words, nothing is to be gained by going back behind the distinctions so carefully achieved by Cassirer and founding fresh confusion by denying Goethe's method a precision and exactitude of its own, suggesting that it only has curiosity interest as the product of his poetic genius.

The original relation between the various manifestations of his mind is much closer, and much more interesting, than that; but it can only be understood if in noting the evident connections we are no less clear about the distinctions. Thus his likening of scientific activity to a game suggests the artistic approach; and it would not be far-fetched to see the psychological origins of his rejection of the spectator-attitude in science in his early emotional crisis over Herder's biting criticism of his own onlooker-attitude in art: 'Es ist alles so Blick bei Euch'.[33] But whatever its origins, the analogy when he uses it in 1823 expresses a conviction which is the fruit of long experience of science and scientists, of mature reflection as to whether man is not altogether too involved with world ever to be able to detach himself from it as pure observer. And its validity will depend entirely on whether it proves to be a more accurate description of what the scientist actually does, and a more appropriate and productive attitude for him to adopt. There are signs that it may. But what is more relevant here is that similar observations are made by thinkers who are not artists at all, and in contexts which have no concern with art. The neurologist, Viktor von Weizsäcker, for example, developing the same train of thought without reference to Goethe at all, uses the identical image of the chess-player.[34]

Again, Goethe's demand for a scientific method combining both induction and deduction in a 'Synthese von Welt und Geist' is one which a poet turned scientist might very well make. There are evident, if fugitive, connections between the young man's knowledge that poetry is the refashioning of outer world by inner and the old man's insistence that mind is constantly at work, selecting, ordering, construing, even in what we tend to think of as pure observation—'und so kann man sagen, dass wir schon bei jedem aufmerksamen Blick in die Welt theoretisieren'.[35] Connections too, on the other hand, between his need as artist for unremitting contact with world, his respect for the laws of his medium, for the reality of the objects whose nature he is always struggling to understand, and his recognition as scientist that the test of all our theories is the answer nature gives,[36] that reason is indeed an essential tool in the pursuit of knowledge but alone can tell us nothing whatsoever; so that alongside Kant's proud claim: 'Der Verstand schöpft seine Gesetze nicht aus der Natur, sondern schreibt sie dieser vor', he can set his own, no less proud, but also humble:

> Freue dich, höchstes Geschöpf der Natur, du fühlest dich fähig,
> Ihr den höchsten Gedanken, zu dem sie schaffend sich aufschwang,
> Nachzudenken. Hier stehe nun still und wende die Blicke
> Rückwärts, prüfe, vergleiche, und nimm vom Munde der Muse,
> Dass du schauest, nicht schwärmst, die liebliche volle Gewissheit.[37]

His scientific *credo*, the conviction that there is a correspondence between the laws of mind and the laws of nature, is here fashioned into verse. But this must not mislead us. It *is* a scientific *credo*, and is just as likely, perhaps more likely, to inspire reflections on the striking coincidence between mathematical logic and the laws discovered by physics, than on the relation of the artist's mind to the forms of the world outside him. Even as the essays in which he weighs the relative merits of induction and deduction can stand in their own right as discourse on scientific method regardless of the fact that they had their origin in the mind of a poet.

It is the same with his relation to philosophy. The poet is much in evidence because it was to his experience of making poetry that the findings of any philosophy were referred. But his rejections were not made in any spirit of retreat into the mistbound fastnesses of the imagination in order to take his stand on a poetic truth deemed the greater for being infinitely more mysterious than that of philosophy. On the contrary. They were made in the spirit of philosophy itself. To begin with, imagination for him was not nebulous at all; it was a quite definite concept, closely related to the equally definite concepts of *Anschauung* and *Gestaltung*. And what he demanded from philosophy was a theory of knowledge which should not have to relegate such important aspects of artistic activity as imagination, intuition, insight gained through sensuous exploration of the medium, to the realm of transcendental reality or the limbo of unreason. With such a conception of mind neither conventional idealism nor conventional realism could provide him, and he had the wit to say 'no thank you' to their findings where they failed to meet his need. True, he found it from time to time convenient, even necessary, to use the language of both; but he was committed to neither and knew the exact point at which he diverged from each. It has been argued[38] that the union of *Erkenntnisidealismus* and *Erkenntnisrealismus* which he consciously represented gave rise to constant conflict within him, that he achieved complete harmony of the two only at odd moments and in isolated works. I find this confusing. On the one hand I doubt whether this particular conflict was ever *in him*; it was a conflict of terms rather than of experience, a question of philosophical concepts available. And as regards the harmony: if what is meant is harmony between the real and the ideal, then he frequently achieved it, because that is what artists are constantly doing; if between the two schools of thought, then he never achieved it, because he very wisely left the job to the philosophers themselves. But if he could not supply the answer, Goethe was certainly philosophically-minded enough to ask the right question. His analysis of the outstanding problem, as he formulated it in the letter to Schiller already quoted,[39] is in essentials the same as that of a philosopher who attemps a solution of it today:

> Unless the *Gestalt*-psychologists are right in their belief that *Gestaltung* is of the very nature of perception, I do not see how the hiatus between perception and conception, sense-organ and mind-organ, chaotic stimulus and logical response, is ever to be closed and welded.[40]

In that same letter to Schiller there is even a hint of how Goethe envisaged the gap being closed: by the unifying concept of *Anschauung*, by which he understood the fundamental activity of construing forms, operative in varying degrees at all levels of human behaviour, from instinctive impulse to the intricate combinations of abstract reasoning:

> From the appetite of a child for an apple hanging on the tree to the fall of same which is said to have aroused in Newton the idea for his theory, there are admittedly very many degrees of perception, and it would be a good thing if they were one day subjected to rigorous analysis and we were made to understand which is the highest and why.

What we are in fact confronted with in Goethe is an outstanding example of a single mind transposing certain basic and implicit assumptions into a variety of modes of thought. His understanding of the nature of form may first have become articulate through making poetry; but the origin of the amazing congruence between his varying modes of thought, and the coherence of the knowledge he arrived at through them, is to be sought outside the sphere of poetry—outside science or philosophy. For what drives and sustains him in all his endeavour is an unshakable conviction that the formative process is one throughout the universe, in nature and in the mind of man, one in all the variety of its manifestations. Such conviction belongs to the realm of belief. This casts no reflection on the validity of his thinking. All thought, all science, is thus rounded with belief, rests on assumptions, more often tacit than avowed, not excluding those of the most personal kind. But to dismiss it therefore as mere rationalization is to fall into the kind of reductive thinking which Goethe himself was so careful to avoid. He could be sceptical enough about progress to coin the aphorism that everything worth thinking has already been thought;[41] but he was sufficiently committed to the human adventure to applaud the unflagging inventiveness of man's mind, to be in no doubt at all that the new methods and symbolisms it constantly devises for the rethinking of old thoughts are, at the same time, a means to genuinely new knowledge. The problem is to discover how the new and the old shall consort together in reasonable peace and harmony.

It can certainly be no easy or simple harmony; differentiation precludes that. It has to be a harmony based on the fullest recognition of differences. The various modes of thought, and the different kinds of knowledge, have to be understood each in their separateness before we can begin to compare their relative achievement and value. This was the procedure that Goethe himself adopted both in his reflections on the nature and scope of the new science of morphology[42] and in his *Farbenlehre* under the rubric 'Neighbourly Relations'. He first sharply distinguishes the specific function and peculiar limitations of each individual science, weighs the merits and demerits of the various symbolisms by means of which man abstracts his manifold pictures of reality: the metaphysical, mathematical, physical, chemical, ethical, religious and mystical. Only after this initial process of differentiating does he embark upon the job of uniting. In a growing collaboration and exchange between men of good-will he sees the only hope of overcoming the inevitable disadvantages of specialization. What we need, he suggests, is a multifarious language which will employ *all* the varying symbolisms, flexibly, and with a clear awareness of the peculiar relation of each to the reality it symbolizes, neither confusing the symbol with the reality nor imagining that any one of the symbolic modes which man has evolved can ever be dispensed with if we are to build our reality as richly and truly as possible. For the picture that each of them presents to us is essentially the real world as construed by that particular mode of abstraction; and the truth about reality is not to be discovered by trying to decide which of them is right and which wrong, but by realizing that each has its part to play in enriching our conception of truth.

And as in the body of knowledge, so in the person of the individual. Goethe's injunction to man to develop all his faculties into a unity[43] is no injunction to return to primal oneness, but to press forward to a new kind

of unity on the other side of specialization. Hence his disagreement with
Hamann's demand that every activity of man, whether in deed or in
word, shall be an expression of the whole man, of the totality of his functions.[44] This, Goethe grants, may be desirable and possible in living and in
art, but not in speech (except when it is poetry) and therefore not in any
kind of analytical thought. Speech, like analysis, is bound to be one-
sided—'Jedes ausgesprochene Wort erregt den Gegensinn'.[45] And indeed,
in view of all the differentiated functions which man has developed,
would it not be one-sidedness of another sort, were he to persist in a state
of undifferentiated wholeness? The wholeness Goethe had in mind was
to be managed in a different way: by being analytical (i.e. one-sided)
where analysis is appropriate, intuitive (i.e. whole) where synthesis is
appropriate. The 'undivided existence' of which he spoke was, in fact, a
unity to be created in succession of time. Any other kind of unity is a
betrayal of what man has become and what he has achieved.

He himself possessed this flexibility of response to a remarkable degree.
And it is at once his great strength and a real obstacle to his being widely
understood. For it seems like vacillation to some that he can conceive of
one and the same reality under different attributes:

> Urphänomen: Ideal–real–symbolisch–identisch.
> Ideal, als das letzte Erkennbare;
> real, als erkannt;
> symbolisch, weil es alle Fälle begreift;
> identisch, mit allen Fällen.[46]

But what saves such vacillation of appearance from being vacillation in
fact is the consistent endeavour which sustains it, the clear awareness that
this weaving of a pattern in time is the only means of giving full play to
the differentiated functions of the mind. The alternative is to renounce
unity of being in favour of uniformity of response, to become fixed in
one particular mode of thinking.

> Ich für mich kann, bei den mannigfaltigen Richtungen meines We-
> sens, nicht an einer Denkweise genug haben; als Dichter und Künstler
> bin ich Polytheist, Pantheist hingegen als Naturforscher, und eins so
> entschieden als das andere. Bedarf ich eines Gottes für meine Persön-
> lichkeit, als sittlicher Mensch, so ist dafür auch schon gesorgt. Die
> himmlischen und irdischen Dinge sind ein so weites Reich, dass die
> Organe aller Wesen zusammen es nur erfassen mögen.[47]

A more intangible, but no less real, obstacle to the understanding of
his thought is his extremely flexible use of language. At any moment,

even in his scientific writings, he is liable to switch from the purely discursive mode to what may perhaps be called the poetical, since—to borrow a working distinction suggested by Paul Valéry—it consists of a piece
of prose which cannot be adequately rendered by any other piece of prose.
These swift changes from one mode to the other can be disconcerting.
But we should not imagine that Goethe himself was the victim of confusion. He was a far too assiduous and conscientious practitioner of language not to know what he was doing. On at least two occasions he explicitly drew attention to the chief difficulty which confronted him in his
scientific work: that of expressing opposites simultaneously. The first of
these was in 1820 in the essay entitled *Bedenken und Ergebung*,[48] where he
deals with the problem in its most fundamental and general form. Thought,
being independent of space and time, can conceive of simultaneity and
succession together; they can only be actually experienced separately.
The scientist seems, therefore, to be faced with an insoluble problem: in
his practice he has to investigate these two aspects of any natural process
one after the other; in trying to render them in his theory he ought,
ideally, to express them both together. But this is more than discursive
thought can contrive; and in the absence of any more adequate symbolism Goethe takes refuge in poetry. But this is no flight inwards, no
despairing retreat from reality. On the contrary, it is open-eyed recourse
to a mode of expression which can in fact render opposites simultaneously, which while stringing out words one after the other can yet create the
illusion of instantaneity.

Just how little Goethe was here turning his back on science, despite the
difficulties it presented, in what unromantic sobriety of spirit he resorted
to poetic symbolism, is borne out by some notes of 1823 headed *Probleme*.[49]
Here he discusses a particular example of the general problem of expressing opposites simultaneously. The two principles at work in the
growth of any form are metamorphosis and specification, the tendency
to constant change, the tendency to persist in specific form. Both are
simultaneously at work and should, therefore, ideally, be presented together in any symbolic formulation of the process of growth—which
seems impossible. Perhaps, Goethe goes on, we can only escape from
this dilemma by again having recourse to 'ein künstliches Verfahren'. He
evokes the analogy of modern musical form, which depends on the dual
principle of a natural progression of notes and the artificially induced
equal temperament obtaining within the octave. The analogy serves a
double purpose; it reflects, on the one hand, the relation between metamorphosis and specification; on the other, the relation of any symbolism
to the experience it symbolizes, the artifice that has to be imposed on a

natural order by any symbolism for explaining it. But of course it is only an analogy. There is no intention of impressing music into the service of science! What Goethe imagines here is the possibility of a new kind of symbolism altogether—characteristically tempering the audacity of his vision with a dash of sceptical irony. What the biologist really needs, he says, is a way of communicating his results which is at once logical *and* presentational, at once artifice *and* art:

A symbolism would have to be devised. But who is to accomplish this? And if accomplished, who recognize its validity?

It is a problem which still remains unsolved today.

IX. Literary Relations in the Light of Goethe's Principle of 'Wiederholte Spiegelungen'

It was Goethe's practice in his later years to express the processes he discerned at work everywhere—not only in nature, but in human life, history, and art—in terms of a few symbols of great simplicity but charged with the cumulative experience of his scientific work. Thus all nature within and without is dominated by the great principles of *Polarität* and *Steigerung*—those two 'grosse Triebräder aller Natur'. Polarity is present, not only in the physical world, as a constant alternation of opposites, but equally in the world of human affairs: head and heart, body and soul, love and hate, sense and reason, conscious and unconscious, the real and the ideal, mind and matter, contemplation and activity, analysis and synthesis, God and the world. For, like breathing-in and breathing-out, it is the very rhythm of life itself. *Steigerung*, or ascent, is in the physical sphere the principle whereby a substance through quantitative intensification undergoes a qualitative change to something of a different order; in the biological sphere it connotes the upward progression observable in nature from the lower to the more highly organized forms of life. And what is true of colours, plants, and animals is equally true of art, of love, even of the culinary processes.[1]

Again, Goethe's intuition of an 'Urphänomen' is primarily associated with the magnet or with his *aperçu* of a primal type-plant, the 'Urpflanze'. But the term is equally applicable to the ballad as the 'Urei' of poetry. Metamorphosis is characteristic of all natural phenomena, but it applies also to things of the mind; its manifestation is changing form, whether in animal, plant, or poem. And metamorphosis is kept from running riot by another basic principle, its counterpoise, the tendency to persist and become specific: the 'Beharrlichkeitsvermögen' or 'Specificationstrieb'. It was the absence of this latter which Goethe so deplored in writers of the Romantic school; for in spite of all their poetic inspiration and talent, it allowed their phantasy to run riot, unformed and uncontrolled.

Extending Linnaeus' theory of prolepsis, or anticipation, according to which the side-shoots of a tree run through all the stages of growth and decay in weeks instead of years,[2] Goethe, in conversation with Eckermann,[3] explains how human knowledge is not confined to what we know through actual experience: our knowledge of fundamental and universal situations we carry within us, and the poet in particular possesses the power of projecting into his work by 'Anticipation' this image of the world within. Thus he, Goethe, as a young man of twenty-two, had been able to write *Götz* and express in it a wealth of emotion which he could, at that time, only have known intuitively. And in *Faust* he could conjure up the depths of the hero's despair and the heights of Gretchen's love out of his own inner consciousness. It is 'anticipation', too, when he maintains to Kestner that the poem, *Der Wandrer*, was written 'Lotten ganz im Herzen',[4] for actually it antedates his acquaintance with her by several months. And as he re-reads *Werther* with the new Lotte, Frau von Stein, in mind, it seems to him that she had been 'anticipated' by the earlier heroine, 'die Lotte, die auf dich vorgespukt'.[5]

Here, already, we are in the presence of that unity in variety which characterizes all Goethe's scientific thought. For 'anticipation' is itself only another aspect of the principle of 'Wiederspiegelung', or reflection and counter-reflection. An 'Erlebnis', Goethe's experience of Lotte Buff, is transmuted into art in *Werthers Leiden*. This, in turn, is seen as anticipatory reflection of his new relation to Charlotte von Stein. There is thus direct reciprocation between life and art and back again to life. This is, in embryo, Goethe's theory of 'Wiederspiegelung', which he set forth in 1823 as a commentary on the Sesenheim idyll.

In 1822 a student of philology, Ferdinand Näke, fired by the fascinating account of Goethe's love for Friederike Brion in *Dichtung und Wahrheit*, had made a literary pilgrimage to Sesenheim in the hope of recapturing on the spot something of the spirit and more of the facts. He related his adventure in a small volume, *Wallfahrt nach Sesenheim*, and sent a copy to Goethe who acknowledged it in a letter of 31 January, 1823, later printed in his posthumous works as *Wiederholte Spiegelungen*.[6] In these somewhat cryptic pages Goethe puts on record the whole relation between literature and life, and life and literature, setting out by means of this early experience that natural process which Sir Richard Livingstone[7] has aptly called the cross-fertilization of life and literature. The sequence of events as Goethe sees them in old age is roughly as follows:

1) A blissful, imaginatively enhanced, episode of his [Goethe's] early life finds a reflection in his mind which is more potently persistent than

he knows [i.e., the Sesenheim episode, including all the imaginative concomitants which awakened it and the poetic productions it inspired].

2) This reflected image not only persists, but is often renewed and hovers in his mind for many years.

3) What he has cherished so long is finally articulated in lively recollection and thereby reflected back to others [i.e., in *Dichtung und Wahrheit*].

4) This reflection of a reflection now sends forth radiance into the world at large, so that some sensitive mind may well be stirred by it as though it were reality, and receive from it a profound impression.

5) From this there develops in such a sensitive mind [i.e., Näke's] an impulse to try to conjure up the past and to give it a new reality.

6) The urge becomes so insistent that, to satisfy it, he must go to the place where it happened in order to assimilate the local atmosphere.

7) Here, by a lucky chance, he finds a sympathetic, well-informed, person on whose mind the image of the original experience has similarly impressed itself.

8) Thus here in this somewhat lifeless locality there arises the possibility of building reality anew, and of creating, from fragments of existence and tradition, a second 'present', a second reality, and of falling in love with the Friederike of olden time in all her original loveliness.

9) So that now, despite all that the years between have brought of new and different experiences, she can through Näke's book be reflected back once again in the soul of her aged lover, and lovingly re-create for him the original experience in all its gracious, living, reality.

In short, Näke, under the impact of *Dichtung und Wahrheit*, fell in love with Friederike's memory and was able by the account he sent to Goethe to rekindle her memory with new vividness in him. Literature and life were as mirrors casting their reflection back and forth, or, as Goethe puts it:

If one considers that repeated reflections in this psychological sense, not only keep the past in lively memory, but actually enhance, intensify, it to a higher degree of vitality, one is reminded of the physical phenomena in entoptics which similarly, as they are reflected back and forth, far from fading away, become rather enkindled. In this way we shall obtain a symbolic picture of what has been, and is being, repeated daily in the history of the arts and sciences, and even in the world of religion and politics.

It is characteristic of the later Goethe that he should thus make use of a scientific metaphor to communicate the process of reflection which he saw at work in every sphere of life. Entoptic images were familiar to him from his studies in optics and colour. They are those images which are caused by something inherent in the structure of the eye itself, not by the reflection on the retina of objects without. Though ophthalmologists may dispute about their cause, their reality is attested by the photographic records made of the eye which sees them. Goethe himself possessed to an unusual degree the gift of producing images when his eyes were closed.[8] Whether these entoptic images really provide a useful parallel at all points with the process Goethe had in mind is immaterial. It seemed to him an illuminating analogy for two reasons: 1. because the images originate in the eye and not in the outside world; 2. because they only acquire vividness and intensity when they are reflected back into the eye again by some reflecting surface outside. These two characteristics made entoptic images seem to him a suitable symbol for the process whereby any experience which comes from within acquires new intensity and new vividness when it is reflected back to us by someone else: as our favourite idea will take on new significance in the responses of a trusted friend; as Goethe's *Natürliche Tochter* seemed to him enhanced in value by Herder's appreciative comments—'wie uns oft im Spiegel ein Gemälde reizender vorkommt als beim unmittelbaren Anschauen';[9] as when we see a familiar landscape through the eyes of a particular painter—'meine alte Gabe, die Welt mit Augen desjenigen Malers zu sehen, dessen Bilder sich mir eben eingedrückt'.[10] This process of reflection and re-reflection from person to person, from community to community, from nation to nation, from age to age, from art and literature to life and back again, seemed to Goethe the basis of our whole growth and development. 'What scientist', he says, 'does not rejoice in the marvels he sees produced by reflection (*Spiegelung*). And what we may call reflection (*Spiegelung*) in the psychological sense, each of us has experienced in himself, even if unconsciously, and he will, once he becomes aware of it, have no difficulty in understanding how much his development in life has owed to this process.'[11] This remark was provoked by the consideration of the foreign periodicals, *Le Globe* and the *Foreign Quarterly Review*. Goethe hoped that easier and better communications would step up this process of international 'Wiederspiegelung' and thereby bring about the creation of a world literature.
Who cannot corroborate Goethe's theory out of his own experience?

Is there any doubt that some of the appeal of the film, *The Young Mr. Pitt*, which was shown soon after Dunkirk, was due to the reflection in the hazards of the Napoleonic wars of our own so recent danger? Similar considerations sufficiently account for the extreme popularity during the last war of Tolstoi's *War and Peace*, which suddenly became unprocurable from either library or bookshop. For us, the retreat of the German armies from Stalingrad seemed mirrored in Napoleon's retreat from Moscow in 1812. And we may note that, at the very time when this retreat from Moscow was an event of immediate reality, Goethe himself felt an impulse to find a mirror for it in history—in the fate of Timur, the Mogul conquer-or, whose defeat in the grip of winter acquired new life and potency be-cause of its reflection in an occurrence which was of immediate import in Goethe's own day. Herder had already led the way by his anonymous translation in 1794 of Jakob Balde's Latin poems, in which 'poetical mirror', as Goethe puts it, [12] his countrymen saw their own troublous times reflected.

As an arrangement of mirrors enhances the vividness of a reflected object, so the potency of the artist's vision is increased as it is reflected back and forth in the life of human beings. Long before Goethe had elabo-rated his principle of 'Wiederspiegelung' by the scientific analogy of entoptic images, he had experienced something very like it intuitively. As early as 1775[13] he had used the image of a lens, or burning-glass, as a symbol of the way art is able to concentrate reality into significant form and so impart to it aesthetic intensity. As Leonore says in *Tasso*:

> Wie reizend ist's, in seinem schönen Geiste,
> Sich selber zu bespiegeln! Wird ein Glück
> Nicht doppelt gross und herrlich, wenn sein Lied
> Uns wie auf Himmelswolken trägt und hebt? *1928-31*

It is, of course, not the specific function of art, nor would Goethe have claimed that it was, to reflect our own experience in this way. It is rather a kind of work of supererogation, the good conscience of art, as Rilke puts it in one of his *Briefe an eine junge Frau*: 'des Kunst-Dings gutes Gewissen, nicht sein Beruf'.

And yet how much poorer our lives would be without 'Wieder-spiegelung' of this kind. For it is our own imaginative, literary, expe-rience which first predisposes us to see the significance of our personal events and relationships, and which in turn enriches them by providing a mirror in which they are enhanced. This experience begins in child-hood when, once we have started to read, the games we play are all a re-enactment of our favourite stories:

F

Unter die lässlichsten Versuche, sich etwas Höheres anzubilden, sich einem Höheren gleichzustellen, gehört wohl der jugendliche Trieb, sich mit Romanenfiguren zu vergleichen. Er ist höchst unschuldig und, was man auch dagegen eifern mag, höchst unschädlich.[14]

The impulse persists into adolescence. Whether we fall in love with this girl or that depends largely on her likeness to some heroine who has imprinted herself deeply upon our imagination. It is indeed a moot point whether fiction is not a more potent factor even in our adult lives than we would readily admit, and whether we are not predisposed to this or that action by having already experienced it in the imaginary world of our reading.

The place assigned to this essay on *Wiederholte Spiegelungen* in some editions—immediately after *Dichtung und Wahrheit*—is supported by what Goethe writes concerning the purpose of a biography:[15]

> For this seems to be the chief purpose of a biography: to present a man against the background of his time, and to show how far he is furthered or hindered by the world without, how he forms out of it for himself his conception of the world and of men, and inasmuch as he is an artist, a poet or a writer, reflects (*spiegelt ab*) his experience of them to others.

If Goethe thought that this was also the function of autobiography, then this would account for the space he devotes in *Dichtung und Wahrheit* to his own poetry, recasting it into a new form, experiencing it anew, and sending it forth again to influence the world once more:

> To the very end of his life the author should not relinquish the advantage of communication, even at a distance, with those whom affection binds to him. And if it is not granted to every one to step forth anew at a certain age with surprising and powerful productions, yet just at that period of his life when knowledge is most perfect, and consciousness most distinct, it must prove a very agreeable and re-animating task to treat former creations as new matter, and work them up into a kind of epilogue which may serve once more for the edification of those who have previously been edified with, and by, the artist.[15]

The title itself, *Dichtung und Wahrheit*, suggests the lability of the relation between poetry and truth, art and life, as Goethe conceived it. The fact that he hesitated between the order, 'Dichtung und Wahrheit', or 'Wahrheit und Dichtung', indicates that it was immaterial which of the two came first in the fructifying of experience by and into art. It has been

a common assumption of literary history that the threads must run from
life to literature, and the 'confessional' element in Goethe's poetry has
been stressed to satiety. The Frankfurt Gretchen, Friederike Brion, the
wretched servant-girl, Susanna Margarete Brandt, who paid with her
life for the murder of her illegitimate child—each has in turn been represented as the prototype of the heroine in *Faust*. But that is not as the affair
is presented to us by Goethe himself. We note how the many threads in
Books IX-XI of *Dichtung und Wahrheit* are gathered up to lead, all of them,
to Sesenheim and Friederike, and how they all, as it were, pass through
Herder's hands. For the whole complex of Herder's influence, and of the
new life in Strassburg and its difference from the atmosphere of Leipzig,
is one and indivisible and cannot be dealt with in separate compartments.
All that Herder had taught him predisposed Goethe to the meeting with
Friederike. The ballads he had collected at Herder's prompting in the
Alsatian countryside mostly treated of the theme of unhappy love. Was
he not, in his relation to Friederike, living out the situation of the squire's
son who wooed a parson's daughter only to leave her to die of a broken
heart? For as he describes her—not once but twice—in her Alsatian costume, she must have seemed to him the living embodiment of a German
Volkslied, 'Des Pfarrers Tochter von Sesenheim'. And as a permanent
background to the idyll there loomed the great pile of the Gothic minster—in Herder's and in Goethe's eyes 'deutsch' like the lovely countryside it dominated, its tower a fitting vantage-point from which to scan
the horizon for the spot which held his beloved. But the chief example
of 'Wiederspiegelung' is the parallelism of the Brion family with Goldsmith's *Vicar of Wakefield*, culminating in the reading of the novel to the
Sesenheim circle: 'So erblickten sie hier sich selbst in einem Spiegel, der
keineswegs verhässlichte'.[16] We note in passing the idealizing tendency of
the mirror.

The account of Goethe's intimacy with the Brion family is condition-
ed, it is well known, by his acquaintance with Goldsmith's novel, which
Herder in actual fact read to him a week or two *after* the first meeting with
them. The departure from chronology in *Dichtung und Wahrheit* is a
combination, as it were, of his two principles of 'Anticipation' and 'Wiederspiegelung'. 'A protestant country-clergyman is perhaps the most
beautiful subject for a modern idyll', he writes, thus preparing the way
for the conclusion of Herbert Schöffler[17] that it was the combination of
Christian piety and rural simplicity of morals and manners which made
English literature the great sensitizing force that it was in Germany. And
there is little doubt that the likeness in the circumstances of the English
and the German vicar was felt by both Goethe and members of the Brion

family. Professor Boyd may not be very far from the truth when he states
that Goethe fell in love, not with Friederike Brion, but with the living
likeness of Sophia Primrose.[18] The whole idyllic situation could only have
been reinforced by that other work of Goldsmith, *The Deserted Village*,
which, because of its background of rural scenes and rustic characters,
was the delight of the Salzmann circle in Strassburg. Not only does
Goethe himself see 'Wiederspiegelung' in the Sesenheim episode; he lets
simple folk like Friederike and her sister see it, and puts into the mouth of
one of the guests at the vicarage the significant phrase, significant because
it adumbrates the whole complex relation between life and art: 'I love
reading novels; there are so many fine people in them whom one would
like to resemble'. When Goethe told them the Melusine story, the Brion
family, the girls in particular, thought they recognised in the personages
of the *Märchen* a married couple from across the Rhine whose circumstances fitted those of the story exactly.

Friederike conspicuously wears 'deutsche Tracht', and Goethe has left
a fascinating account of the charmingly alluring impression she made in
her national costume: 'A short, white, full, skirt, with a furbelow, not so
long but that the neatest little feet were visible up to the ankle'. Predisposed as he was by Herder to all things German, it was only natural that
he should fall in love with her rather than with the daughters of the French
dancing-master in Strassburg who met him more than half way. But once
away from the naive rustic surroundings of village life, amidst the
sophisticated artificialities of the city, in the world of tapestries, mirrors,
grandfather-clocks and porcelain figures', the dress and manners of the
country-girl seemed just a little ridiculous. That at least is the impression
that Goethe is at pains to evoke in his account of Friederike's visit to her
town cousins, the Schoells. Friederike, intent upon showing off her lover,
prevailed upon him to read aloud to the assembled company, as he was
wont to do in Sesenheim. The German influence which radiated from
her was still strong enough amidst these French surroundings for him to
choose an English author, the 'Gothic' Shakespeare, and to read *Hamlet*
straight through at one sitting with great success. He tells us of Friederike's response: 'She had sighed deeply from time to time, and her cheeks
had been suffused by fleeting blushes', thus delicately insinuating that she
had some sense of the 'Wiederspiegelung', of the similarity of her own
situation to Ophelia's. Critics have been swift enough to seize on the similarity, and to transfer it from Ophelia to Gretchen. Were not both the victims of a faithless lover? Did not both go mad under the stress of betrayal?
Does not Gretchen in her madness sing a coarse song? And are not the
very words of Ophelia's song echoed by Mephistopheles in order to goad

Valentin to the attack? The verbal and factual influences are patent and need no stressing. But what is much more interesting, and less immediately apparent, is the process by which the Goethe-Friederike, Hamlet-Ophelia, Faust-Gretchen pattern of relationship is evolved, and the 'Wiederspiegelung' of life into poetry (Goethe-Hamlet), and its further reflection from one poem into another (*Hamlet-Faust*), is revealed. The only motif common to all three pairs is the feeling of guilt induced in the man. This is painfully confessed in that seemingly callous avowal of Goethe as the Brion girls left Strassburg to return to their village: 'At last I saw them go, and it seemed like a great weight off my heart'. But on his return to Frankfurt he realised the extent of his loss and the burden of his guilt; 'I had wounded the fairest heart to its depths and thus this period of dark repentance . . . . became almost insupportable . . . I sought to find an outlet in my poetry'. It is the *feeling* of guilt, the emotion and not the *situation*, which Goethe, Hamlet, and Faust have in common. In this amalgam of literature and life we have the raw material of the Gretchen tragedy. It is only when the experience of life is lit up by poetic imagination that a new creation is born—something which owes as much to literature as to life. For Friederike did not bear an illegitimate child, did not murder it, and did not go mad; and the only thing in common between the two lovers, Goethe and Faust, is their guilt-feeling. It was like death in Goethe's heart as he felt the breach approaching, relentlessly, inevitably, even as he carved his name with his beloved's in the beech grove at Sesenheim, or as he wrote despairingly, making use of a favourite image: 'ehe ich mein geflicktes Schiffchen wieder auf den Ocean wage, wahrscheinlicher dem Tod als dem Gewinst entgegen'.[19] In 'anticipation' of his betrayal he is already seized by the pangs of remorse which were to torture him for years to come. As Professor Beutler well remarks,[20] it was of this death-urge that *Faust* was born.

It is obvious that an autobiography lends itself to 'Wiederspiegelung' as does no other form of literature, and the examples in *Dichtung und Wahrheit* are numerous and arresting. R. M. Meyer pointed out[21] how the Frankfurt Gretchen grew in poetic stature by being associated in Goethe's mind with Manon Lescaut. In the fluent ease with which he related to her the picturesque ceremonies of the imperial coronation he saw himself in the role of Abélard. His sister Cornelia seemed to require the setting of a Richardsonian novel to do her full justice.[22] Nor are the 'Wiederspiegelungen' by any means all of a literary character. The Gobelins tapestries of Medea murdering her children, which adorned the 'maison d'échange' on the Rhine where Marie Antoinette was received by the French authorities, seemed to Goethe redolent of impending disaster, and the new Dauphine herself is reported to have commented on their sinister character. But such cross-fertilization is not restricted to any one work or to any particular period. The old ballad of the Graf von Gleichen, the account of Dean Swift's entanglement with Stella and Vanessa, Bürger's and Fritz Jacobi's matrimonial embarrassments, as well as his own vacillation between Lili and Gustchen von Stolberg, were all reflected in *Stella*. As Lotte and Werther watch the storm from the open window and sniff the refreshing scent of wet earth, Lotte lays her hand on his and cries: 'Klopstock!' In the second version of 1787, Goethe deliberately drew attention to this 'Wiederspiegelung' by inserting: 'Ich erinnerte mich sogleich der herrlichen Ode [i.e., *Die Frühlingsfeier*], die ihr in Gedanken lag'. Lili von Türkheim's painful odyssey from Strassburg to Frankfurt under the stress of war and revolution was amalgamated in Goethe's mind with an account of the expulsion by the Archbishop of Salzburg of his Protestant subjects in 1731, both elements, *Wahrheit* and *Dichtung*, to become reflected in the political background of *Hermann und Dorothea*. The sentimental ballad, *Edwin and Angelina*, which he had read in the *Vicar of Wakefield*, was recalled by the artificialities and conventions of Lili's circle and, suitably recast in a rococo setting, reborn as the 'Singspiel', *Erwin und Elmire*. The title itself reflects Goethe's own pull between nature and convention—Erwin is a reminiscence of the builder of the Strassburg minster, Elmire a typical name from pastoral poetry. His own Iphigenie is a patent amalgamation of literary Iphigenias with both his sister and with Frau von Stein; and the historical Tasso has been joined by both the hypochondriac Lenz and his own Werther to be 'intensified' into a qualitatively different hero. It is generally accepted that his erotic experiences in Rome, plus the reading of Ovid and Propertius, predisposed him to see in the fresh beauty of Christiane Vulpius the living embodiment of his newly awakened sensuousness, and it is in this sense only that she can be called the real begetter of the *Roman Elegies*. The reader who feels a little confused in reading of these reflections and re-reflections need not be unduly perturbed. That is how he is meant to feel. For the whole effect of 'Wiederspiegelung' is akin to that mazed delight we might experience in a hall of mirrors. Real and imaginative experience are no longer distinct, cause and effect cease to matter, and time itself is annulled. All that remains is the quintessence of experience, not the accidental externals of chronology and fact. Might it not perhaps be more fruitful to study literary influences as such 'repeated reflections', seeing their increasing concentration as one of the major excitements of the poet's imagination?

If 'Wiederspiegelung' plays so important a part in the making and interpretation of poetry, it is because the image of the mirror, the *Spiegel*, has such distinctly aesthetic connotations. Its early symbolic meaning is attested by the Greek myths of Narcissus and Dionysos. For the Neoplatonists God had created in the souls of men blessed mirrors of his own blessedness. 'The soul', Plotinus wrote,[23] 'gives forth images like one face in many mirrors'. For the 'schöne Seele' in *Wilhelm Meister* the soul of man is similarly a mirror to reflect the eternal soul of God,[24] and in the disputation scene in *Faust*—planned but never completed—Faust was to have reduced the sterile Mephisto to silence by his query concerning the 'schaffender Spiegel' which was the Godhead.[25] But it is not only, and not primarily, as a metaphysical-religious symbol that Goethe uses the mirror, but as a symbol of art and of aesthetic experience. For his Werther it is a simple matter of analogy: he would like his painting to be so transparently expressive of his feeling that it would be the mirror of his soul, 'wie deine Seele ist der Spiegel des unendlichen Gottes'.[26] Like his Neoplatonic prototype, the painter in *Emilia Galotti*, he would fain create directly with his mind, without intervention of hand or medium. His more sophisticated creator knows very well that the mirror is only an appropriate symbol for the finished products of art and from the point of view of the beholder. Itself a non-organic substance, unmalleable and unchanging, it yet reflects in its bright unclouded surface the changeful forms and processes of life, turning them into something timeless and imperishable, beautiful but barren—and wholly non-naturalistic. For, *pace* the more literal followers of Plato, art does not just 'hold the mirror up to nature' as though it were a brilliant form of imitation.[27] It reflects nature in its own way, transforming it into something which is the same and yet different. Seen through the looking-glass, the world takes on a new aspect in which everything appears strange, and goes contrary to the accepted notions of common sense, in which right becomes left and left right, and it is not the same face which is reflected back again: 'Wir sehen unser Angesicht niemals ganz richtig darin, ja der Spiegel kehrt unsre Gestalt um und macht unsre linke Hand zur rechten'.[28] That was why Goethe bade the actor offer his left hand if his position on the stage warranted it, 'denn auf der Bühne [i.e., in the world of art] gilt kein Rechts oder Links'.[29] And when Eduard and Ottilie, in the *Wahlverwandtschaften*, have so grown together that their very pains are reflected in each other, it seems only natural that their headaches should be felt on different sides of the face.

It is understandable that more than half the examples of the mirror-image should come from *Wilhelm Meister*, the chief confession of Goethe's artistic faith. The effect of a mirror is threefold. It can give aesthetic distance to scenes or persons by isolating them in a framed surface and transposing them into a different dimension. Thus Wilhelm Meister carries his child to the mirror in the hope of discovering his likeness to it and so resolving the doubts in his mind concerning its paternity.[30] But the mirror, too, divests experience of its practical implications and invites us to contemplate it for its own sake. Lucidor, in *Wilhelm Meisters Wanderjahre*,[31] pauses for a moment in the tumult of his love-making as he catches sight of himself and his beloved in the mirror, and reflects that his whole life has culminated in this moment of enhanced awareness. And the mirror is clearly a symbol of contemplation when Faust, looking at the rainbow, sees life mirrored back in its manifold variety, its transience and change given permanence in the moment of reflection—'des bunten Bogens Wechseldauer' but as a symbol of art and of aesthetic experience. For his

> Der spiegelt ab das menschliche Bestreben.
> Ihm sinne nach, und du begreifst genauer:
> Am farbigen Abglanz haben wir das Leben.   4725-7

The effect of the mirror is, moreover, to enhance and beautify reality. In *Der Fischer* the moon seems doubly beautiful as it is reflected in the mirror of the water:

> Kehrt wellenatmend ihr Gesicht
> Nicht doppelt schöner her?

Gretchen, or 'die schöne Seele',[32] or the Lilie of the *Märchen*[33] have only to preen themselves in their jewellery before the mirror to increase its effect and their satisfaction. Goethe imagines Friederike stepping up to the mirror to admire herself in all the finery of the embroidered sash he has sent her:

> Und so tritt sie vor den Spiegel
> All in ihrer Munterkeit.[34]

While at Einsiedeln in 1775 he picks up a crown out of the monastic treasury and, in imagination, places it upon the head of Lili Schönemann, leading her by the hand before a mirror. Such a theme, he declares, would be worthy of the brush of a talented artist.[35] The magic mirror in *Faust* is of literary origin, as Byron perceived;[36] but it is invested by Goethe with the power of bringing out the ideal in the real, of piercing through to the inner significance behind the outward appearance of things. The 'magic play' of Marie's obsequies brings home to Clavigo, 'as in a mirror', the sum and summit of all his crimes. The wise woman of the *Wanderjahre*,[37] Makarie, by holding up a 'sittlich-magischer Spiegel', an image of inward harmony, to such as are confused and disoriented, is able to restore them to new life. When we remember that Goethe uses 'sittlich' more often to denote man's whole psyche than his moral sense, it becomes clear that he is here symbolizing the beneficial effect of bringing hidden problems to awareness and contemplating them with a measure of objectivity. In other contexts the 'magischer Spiegel' is used, somewhat as the magic mirror in the fairy-tale of Snow White, to invoke a distant person or scene. This is one aspect of its effect in *Reineke Fuchs*, the other being the curative:

Alles zeigte sich drin, und wenn es meilenweit vorging,
War es Tag oder Nacht. Und hatte jemand im Antlitz
Einen Fehler, wie er auch war, ein Flecken im Auge,
Durft' er sich nur im Spiegel besehn, so gingen von Stund' an
Alle Mängel hinweg und alle fremden Gebrechen.   *X, 114-8*

Goethe also uses the image of the magic mirror in *Dichtung und Wahrheit* to recall such long-dead figures as his beloved sister, Cornelie, or Fräulein von Klettenberg.[38]

Thus, from being a philosophic image of divine creation as it is reflected in the human soul, the 'Spiegel' takes on aesthetic value, until it is finally assimilated into the all-embracing principle of 'Wiederspiegelung' to express the interpenetration of art and life. We can see the whole process at work in the words which Goethe wrote[39] under a silhouette of Frau von Stein before he had actually met her in the flesh: 'Es wäre ein herrliches Schauspiel zu sehen, wie die Welt sich in dieser Seele spiegelt. Sie sieht die Welt, wie sie ist, und doch durchs Medium der Liebe'. Here already are the germs of 'Wiederspiegelung'. Though a human soul here takes the place of an actual mirror, the image yet evokes reflection in both its philosophic and aesthetic connotation. It is both a symbol of life and a symbol of art, the one transforming itself so imperceptibly into the other as to be indistinguishable. The world as mirrored in her soul would be an enhanced world, and the implication is that this heightened picture of life would excite to further living. 'Wir bespiegeln uns in einander ... und teilen Freud und Langweile auf dieser Lebensbahn', Goethe had written to Herder as early as 1772.[40] 'Die Existenzen fremder Menschen sind die besten Spiegel, worin wir die unsrige erkennen können', he was still writing in 1783;[41] and from Rome in 1787, 'Moritz wird mir wie ein Spiegel vorgehalten';[42] and, again, this time in his poetry: 'War dir mein Leben ein Spiegel, in welchem du dich gerne betrachtetest', he makes Egmont say to Ferdinand, 'so sei es auch mein Tod'.[43]

At Goethe's death there were found among his papers certain lines in

F*

which he, like his dying Faust, casts up the sum of his existence.[44] They fittingly end with the injunction that others should see their fate mirrored in his:

'Und so ging mein Leben hin unter Tun und Geniessen, Leiden und Widerstreben, unter Liebe, Zufriedenheit, Hass und Missfallen anderer. Hieran spiegele sich, dem das gleiche Schicksal geworden'.

x. Goethe's Conception of Form

'In the sciences', Goethe observes, 'it is greatly rewarding to seek out the inadequate truths already possessed by the Ancients and develop them further'.[1] With this seeming paradox we are at the heart of his attitude to intellectual inquiry. In what sense may a truth be said to be inadequate? It is here said to be so in the more immediate sense that some insight of a man of science may not quicken, or may not survive long enough in the intellectual climate of his age, for its implications to be fully explored. Before its generative force is spent, it is elbowed out by others which more nearly meet the needs of the moment. It remains inadequate because it still awaits clarification in detail and the test of precise application. But implicit in this paradox, too, is Goethe's conviction that the perception of truth is not the monopoly of any one mode of thinking. Ritual, myth, religion, philosophy, as well as earlier, more naïve, epochs of scientific inquiry, have all bequeathed truths to mankind. It is one of the secrets of Goethe's successful living that he did not withdraw his allegiance from these just because they could not command the assent of his purely discursive intelligence. They had been discovered as answers to older needs of the human mind, and some unerring wisdom taught him that these do not atrophy as new needs develop. They live on side by side, not essentially incompatible, but at war, even to the point where sanity is threatened, unless appropriate satisfaction can be found for both. Goethe found it by transforming his mode of assent. Much that could no longer, without intellectual dishonesty, be accepted literally, as fact, he accepted transliterally, as symbol. In this, as in much else, the Either/Or attitude was repugnant to him in its crudity. He reserved the right, and developed the mastery, of free movement among the mansions of his mind, weaving his way, with immense flexibility of response, between the symbolic and the factual: between memories of childhood piety, or intimations of the divine, and sober investigation of natural process, between metaphysical insights and robust common sense, between literal truths and those transformations of myth and ritual which live on in art and in the sense of occasion.

Thus reason was safeguarded. But not by the denial of rationality. To mistake this flexibility for indeterminate vagueness, a kind of intellectual chiaroscuro, is to court disaster from the unexpected sharpness of some of his distinctions. The swiftness of his transitions from one mode of response to another, at the sovereign instance of appropriateness, may dazzle the eye of the beholder; the responses themselves are differentiated to a fine degree. Thus he insisted[2] that myth and legend have no place in science; or if used for purposes of illustration, then it must be, like all analogy, with clearly metaphorical, not factual, reference—a distinction not always strictly observed by more orthodox scientists. To confuse these symbols with the objects or processes they symbolize is to foster superstition, which, he allowed, has indeed its place in life, but in the realm of poetry and imagination,[3] not among the abstractive techniques of rationalized knowledge. In other words, one mode of thought may illuminate and support another; it can never do duty for it. A famous aphorism of his begins: 'Everything worth thinking has already been thought'; but it continues: 'our endeavour must be to think it through again'.[4] And this rethinking proceeds by what Goethe called successive transpositions. From time to time the human mind evolves new leading concepts, develops new methods, which by their very nature are provisional, to be superseded by others when their work is done.[5] But only in this way are new insights ever achieved, old 'inadequate' truths given precision and application, and the challenge of the present moment answered. To those who, appalled by some of its accompanying effects, would call a halt to the physicist's method of exploring the universe, Goethe offers no genuine support. They may invoke, and it is salutary to do so, his misgivings about the rise of technology, his suspicion of the atomistic reduction of nature to quantitative symbols, his concern at the decline in man's power to apprehend, through disciplined and concrete intuition, the forms of natural phenomena as they present themselves, in all the fulness of their qualitative variety, to sense-experience. But the picture is misleadingly incomplete if it includes no indication of his undismayed acceptance that good and evil are fatefully interlinked, and that truth may well arise as a by-product of error.[6] Thus we might construe as an illiberal setting of his face against further inquiry the dictum that 'even discerning minds do not see that what they are trying to *explain* are in reality primary facts of experience, incapable of further reduction', were it not followed *at once* by the saving corollary: 'Yet this pursuit of explanations may be all to the good, for without it the search for knowledge would be abandoned far too soon'.[7] The style of his thinking is, in fact, essentially dramatistic, and in presenting it we must see to it that both antagonist and protagonist have their say. To his insistence that science is held back by its preoccupation with what is neither knowable, nor worth knowing,[8] we must oppose his categorical resistance to the dangerous prejudice of putting any mode of scientific inquiry under a ban.[9] His contention that the highest happiness of a rational being is to have explored the accessible, and quietly to revere the inaccessible,[10] has to be parried with its evident counterpart that man must persist in his belief that the incomprehensible is comprehensible, for otherwise he would cease to explore.[11] And we must make it clear that when the author of this unending dialogue speaks to us *directly*, he does so in statements which either synthesize, or hold in balance, the contraries involved. As in the aphorism: 'Whatever emancipates the mind without giving us control over ourselves is dangerous',[12] where explicit statement of the reserves in his loyalty to intellectual enlightenment conceals implicit exhortation to render it foolproof by enlightenment of another sort. Or in these concerning man's proper relation to the past: 'Authority—without it man cannot exist, yet it brings error as well as truth in its train',[13] or 'Ancient fundaments one respects, but one must never forfeit the right to start laying fresh foundations elsewhere'.[14]

'The mighty taker', Klopstock once called Goethe in a moment of acrimony. And so he was. But his strength, and his originality, derive from the productive tension between taking and rejecting. Indeed we might get a fresh angle on this Teutonic sage by applying the concept of 'perspective by incongruity' and assigning him to what Mr. Kenneth Burke[15] calls the 'comic' order of thinkers—by which synonym for sceptical, dialectic, humanistic, he would suggest that to be an accepter-rejecter in a world which goes in for whole-hearted accepters or out-and-out rejecters is a pretty funny thing to be.[16] I don't know that Mr. Burke has ever thought of including Goethe in his 'comic' frame. But it's where he belongs. For he is neither wholly orthodox nor wholly heretical. He moves dialectically between ironic scepticism about progress and unshakable devotion to the further adventuring of the human spirit, between steady conviction of the hypothetical nature of all knowledge and firm belief in truth, between the sanction of authority and wholesome reaction against it, between allegiance to the past and assent to the future.

It is in something of this same spirit, I suggest, that it would be profitable to re-examine his own conception of form at this particular point of time. For form is in the air—indeed on the air. Whether we tune in to a talk on the molecular structure of synthetic fibres, the processes of the human brain, the making of history, or recent work in sociology and linguistics, this powerful medium for the popularization of ideas speaks to us of *patterns*. The scientist, it seems, no longer thinks only atomistically, in terms of ever more precise analysis into smaller and smaller particles of matter, but also formally, in terms of complex systems of relationships, systems from which the observer himself can no longer be rigorously excluded. By 'explanations' he no longer means tracing the very springs of nature, but, more modestly, arranging nature in a coherent *order*. The symbols for communicating these notions have changed accordingly. The layman is invited to think of nature less as an engine than as an algebra,[17] and of himself less as an animated machine than as a pattern. He hears this word so often that, as J. Z. Young suggested in his Reith Lectures, he could easily fall to thinking of himself as a carpet—Sherrington's likening of brain-activity to an 'enchanted loom' might support the fancy—and this error has to be forestalled by frequent reminder that it is a pattern of constantly *changing* relations. Stability of structure, individual identity is, it seems, a property not of material particles, but of *form*. It is perhaps not surprising that in this climate of thought the arts and the sciences, after a longish estrangement, should show signs of drawing together again. The artistic and the scientific imagination are compared now as much as they are contrasted. A poet and an astrophysicist[18] can find common ground for an exchange of their views of nature. And there is at this moment[19] an exhibition of the natural shapes and structures revealed by modern science, entitled 'Growth and Form' in tribute to that great scientist D'Arcy Thompson, but arranged by the Institute of Contemporary Arts.

I often catch myself thinking: 'Goethe said as much'. I may remember that the loom was his favourite symbol for the processes of nature, within man and without; recall his aphorism: 'The phenomenon is not severed from the observer but inextricably implicated and involved in him';[20] or 'Pushing problems aside which can only be explained dynamically is bound to result in mechanistic modes of explanation';[21] or his unwavering conviction that the laws of art and nature are fundamentally the same. But, of course, he did not say *as much*. He said either more or less—according to how you look at it. His knowledge was more varied, and far more coherent, than that of any specialist today; but it was less exact—in the scientific sense of the word 'exact'. For what we now call exact knowledge can only be obtained by an approach to nature which is the very antithesis of his; by isolating and immobilizing things under the artificial conditions of experiment, and analyzing them with the precision of mathematical calculation. But thereby phenomena which he deemed incapable of further reduction *have* been further reduced. The pursuit of 'explanations', in the older sense of a search for ultimate causes, has, in fact, as he foresaw, given man immense control over nature, for good, and not only for evil. And if thought seems to be swinging round to what preoccupied him, dynamic explanations of forms in movement, it is a swing *round*, not back—the appropriate image is Goethe's spiral, not Nietzsche's cyclic recurrence—round at a level of far greater exactitude and detail. Nevertheless, this turn of events does mean that his insights have new actuality, that he speaks to us in accents more urgent than perhaps to any generation, during his lifetime or since.

Inside Germany there has been growing awareness of this for thirty years or more. No less than four editions of his scientific works were prepared independently during the twenties.[22] His concepts and methods have been developed in the field of botany by Wilhelm Troll and his pupils and in the field of literary criticism by Günther Müller and the morphological school. The impulse they gave to the theory of perception evolved by the *Gestalt* psychologists and to Viktor von Weizsäcker's work on the relation between sense-perception and motor-activity, if less explicitly acknowledged, is none the less apparent. Of the value of much of this work there can be no doubt, though one feels that some of Goethe's own warnings can never be too often invoked: warnings about the danger, always imminent in our longing for order, of leaping from observable fact to inadequate theory, of mistaking the scaffolding for the building, the hypothesis for knowledge, of succumbing to the domination of phrases and substituting analogies for phenomena, of generalizing prematurely from one field to another.[23]

Outside of Germany the tendency is all the other way, and as thinker he is usually relegated to a position of at most historical interest. The language barrier is of moment. Few are equipped to offer us, as the late Agnes Arber did,[24] both an impeccable translation of his *Metamorphosis of Plants* and an expert assessment of its standing as botany; fewer still to transcend the technical details of their subject and, in a survey ranging from Aristotle to the present day, to show us, as she has shown, Goethe's contribution to the natural philosophy of plant form.[25] The non-German scientist tends on the whole to be more chary of relating his findings to a general theory of knowledge. But a too ardent scepticism is no less inept than over-enthusiasm. Where separate fields of study are moving independently to conclusions similar enough to provide a point of contact, it seems almost perverse not to explore possibilities of integration. For, as Goethe says,[26] we should not call our knowledge a mere patchwork of disjointed fragments if we did not possess the concept of wholeness. And at such moments of convergence thinkers of the past, with their more unified and less distracted vision, may well provide us with principles for organizing the scattered results of experimental knowledge. What is needed is a blend of boldness and caution. In borrowing Goethe's eye for connections, we must proceed with nothing less than his care for distinctions; knowing how to separate not only the false from the true, but adequate truths from those still awaiting demonstration; remembering that to elevate him into dogma is not only alien to the profoundly undogmatic temper of his own mind (despite his blind spot about Newton) but comes uncomfortably near to fulfilling his ironic prophecy that it would not be long before people started believing in him and quoting him as if he were gospel.[27]

But why should we turn to Goethe in particular? Has he anything more to offer us than, say, Aristotle for whom form was a master concept in all branches of knowledge? I think he has. For Goethe was not only a discerner of form; he was a maker of it, and a maker of an immense variety of forms. It has been said, by no less an authority than Sir Charles Sherrington, that if it were not for Goethe's poetry we should not trouble about his science.[28] And this is true. But not in the sense intended. His poetic mind does indeed constitute the interest of his scientific work, not because he thinks as a poet when he is supposed to be thinking as a scientist—he moves freely between both these modes of thought,—but because his extensive first-hand experience in the two spheres makes him uniquely qualified to evolve a conception of form embracing both art and nature.

And he has yet a further qualification which is often overlooked in treating of his view of form: his profound comprehension of *how* he made it. This is not to say that he plucked the mystery out of creation. The 'mighty visitation unimplored' remained to the end a token of grace before which he bowed his head in awe. But if the cause of inspiration was not to be explained, the form of its operations could still be explored. His lucidity about the creative act is reminiscent of a Flaubert, a Gide, or a Valéry—and all three were, in fact, fascinated by the records of it he has left. But the marvel is that in him this knowledge was not destructive of spontaneity. The muse who in his youth 'dictated to him slumb'ring', so that he must leap from his bed and scrawl his 'unpremeditated verse' diagonally across the page,[29] still deigned to bless him at sixty with lyrics of such mysterious power that we are not surprised when he tells us that one of them 'came' to him at midnight, unheralded and unsought.[30] But she was more gracious still. Perhaps as a reward for long years of unremitting poetic labour, she granted him, just before his death, a measure of power to 'command' his inspiration, to descend, fully waking, into that unconscious stream where poetry has its source—'a mysterious psychological development which might be worth looking into' was his comment upon this new mode of productivity in a letter to Wilhelm von Humboldt.[31] But he had been preparing for it since his late twenties when he first began to turn a watchful eye on the involuntary movements of his mind, fostering in himself a kind of awareness which could *observe* his spontaneous activity without inhibiting it.[32] 'I must observe more closely the cycle in me of good and bad days', he wrote in his diary when he was thirty;[33] 'inspiration, technical working out, ordering—it all alternates and follows a regular course'. His interest clearly embraced more than the activity of composition; he was intent on discerning the whole pattern of his mental processes. For the same diary entry continues: 'Good humour, depression, strength, elasticity, weakness, composure, and desire, likewise. With patience I ought to be able to discover the time and order of my own cycle'. And the last words he ever wrote[34] are still concerned with what he calls these 'ultimate mysteries', with the secret, intricate connections between conscious and unconscious, awareness and spontaneity, with the strange duality of man, whereby, to be wise, he must never cease to hearken to the involuntary promptings of his nature and yet, by taking thought, can learn, in some measure, to guide their direction and so bring to full realization the inherent *form* of his being.

What Goethe, then, brought to the investigation of forms outside himself, whether of art or of nature—rock, cloud, or crystal formations, plant metamorphosis or comparative anatomy—was inside knowledge of the formative process at work in his own mind, an objective awareness of his own subjectivity. Looking at nature within himself he found that the psychological laws operating there were not a denial of the laws of external nature, but their fulfilment, and what he offers us is a unified conception of a formative principle transcending the dichotomy of subjective and objective experience.

But Goethe has also something different to say to us from Aristotle because, by virtue of his historical position, many of the problems which preoccupied him were already conceived in terms in which we still conceive them today. He lived, as a young man, through the surging excitement of the revolution which was taking place in man's whole way of thinking: the change to a dynamic view of the universe. The world into which he was born was a world of static forms. The established sciences were the separating ones—*Scheidekunst* the eighteenth century called chemistry—which immobilized in order to weigh and measure, and, with the precision instruments of Newtonian physics, translated the moving forms of sense-experience into the immutable formulae of mathematics. But the coming sciences were those dealing with the continuity of living organisms—not with being, but with becoming. The venerable idea of an unbroken hierarchy of forms, from the lowest to the highest, the Great Chain of Being, had been transferred from philosophy to the fields of biology and history, and there was shaping in men's minds, not so much a *theory* of evolution—the theory came later and is far less of a change than this imaginative revolution which prepared it—but a mental image, a view of the world in which process, growth, and development are basic. Before this time to speak of evolution meant simply increase of size, the swelling of the primary cell which, according to the doctrine of pre-formation, or *emboîtement*, already contained in miniature the entire animal or entire homunculus. But from now on it began to mean the changes in the life-cycle of an individual organism, and the idea, familiar to us now, but not in itself easy to grasp, of one form gradually changing into another and yet somehow retaining identity.

And the society Goethe moved in as a boy was a society still dominated by the forms and conventions of French classicism: finite forms, of static grace and symmetrical proportions, produced by artists who thought of themselves as craftsmen, modestly imitating the finished products of nature, or improving upon them in accordance with traditional rules to evolve what they charmingly termed a copy of *la belle nature*; an art to be measured against fixed norms and judged by the prevailing standards of good taste and good sense. But by the time he was twenty he was caught in the flood-tide of the new dynamic mode of thinking and the morphological approach to the study of cultures originated by Vico in his *Scienza Nuova*, but which Goethe had straight from the mouth of that other great progenitor of the historical method, Johann Gottfried Herder. From him he learnt to appreciate works of art in appearance so irregular, fragmentary, individual, even idiosyncratic, that by rationalistic standards they had been reckoned formless and barbaric: Gothic architecture and the Gothic Shakespeare, the primitive songs of backward peoples, the Dionysiac origins of the Greek dithyramb. Once referred back to their origins, however, seen in historical perspective as products of a certain soil, climate, and cultural environment, these could be understood as highly characteristic organisms, forms not finished perhaps, but becoming. The artist, he now heard, was no mere imitator, but an original genius, manifesting in his activity the very processes of natural creation; and the standards for judging his work were no longer absolute norms, external to the individual work in question, but laws inherent within it, relative, and accessible only to the genetic method.

Goethe was thus the immediate heir of various, and conflicting, conceptions of form. From each he took what he needed and rejected what was alien to him. What attracted him in the doctrine of 'inward form',

deriving from Plotinus, and just then made available through its revival
by Shaftesbury (though he also came across it in his reading of Giordano
Bruno), was the idea that form is itself the principle at work in a living
organism. It enabled him to dispense with the thought, repugnant to any
artist, of form as a mere vessel for the containing of essence or spirit; or
the related theory, proceeding from the mechanistic sciences, of the form
of anything being the purely passive configuration of the elements com-
posing it, produced by an agency which is something other than form, by
energy or forces. It taught him, too, that form is something different
from symmetry, and so provided him with a new criterion for judging
works of art. But his encounter with this exciting new notion did not
oust his appreciation of traditional outward forms; it revitalized it. It
never led him into excusing sheer formlessness on the grounds that a
work had plenty of content! After his first brief and intense surrender the
unifying activity of his mind prevailed, and by the time he was twenty-
five he was pointing out to his more formless contemporaries of the
Storm-and-Stress movement that 'inner form is the form embracing all
forms', transcending, but including, outer form.[35] He might agree that, in
Sir Thomas Browne's phrase, 'the outward figures of a thing, plant or
person hang as signs or bushes of their inward form'; but never with that
more extravagant Neoplatonism which thought such outward figures
mere reflections of inward essence. Nor did he ever fall victim to those
implications of the doctrine, which still dominated the Romantics and
have been the bane of much German criticism and aesthetics since: the
notion that form, as the principle of mind, suffers an inevitable loss of
perfection when, as Plotinus has it, it *descends* into matter, or, as Shelley
puts it: 'the most glorious poetry ever communicated to the world is
but a feeble shadow of the original conception of the poet'. Goethe's
answer to this is already implicit in the brief comments he wrote in 1775
for the German translation of that impudent challenge to classicism,
Louis Sébastien Mercier's *Nouvel essai sur l'art dramatique*; it is explicit in
his late criticism of Plotinus himself: 'The created product is not less than
the creating mind. It is the advantage of living creation that what is
created can be of greater excellence than its creator'.[36] His awareness of
his own creative process taught him early that an artist's material medium
is already a factor in his original conception, that a form is not there,
complete and insubstantial in his mind; if it comes to him, whole, by
sudden inspiration, then it is already in terms of his medium; otherwise
he wrestles with his medium until he discovers and realizes a form.

What Goethe, then, did was to take over from the Neoplatonists the
idea of form as a process at work even in the inmost parts of an organism,

and fuse it completely with the idea of form as outward shape. The one is not the *cause* of the other; they are completely reciprocal. Inner structure determines outward shape and outward shape inner structure.[37] As he puts it in his *Lectures on Comparative Anatomy*,[38] the development or non-development of any one member affects the whole body, as this and its needs affect each single member. All the parts work in and through each other.

And if inner form is not separable from outer form neither is organism from environment. A living thing, he says in the preface to his *Morphology*,[39] is not a single unit but a plurality. Some of its elements are already joined together when it comes into being. But growth consists of a constant interchange of its own elements with elements of the environment, a taking-in and a giving-out, an incessant re-arrangement of patterns in all directions. What is formed is immediately broken down and re-formed. Stable identity derives not from the unchanging elements, but from the pattern which survives all their changes. Thus there is no hard and fast boundary between an organism and its surroundings, but a continuity. Again, Goethe took all he could from the new genetic method with its emphasis on environmental conditions; but he never fell into what Coleridge calls the 'sophism' of mistaking conditions for causes. He points out[40] that neither the statement that the fish is fashioned for living in water, nor the statement that it adapts itself to living in water, really reflects the actual state of affairs. It is better to say that the fish exists in and through water. There is no before or after in this formative process, in the sense of cause and effect. Nature fashions from outside inwards and from inside outwards, and the study of any living thing involves a study of all the reciprocal relations between organism and environment, considered not only genetically but *sub specie formae*.

The only actual definition Goethe ever gives of 'form' is tackled on semantic lines: 'For the whole complexity of existence of an actual being German has the word *Gestalt*'.[41] Alive to the static quality of this word of past-participle origin, he continues: 'In using this expression, however, we abstract from what is in constant flux and assume that the collection of parts we call an identity is finished and fixed in its character. But if we consider natural forms, we find that nowhere does anything stable or completed occur. Rather is everything suspended in precarious balance. Wherefore the German language is wont to use, appropriately enough, the word *Bildung* both of the form produced and of the process of formation'. But here is no niggling obsession with the problem of the meaning of meaning! Having made his distinction with care, he at once sanctions the use of the word *Gestalt*, provided that we always remember that it is an abstraction of something which in actual experience is never stable for more than a moment.

The subject Goethe developed, and christened, for the study of living forms in process of constant change and transformation was *Morphology*. By it he understood not only a branch of botany or biology, which is the meaning it still has today, but an independent science. It would, as he conceived it, make use of the findings of all the other sciences, including the quantitative results of physics and chemistry. For he was not, as is often asserted, opposed to analytical methods. On the contrary, he states explicitly, and on many occasions, that every means of investigating nature is legitimate and useful. But what he himself was interested in was not the identical elements, the atoms or nuclei, which are nature's material, but the multifarious patterns in which they manifest themselves, so that what is identical in substance can appear in forms utterly dissimilar;[42] just as in his study of plants and animals he never ceased to marvel at nature's power to modify identical organs, so that in form and function they appear not only different, but even opposed.[43] The business of morphology was what he called 'synthesis'; by which he did not mean putting together again all the parts that analysis had laid out side by side, but starting with living wholes and studying them in the light of the information about them that other sciences can provide; or, put the other way round, co-ordinating the scattered findings of the other sciences under the unifying aspect of form.[44]

The problems of morphology are so difficult precisely because of the great demands they make on the personality of the scientist. By what means is one to grasp the full complexity of an organism—not just its external appearance but its internal organization, the interworking of all the parts in and through the whole? And not just the organism as we see it at any given moment of time but the cycle of its development from the beginning of its life-history till its end, including transformation into something totally unlike in appearance, as, for instance, the metamorphosis of a chrysalis into a butterfly? Goethe thought it could only be done by what he called *Anschauung*, intuitive contemplation, if you like, though both these words have something misleading about them. It involved first a subtle technique of the eye, indispensable for the apprehension of developmental processes; but the role of the mind's eye is no less important. The analytical thought involved is considerable too; for all the findings of the physico-chemical study of organisms have to be borne in mind. It is, as Agnes Arber puts it in an illuminating discussion of this tricky problem,[45] a combination of mediate knowledge *about* with the immediacy of knowledge *of*, a fusion of conceptual reason with thought which is visual and tactual. Intuition, on the other hand, might suggest the sudden flash out of the blue. But, vital and indispensable as that is, it is but one moment in the sustained process of *Anschauung*, a moment for which Goethe reserved the term *aperçu*, defining this as one link in a chain of observation and thought.[46] Goethe developed the technique of *Anschauung* into a methodical discipline and a fine art; it was by means of it that he made the discoveries he did about the forms of animals and plants.

The bringing of order into all the variety of individual forms thus grasped was achieved by Goethe in two complementary ways: by comparison and by the use of type concepts, the former a source of genuine inspiration to later workers in the field, the latter still a subject of much dispute. The archetypal concept, as *he* used it, involved a free movement between deduction and induction, even as *Anschauung* involved a constant alternation between analysis and synthesis. The procedure was to compare individual forms until the mind was sufficiently saturated with them for an archetype to emerge which then, in its turn, served as a regulative organ of perception in the comparison and ordering of further forms. Though abstractions, therefore, these archetypes or, as he called them, *Urphänomene*, were never purely mental abstractions; they still partook of sensuous experience. Nor were they static conceptions like Platonic ideas; they were capable of modification as new forms were investigated. Goethe could never linger long in a schematic world. His immediate impulse was to find sensuous embodiment for his abstractions. Hence his instinctive movement to *sketch* his *Urpflanze*, that essence of 'plantness', a gesture incomprehensible to Schiller who was more at home in the realm of abstractions and could not imagine such an apparent contradiction in terms as a sensuous idea.[47] But so sensuous were Goethe's ideas that he—naïvely in the view of idealist philosophers—half hoped, though never in all seriousness, that he might come across his type-plant in the gardens of Palermo. Hence, too, his passionate attachment to that garden-love of his—which had come all the way from Kew!—*Bryophyllum calycinum*, because, in its strange mode of reproduction, it seemed to him the very image and symbol of the activity of metamorphosis.

Obviously the natural sciences can achieve results without considering the problem of *Gestalt*. They have done. Whether they will ever be able to effect any unification of their knowledge without coming to grips with questions of form in a systematic way is another matter. But in criticism and aesthetics form is the central issue, which it is impossible to avoid. And in the present chaotic state of literary studies in particular, Goethe's morphological principles could have both clarifying and unifying effect—provided they are applied with discrimination. It is all very well to say that he realized that there is no essential difference between form, not only in the crystal and the bone, in the leaf and in the cloud, but also in the painting and in the poem. But this is misleading. True, he is always coupling art and nature, once even with a single article, which in German almost has the effect of hyphening them: 'Die höchste und einzige Operation der Natur und Kunst ist die Gestaltung'.[48] But just as often he insists that art has its own laws. It is the handling of likeness and difference that he manages so superbly. There is no question of an identity of art and nature. It is a matter of analogy, or homology, as the scientist would say today; and analogies, as Goethe is always insisting, though indispensable for the communication, and even for the acquiring, of knowledge, defeat their own ends if pressed too far.

We should do well to clear our minds first of what he did not mean when he said that a work of art is like a work of nature. He did not mean such biologization of art as can be found, for instance, in the *Avant-propos* to the *Comédie Humaine*—the contrast is appropriate since Balzac is there drawing explicitly on the theories of Geoffroy Saint-Hilaire, the French biologist whose methods of tackling nature were, as Goethe publicly acknowledged, so like his own. Nor did he mean the rendering in art of the visual forms of nature, neither of external shapes nor of internal structures. Such forms may indeed inspire the artist. They inspired Goethe himself in his middle period. But that is not what he had in mind when he said that the laws of art and nature are fundamentally the same.

What he did mean was, firstly, that a work of art must be treated as an unalterable fact.[49] 'What the poet has created must be taken *as he has* created it', he said in one famous conversation;[50] 'as he made his world, so it is'. The Abbé in *Wilhelm Meisters Lehrjahre*[51] gives us an all too familiar picture of the opposite procedure: 'Most people treat finished works of art as though they were made of putty. According to their own preferences, prejudices and whims, they would have the chiselled marble remodelled, massive walls pulled out or in; a painting must teach, a drama edify, and everything must be anything but what it is . . . They reduce it all to what they call effect, and everything is relative to their own feeling and taste'.

Secondly, in a work of art as in a natural organism the organization of the parts is always according to the principle of what Goethe calls subordination. The relationships are never those of mere succession or coexistence, the single part affected only by its immediate neighbours. Each several one not only determines, but is determined by, all the others, and all are subordinated to a dominant tendency which is more than their simple agglomeration. The pattern they make has a mysterious life of its own; for the whole is more than, and different from, the sum of all its parts.

Hence no examination of a part in isolation can ever be valid in its conclusions; nor an account of external proportions ever do justice to the
form. For no more than in a work of nature is outward shape separable
from inner patterning.

But for such principles to be fruitful in their application the critic must
have the differences between art and nature constantly in mind. First and
most important is the difference of material. Morphological criticism
which, in discussing a work of art, does not take account of the *substance*
in which the formative principle is there at work lands itself in that species of organism aesthetics which is content to speak in terms of cells and
fibres and never gets down to talking in terms of words and tones, paint
and canvas, clay or stone. Not that there is anything wrong with biological analogies for purposes of illumination. But they can never yield any
measure of precision.

Secondly, the relations of natural forms are in constant flux and change.
Those of art-forms are stable. As Goethe puts it in his essay on Winckelmann,[32] man, the victim of transience in himself and in the forms among
which he dwells, is yet endowed with the power to create forms which
endure. It is perhaps ironical that we can only continue to live in the
world we inhabit by abstracting stability from the forms of change;
whereas we endow art with life by attributing movement, growth, and
function to relations which are in fact stable. It is this illusion of movement
which makes it possible to apply to art the same morphological principles
as to nature; and the sense of its being an illusion—a frank, an honest
illusion, as Schiller would say—must never be absent from criticism.

And thirdly, art has what Goethe called *Gehalt*. This is perhaps best
rendered by *import*, for it is not to be confused with content, as this is
often understood. The objects, figures, and scenes represented, the para-
phrasable prose sense which can be abstracted from literature, these, for
Goethe, are all as much a part of the artist's material, his *Stoff*, as the stone
or the clay, the brush, paint, and canvas, the words and the tones. They
are the potential which takes on the specific actuality of form. Once all
this heterogeneous material is fashioned by the artist it constitutes *Gestalt*
—all of it. *All* the patterns, or systems of relations, work on each other.
Sound patterns, rhyme, rhythm, colour, and shape do not simply work
together as form and *contain* images, ideas, characters, objects, and themes
which are to be thought of as meaning or content patterns. What, then, is
Gehalt? A *Gestalt* of nature has no import. Its whole complex of existence
is its *Gestalt*, which is expressive of nothing but itself. It is, if you like, its
own import. But a *Gestalt* which is a work of art is expressive of feeling,
of the elusive but familiar patterns of our inner life, those transient ex-

periences which are expressible in no other way. This is its *Gehalt*. And this import is immanent within the *Gestalt*, implicit in it, and never to be made explicit by being translated into any other set of terms.[53]

Must we, then, despair of saying anything about a work of art at all? Goethe encourages us to think that we need not. 'The true mediator', he says,[54] 'is art itself. To speak about art, therefore, would seem like trying to mediate the mediator; and yet by doing so, much that is valuable has accumulated.' For what we *can* speak of is not the *Gehalt* but the *Gestalt*— and that is the whole value of the analogy with works of nature. We can try to discover the relations of the parts to each other and to the whole; partly by *Anschauung*, and partly by analysis. Again with his approval: 'Don't be discouraged by having to take the poem to pieces as it were', he wrote to a friend,[55] 'I know of no other way of proceeding from a general to a specific appreciation.' The procedure advocated was essentially the same as for works of nature: a constant to and fro between analysis and synthesis—synthesis not in the sense of putting together the results attained by attending to the parts, but in the sense of looking at the whole again in the light of all the detail discovered.

When I tell the young people I teach that form is essence, they raise a sceptical eyebrow or become vocally querulous. And it is understandable; for we are at the tail end of a reaction against that attenuation of the meaning of the word *form* which was the result, though not the intention, of the movement of art for art's sake. But if one comes from Goethe's conception of form it is impossible to think otherwise. For it embraces all the forms of the natural world, animate and inanimate. And because for him the habitual distinction between form and function has no reality —function, he says, is existence thought of as activity[56]—it also comprises all modes of animal and human behaviour; not only that non-spatial structure, the form of the individual personality, but social forms, the art of living one with another, that delicate, indefinable, and easily disturbed pattern of relationships which we call 'good form', and which Goethe so much admired in those young Englishmen who frequented his house[57]— more for the sake of his daughter-in-law's charms than for the privilege of consorting with the greatest mind of Europe! It is wide enough to include the harmonious proportions and exquisite symmetry of his *Tasso* and the jumble of styles and verse which is *Faust*. His definition of *Gestalt* has been described as peculiarly anti-Classical. It would be truer to say that it includes and transcends the Classical. There is room in it for the Romantic and even for the Surrealist. And it does not force us into tiresome arguments about the relative value of form and content. For if Goethe insists that form is everything, he does not do so because he thinks it more important than content, but because it is the *condition* of content, because he knows that without form there can be no artistic content. Nor does it impose on us a false opposition between the formal and the genetic approach to works of art. On the contrary, his morphological approach takes up into itself the genetic method by examining questions of origin in the light of all-predominating considerations of form. At the moment at which he lived it would have been easy for him to fall into that exclusive preoccupation with sources and influences, with the biographical and social conditions of literature, which prevailed during the nineteenth century, and to become a prey to the critical relativism which ensued therefrom. He did not. Just because of his preoccupation with form as a dynamic, developing, system of relationships, he achieved what Hugo von Hofmannsthal has called 'the majestic equipoise of his mind between the relative and the absolute', and so anticipated the balance which a present generation of critics is still struggling to effect.

But to set forth Goethe's conception of form in summary fashion gives no hint of its resonance in his actual work. For it pervades all his writings, verse as well as prose, not only in the sense that conceptual statements of it are incorporated into his philosophical poems; it is implicit in the structural relations of the language itself. Consider those verses in which an infinity of personal experience of metamorphosis had coupled with ancient memories of Heraclitus, and with more recent reading of the work of a Basel brain-specialist on the unstable flux of bodily and mental states,[58] to precipitate a poetic statement of the transience of all things, in which romantic melancholy modulates into classical acceptance. In the fourth verse he comes, then, to the changefulness of our own body. This hand which even now in generous impulse stretched forth to bring solace, even that has changed:

> Jene Hand, die gern und milde
> Sich bewegte, wohlzutun
> Das gegliederte Gebilde
> Alles ist ein andres nun.

This articulated structure—'das gegliederte Gebilde'. The feeling of completion in the past participle combines with the collective *Ge-bilde* to give the sense of a complex finished structure; and yet all the movement of *bilden*, the activity of formation, is retained in *Gebilde*. Does poetic language here not in fact render that simultaneity of changefulness and continuing identity for which he despaired of ever finding an adequate symbolism?

Or think how he elevates the rhetorical device of oxymoron into an instrument of philosophical thought, as when he speaks of 'innate merits'—'angeborene Verdienste'[59]—as masterly a rendering of the paradox of personal development as is Keats's 'negative capability' of the paradox of artistic power. What questions it raises of whether we can achieve anything at all unless we are right by nature! What recognition of the arduous responsibility of realizing native endowments! There lies the merit. In this phrase, grace and endeavour both receive their meed, even as they do in *Faust*.

Nor can such abstractive exposition convey the ironic reservations, or the mild acceptance of our human condition, which kept him from ever becoming the slave of his theories. It is characteristic that his finest distinctions are usually followed by a saving 'And yet' or its equivalent—as in this concession to popular appreciation: 'Form is a mystery to most people . . . hence they pick out the odd line to quote or discuss; and yet this has its value, for something of the whole is in every part'.[60] Or this, on the necessity for patience in the academic teacher: 'We young students listened all agog for the story'—it was Herder reading *The Vicar of Wakefield*. 'To me it was all real and alive. But he was impatient that we had no eye for the form, and had missed the significance of a change from the third to the first person. He would have had us regard it strictly as a work of art; but we were still at that youthful stage when it is appropriate to respond to a work of art as if it were a work of nature.'[61]

But above all such an account misses the dramatic tension of Goethe's quest for forms. It leaves us with the impression of a mild old gentleman sitting there in the backwater of a small German capital with his collection of plants and bones, emitting from time to time exhortations about the importance of form to a Romantic generation which rarely heeded them. But what gives depth and tension to his love of order is his experience of chaos. Still at seventy-three he knew what it was, in anguish of heart, to feel the world of forms he loved so well and had done so much to discover—dissolve, more than that, cease to matter. Let someone else get on with the job of exploring the forms of nature is what he really says at the end of his great Marienbad Elegy, and leave me to my affliction of soul. But this experience of a world bereft of forms, when time and place shivered to atoms and the normal congruence between self and surroundings snapped, found its precipitate not, as with our present-day Existentialists, in his thought, but in his poetry. His Werther, when misery overcomes him, feels as though a curtain has been rent before his soul, and that same landscape which was even now filled with significant forms, turns into a meaningless flux, a self-devouring monster. His Tasso in extremity feels the edifice of his existence crumble into a terrifying heap of rubble and doubts his very identity. And Faust in his descent to the Mothers must traverse a void of nothingness. Mephisto tries to give him an idea of what it means: Can you imagine the final desolation of utter solitude? Were you to swim to the boundless ends of the ocean, you would still see *something*—sun, moon, and stars, and the waves, those most transient of forms, each moment taking shape and surrendering it again. But down there on the way to the Mothers—nothing.

> Und hättest du den Ozean durchschwommen,
> Das Grenzenlose dort geschaut,
> So sähst du dort doch Well' auf Welle kommen,
> Selbst wenn es dir vorm Untergange graut.
> Du sähst doch *etwas*. Sähst wohl in der Grüne
> Gestillter Meere streichende Delphine;
> Sähst Wolken ziehen, Sonne, Mond und Sterne;
> *Nichts* wirst du sehn in ewig leerer Ferne . . .   *6239-46*

Yet this passage through waste and desolation is to the very archetypes of formation and transformation. For that is what the Mothers are. A strange word! And it moves Faust strangely too. The implication is that the source of forms lies partly in man himself. In searching for them he must search too within himself, and at his most original depths. And that, indeed, is how Goethe saw it. We are committed to the world in which we find ourselves—*angewiesen* is the word he uses—'engaged' in existence. And existence throws out a challenge to us to create forms in collaboration with nature. It is an unending dialogue between us. Nature speaks to us;[62] but what we discover depends also on how we respond. To understand her language, just as to appreciate the language of art, we have to see to it that our minds are flexible and formative too.[63] For if there is no form within us, we shall not find it outside us.[64] What this view implies is an increase of responsibility in our encounter with the world. And a responsibility chiefly towards ourselves. The discovery of forms, Goethe is always insisting, is a matter of choice no less than a matter of understanding. And if we do not discover them, the loss is ours. For where there is no form, there is no meaning. And it is significant that at those moments of crisis when his heroes experience a loss of meaning through the disintegration of forms, they simultaneously experience a loss of power. For where there is no form there is no power either. Which perhaps explains Goethe's affection for a phrase from the *Liber Basiorum* of the sixteenth-century poet, Johannes Secundus:

Vis superba formae.

XI. 'Tasso—ein Gesteigerter Werther' in the Light of Goethe's Principle of 'Steigerung'

Some Reflections on Critical Method

It is a moot point whether criticism of Goethe's poetical works has not been more hindered than helped by the fulness of biographical and auto-biographical material made available in ever more convenient form by patient and devoted research. Certainly as one reads one's way through the vast literature on *Torquato Tasso*, and observes to what indiscriminate and often irresponsible use this material has been put, one is inclined to envy the Shakespeare critic who is denied such doubtful blessings. The single fact that Goethe is known to have referred to Tasso as 'ein gestei-gerter Werther' has proved as useful to those who would see the play end-ing in an abyss of unmitigated tragedy as to those who conceive it as yet another example of his conciliatory optimism. And it is not difficult to see why when one considers the divers interpretations to which the re-mark can lend itself once it is divorced from the context in which it was originally made. The critic's conclusion will depend on

1. whether he takes it to refer to the two works or to the two charac-ters; if to the works, whether (a) to their themes or (b) to their form; if to the characters, whether (a) to positive characteristics or (b) to negative characteristics.

2. which inflection of meaning in the verb *steigern* he singles out for attention. Clearly the possibilities of combination and permutation are endless. But it is perhaps a significant commentary on the primitive nature of the instruments and techniques of literary criticism that no one has yet ventured upon an investigation of the formal relation between the two works in the light of this statement. By contrast it has been applied with zest to both characters and themes and has brought forth, not simply a fruitful plenitude of varied interpretations, but a stultifying chaos of conclusions so conflicting that they cancel each other out. Attending rather to the spatial image implicit in *steigern*, i. e. raising to a higher *level*, upward gradation, some have seen in Tasso a more highly developed Werther, 'developed' implying here a judgment of value. Werther, they

contend, is a would-be artist, while Tasso is an artist in fact; he achieves, where Werther only dabbles; herein lies his power of salvation, his source of spiritual health. Equally optimistic conclusions concerning the educative power of artistic creation could, of course, be reached by stressing the other inflection of meaning in *steigern*, i.e. stepping-up of inner potency, rasing to a higher *power*, intensification, and applying this to Werther's positive characteristics, seeing his artistic potentialities so intensified in Tasso that they become a source of strength rather than of weakness. But on the whole it is Werther's negative characteristics, his pathological qualities, which have received most attention from those who use *steigern* in this latter sense, and Tasso has been seen as more Wertherish than Werther, more acutely suspicious, egocentric, hypersensitive, and therefore even more likely to come to a bad end.

As one reads one wonders which, if any, of these meanings Goethe could have had in mind, and whether any useful purpose is served by offering in support of some interpretation of a work a judgment by the author which has itself been interpreted by the critic to suit his own view. Not that we would wish to diminish the potency of Goethe's sayings by setting limits to their meaning. It is the general direction of his meaning we should like to know, not its bounds. Nor do we exclude the possibility that this meaning, if discovered, will hold within it contradictory elements. Indeed, we should be surprised to find that it did not. But they must be contradictions which make sense in the light of the whole, a significant paradox, not some inadvertent ambiguity. The same holds for any single utterance, however oracular its form. Before deciding that 'ein gesteigerter Werther' can mean anything, and therefore nothing, let us see whether there is any means of determining more precisely in what sense Goethe was using the word *gesteigert* here. We shall then be in a more favourable position for considering the wider question of how this comment may profitably be used in critical interpretation of the two works *Werther* and *Tasso*.

It might be well to begin by recalling whose comment it really is. This is neither as idle nor as redundant as it sounds. It is common knowledge that Goethe, in conversation with Eckermann,[1] attributed it to the French Romantic critic, J.-J. Ampère. Recalling the drift of Ampère's review of his dramatic works which had appeared in *Le Globe*[2] the previous year, he puts the seal of his approval upon its conclusions: 'Sehr treffend nennt er daher auch den Tasso einen gesteigerten Werther'.

Critics accepted without question that he must be quoting verbatim from Ampère's review—had he not, after all, translated most of it for *Kunst und Altertum*[3] only a few months before?—and with few exceptions they were at pains to give the appearance of academic precision by finding some turn of phrase which would show that they knew the original author of this critical judgment: 'das von Goethe gebilligte Urteil Ampères' or 'dem Urteil Ampères beipflichtend'. Their efforts were misplaced, for it did not derive from Ampère at all.[4] What Ampère had really said was: 'et dans cette poésie si harmonieuse, si délicate, il y a du *Verther*'. To note this is not mere pedantry. For had not these same critics always assumed that the expression 'ein gesteigerter Werther' originated in a mind other than Goethe's own, surely one or other of them would have been provoked to inquire whether it did not carry some peculiarly personal inflection, whether it was not one of the many words to which he imparted a pregnant significance over and above the ordinary dictionary meaning. Once it is realized that the phrase is not just translated from the French, but represents a personal judgment couched in Goethe's own terms, it seems natural to examine his use of *steigern* at this period of his life and the circumstances which gave rise to its use in this particular context. And this means that the reference to Ampère is not irrelevant. Because he did not make the remark, it does not mean that he can now drop out of our investigation. On the contrary; it is, as we shall see, the two facts taken in conjunction—that Ampère did *not* say it and that Goethe nevertheless attributed it to him—that afford the clue to the more precise meaning of this much used and abused phrase.

As soon as he starts on work of this kind the scholar at once feels the lack of any comprehensive work on Goethe's language. Fischer's *Goethe-Wortschatz* leaves us in the lurch as soon as we inquire about *development* of meaning. And there is much more that we should like to know which is beyond the scope of a small dictionary: the prevalence of a word and its dominant meaning at different periods, the overtones it carries in particular contexts, and—this is of the utmost importance in view of the organic unity of Goethe's thought—its relation to other words within the same complex of associations. A beginning has been made on these lines by R.M. Meyer and E. A. Boucke,[5] though their work touches only the fringe of the subject. In the case of *steigern*, Fischer records no single instance of its frequent occurrence in the scientific writings: the noun *Steigerung* is not even mentioned; and it is not one of the words discussed by Meyer. Boucke, on the other hand, affords invaluable help precisely by showing that the individual stamp given to this word by Goethe, the deepening of its ordinary meaning, derives from a quite specific scientific concept closely connected with his theory of metamorphosis; and out of his intimate knowledge of Goethe's thought he is able to con-

clude that in his later period one can rarely be certain that his use of the
word, even in seemingly remote contexts, is wholly free of this scientific
colouring. This is borne out by F. Weinhandl's more recent book on
Goethe's metaphysics,[6] which, although it comes to the problem of
Steigerung from a quite different angle, nevertheless offers a most useful
collection of examples drawn from that borderland of thought where
science and philosophy meet. Neither he nor Boucke considers the particular case of 'ein gesteigerter Werther', and in order to bring out the
shades of meaning which may well be implicit here I have found it
advisable in the following account to present the material rather differently, and to supplement their examples by others which illuminate the
peculiar problems involved, more especially the relation between poetry
and science. On the other hand, I have selected only what is strictly
relevant to my present purpose, and for much that is of cognate interest
the reader is referred to both these authorities.

The passage which possibly reveals more clearly than any other the
immensities of meaning contained in the principle of *Steigerung*, and the
quite central position it occupied in Goethe's later thought, is in the letter
written to Kanzler von Müller on 24 May 1828,[7] that is just a year after
he had called Tasso 'ein gesteigerter Werther'. Discussing the authorship
of the *Fragment über die Natur* of 1782, the manuscript of which had just
come to light, Goethe frankly confesses that he cannot remember having
actually written that essay; but he recognizes the view of nature expressed
there as characteristic of his own in the early eighties, and goes on to
estimate its place in the development of his thought:

Die Erfüllung aber, die ihm [dem Aufsatz] fehlt, ist die Anschauung
der zwei grossen Triebräder aller Natur: der Begriff von *Polarität* und
von *Steigerung*, jene der Materie, insofern wir sie materiell, diese ihr
dagegen, insofern wir sie geistig denken, angehörig; jene ist in immer-
währendem Anziehen und Abstossen, diese in immerstrebendem Auf-
steigen. Weil aber die Materie nie ohne Geist, der Geist nie ohne
Materie existirt und wirksam sein kann, so vermag auch die Materie
sich zu steigern, so wie sich's der Geist nicht nehmen lässt, anzuziehen
und abzustossen . . .

What strikes us at once here is the intimate connection of the two concepts, polarity and ascending progress, the impression of an interweaving
of interdependent forces. We may note that Goethe calls these two principles the 'Triebräder *aller* Natur'; and if his eye was sharpened to perceive them at work everywhere, often symbolically beyond the point
where they are scientifically observable, it was because he had first known

them with that immediacy of knowledge which derives from the sensations and functioning of our own being. He may not in the early days of his scientific studies have perceived them as laws of external nature; but he had already felt the necessity of their workings from within and recognized them as the mainsprings of his own innermost nature. This is how he had expressed the characteristic form of his own process of growth in a letter of 1775:[8]

> Aber nun gibts noch einen [Goethe], der . . . , weder rechts noch links fragt: was von dem gehalten werde was er machte? weil er arbeitend immer gleich eine Stufe höher steigt, weil er nach keinem Ideale springen, sondern seine Gefühle sich zu Fähigkeiten, kämpfend und spielend, entwickeln lassen will.

Here is the idea of a progress organic and slow, achieved not by a soaring leap, but gradually, stage by stage, not by reaching out towards some ideal conceived in the mind, but by realizing, through activity, the potentialities of one's own nature. Here, too, is the intimate connection of ascent with polarity, for in 'kämpfend und spielend' we recognize that rhythm of tension and release which Goethe later felt to be the very pulse of the universe, made palpable to us in our breathing in and breathing out. And already he is feeling towards the idea of what he was to call 'Specification', the differentiation of what is vague and inchoate (here *Gefühle*) into something of clearly defined form and function (*Fähigkeiten*). Well over fifty years later, in the last letter of his life,[9] he is concerned with the same problem in essentially the same form:

> Zu jedem Tun, daher zu jedem Talent, wird ein Angebornes gefordert, das von selbst wirkt und die nötigen Anlagen unbewusst mit sich führt, deswegen auch so geradehin fortwirkt, dass, ob es gleich die Regel in sich hat, es doch zuletzt ziel- und zwecklos ablaufen kann. Je früher der Mensch gewahr wird dass es ein Handwerk, dass es eine Kunst gibt, die ihm zur geregelten *Steigerung* seiner natürlichen Anlagen verhelfen, desto glücklicher ist er . . . Die Organe des Menschen durch Übung, Lehre, Nachdenken, Gelingen, Misslingen, Fördernis und Widerstand und immer wieder Nachdenken verknüpfen ohne Bewusstsein in einer freien Tätigkeit das Erworbene mit dem Angebornen . . . Ich habe nichts angelegentlicher zu tun als dasjenige was an mir ist und geblieben ist wo möglich zu *steigern* und meine Eigentümlichkeiten zu cohobiren . . .

It is still, we see, a question of realizing inborn potentialities, of an upward progression through activity manifesting itself in a polarity of opposing forces, of increasingly differentiated characteristics. But now the process of differentiation is defined more closely. It is to be achieved by *cohobiren*, a term of Arabic origin used in alchemy to denote repeated distillation in order to obtain a more refined and concentrated essence. And it is no longer enough simply to recognize the processes of nature, just to *let* 'Gefühle sich zu Fähigkeiten entwickeln'. One must take a hand in the direction. The emphasis now is on the relation between nature and nurture, between the unconscious activity of an organism containing the law of its development within itself and the conscious fostering of this development in accordance with that law.

This relation, as Goethe says elsewhere in this letter, is as close as the relation of weft and woof. Just how close is reflected in his use of *steigern* and *Steigerung*. Whereas in the early letter the upward movement of the organism, and the differentiation of its innate powers into distinct capacities, were ideas associated in the comparatively loose relation of simple apposition, and required for their expression two separate verbs, the intransitive *steigen* and the permissive *entwickeln lassen*, here they are bound so intimately together that they can be rendered by the single *steigern*, a factitive implying an agent and directed activity. The upward progression of the organism is now seen to consist precisely in the differentiation of its natural tendencies, and in this late phase of Goethe's thought one term suffices to express the whole complex process.

These three quotations mark out the vast territories to be explored by anyone pursuing Goethe's principle of *Steigerung* into all its ramifications: the whole of nature within and without, the realms of matter and spirit alike. They do more. They give a hint of how his mind worked when he extended this principle to art and poetry, or to the development of human personality. There is clearly no question of his simply taking findings from his scientific studies and applying them wholesale to other spheres of life and thought. The process is much less mechanical than that. It is rather that such 'produktive Naturmaxime' became, by a kind of inner possession, part of the structure of his mind, new organs of his thought, in the light of which he was then able to apprehend the significant relation between other phenomena of existence. These three letters considered together lift the veil upon that secret correspondence between the human mind and the laws of nature, which, as the older Goethe was never tired of proclaiming, is the source of all our knowledge of the structure of the universe.[10] For the early one of 1775 reveals unmistakably that his natural mode of experiencing was in a double rhythm of oscillation and upward movement, that his mind was in fact organized to perceive these rhythms in the world outside. But the two later letters make it equally clear that his close observation of the world outside in turn adjusted and modified this natural mode of experiencing, transforming vague intuitions into precise instruments of thought. When in his last letter he returns to that problem of personal growth which was the subject of the early one, we are struck as much by the difference as by the similarity: his long study of the growth of plants and animals has clearly left its mark on both concepts and terminology. Between these two letters lies the whole history of his scientific investigations; between them, too, lies an interesting chapter of semantic development. For the intense concentration of meaning in the verb *steigern* is the residue of its cumulative use in precise scientific contexts. Through the need for precision the more delicate nuances of meaning have been recovered, those middle shades which tend to get lost in the rougher handling of ordinary verbal commerce, where it is enough to indicate the general meaning. Goethe has filled the word with a significance beyond its dictionary sense. How much of this individual enrichment has since passed over into ordinary usage is a matter for separate investigation; but such an investigation would probably show that *steigern* has not only become more common since Goethe's day, but that its meaning has also been affected.

It was in his morphological writings that Goethe first began to use *steigern* with specially pregnant significance; but it is in the *·Farbenlehre* that the sensuous element in the concept is most palpable, and it will therefore be more appropriate to abandon strict chronology and examine it first in a context where it is free of any metaphorical flavour. After all, the general idea of ascent, upward development, perfectibility, is present, more or less explicitly, in all philosophies which interpret the universe as an activation of potential forces. Herder was even then concerned with the problem from the historical and religious point of view. What Goethe did was to move away from the metaphysical and to follow it up in the physical and biological spheres, trying to discover how exactly the development of new, more highly organized, forms takes place.

In his experiments on colours, then, he notes that when a piece of paper is treated with repeated coats of yellow or blue a point is reached when we can no longer simply speak of the yellow or blue becoming deeper; they each take on a new, reddish tone.[11] Similarly if a yellow or a blue liquid is poured into a vessel of white porcelain which is stepped at the bottom, the colour varies according to the thickness of the liquid, assuming a reddish tinge as the vessel deepens, until at the deepest part, where the thickness is greatest, it appears as orange or violet.[12] In both cases we may observe how a difference in degree becomes a difference in kind, not by essential opposition, but by intensification of the original characteristics.[13] This process of concentration or saturation it is which Goethe calls *Steigerung*, defining it in the *Farbenlehre* as follows:

> Die Steigerung erscheint uns als eine in sich selbst Drängung, Sätti-gung, Beschattung der Farben.[14]

If the process of intensification is continued, we finally obtain a clear red in which there is no trace of either yellow or blue;[15] but the most splen-did red (*Purpur*) is to be obtained by mixing the red derived from yellow with that derived from blue, i.e. through the 'Vereinigung der *gesteiger-ten Pole*'.[16] The intimate connection of *Polarität* and *Steigerung* is at once apparent. It is, according to Goethe, through the interaction of these two forces that, out of the oneness that is light, the manifold variety of colour is made manifest to our senses. The primary colour, yellow, we become aware of directly through light, while the other primary colour, blue, arises at the opposite pole of darkness. Combined, these simple opposites give green; but each is capable of intensification, whereby it progressive-ly assumes a different hue, and the union of the two intensified opposites gives red. However varied the phenomena of nature, its elements are al-ways the same:

> Das Geeinte zu entzweien, das Entzweite zu einigen, ist das Leben der Natur . . . Man vergleiche das Mannigfaltige, das aus einer *Steige-rung* des Gelben und Blauen zum Roten, aus der Verknüpfung dieser beiden *höheren* Enden zum Purpur, aus der Vermischung der beiden niedern Enden zum Grün entsteht.[17]

It is through the interaction of these same two factors, *Polarität* and *Steigerung*, that Goethe tries to account for the phenomena of change and mutation in the organic world. He is not satisfied to observe the outward signs of metamorphosis; he wants to understand its mechanism. Thus in tracing the successive changes occurring in the lateral appendages of the plant, from the cotyledons, through the foliage leaves and bracts, to the final reproductive goal in the fruit, he believed he could discern two principles governing its inner economy. The one he terms a force of expansion and contraction, freely admitting that these words are inade-quate to describe all that he means by it:

> Bei der fortschreitenden Veränderung der Pflanzenteile wirkt eine Kraft, die ich nur uneigentlich Ausdehnung und Zusammenziehung nennen darf. Besser wäre es ihr ein *x* oder *y* nach algebraischer Weise zu geben, denn die Worte Ausdehnung und Zusammenziehung

drücken diese Wirkung nicht in ihrem ganzen Umfange aus. Sie zieht zusammen, dehnt aus, bildet aus, bildet um, verbindet, sondert, färbt, entfärbt, verbreitet, verlängt, erweicht, verhärtet, teilt mit, entzieht und nur allein, wenn wir alle ihre verschiedenen Wirkungen in Einem sehen, dann können wir das anschaulicher kennen, was ich durch diese vielen Worte zu erklären und auseinander zu setzen gedacht habe. Sie tut das alles so stückweise, so sacht, so unmerklich, dass sie zuletzt uns vor unseren Augen einen Körper in den andern verwandelt, ohne dass wir es gewahr werden.[18]

Polarity manifests itself here not as oscillation between two poles simultaneously existing in space, but rather as a sequence of opposing tendencies in time. But such periodic oscillation would not of itself account for growth, for developing form. There is another tendency at work in the organism. In the journey from the root upwards to the reproductive appendages there is, in Goethe's view, a process of repeated filtration going on, which results in a progressive elaboration and refinement of the sap as it travels from node to node. The moisture transmitted from the roots is constantly being modified in the leaves through the action of light and air: vapours are given off, and the sap that is handed on to the higher vessels is a more concentrated and refined essence.[19] It is in this modification and elaboration of what it assimilates from the environment that the upward tendency of the plant manifests itself, so affecting the rhythmic oscillation of expansion and contraction that, instead of a never ending seesaw, a spiral movement results—a return to the original position but at a higher level. Goethe later made an explicit distinction between a vertical and a spiral tendency in vegetative growth, at the same time insisting that the two are not to be thought of apart, since they operate only in and through each other. The spiral tendency covers everything in the economy of the plant which is directed towards change and transformation through ever renewed contact with the environment. The vertical tendency is concerned with continuity, with consolidating what is assimilated, converting it into a solid structure, which persists as recognizable form. It is

... dieselbe Naturkraft, welche unaufhaltsam von Knoten zu Knoten in die Höhe oder sonst fortschiebt, die einzelnen Spiralgefässe mit sich fortreisst und so, indem sie Leben nach Leben fördert und *steigert*, eine Continuität des Ganzen sogar in rankenden und kriechenden Gewächsen folgerecht hervorbringt.[20]

In the sphere of vegetative growth, then, *Steigerung* denotes the upward tendency of the plant. But it denotes, too, the mechanism by which this is achieved: the progressive concentration and refinement of the sap. And although in Goethe's time there were no means of developing this theory in detail, the view he was trying to express may well be regarded as foreshadowing modern ideas upon the relation between chemistry and plant-form.[21] I note this here, not because it is important to show that his theory is borne out by later scientific discovery—for the purpose of this investigation that is totally irrelevant—but because his use of the word *steigern* can only be properly understood if we fully realize the concrete, physical, nature of the perception which underlies it.

In the animal kingdom, where there was even less possibility of exploring the mechanism of developing form, Goethe's theory bears more clearly the stamp of speculation, though speculation of a concrete enough kind, as is evident from one of the Paralipomena to his *Morphologie*:

> Weg der Pflanzen Metamorphose—Identität der Teile—Aperçu dass das Haupt aus verwandelten Wirbelknochen besteht ... *Os ethmoideum* wird nun die Blüte des ganzen ... Die Gehirnknochen entstehen aus Wirbelknochen. Durch *Steigerung* erheben sich zu Sinneswerkzeugen.[22]

The similarity between the changes observable in the vertebrae of the spinal column and the successive modification of a 'type-leaf' in the plant seemed to point to a similarity in the inner mechanism which produced such metamorphosis: to a progressive elaboration and refinement, culminating in the brain in an extreme contraction similar to that which occurs in the flower. When, on the other hand, he uses *Steigerung* of the general evolution of species, this more concrete hypothesis is replaced by the much wider, but also more abstract, idea of an ascent stage by stage to more highly organized forms. How he conceived this 'allmähliche Steigerung organischer Wesen'[23] is most clearly set out in his lectures on comparative anatomy (1796), where with a masterly sweep he runs through the scale of being in a brief ten pages[24] in order to bring out the gradual change in the principle governing the organization of the parts: from inorganic bodies, where the parts are loosely co-ordinated in a state of 'suspendirten Gleichgültigkeit', easily disintegrating but as easily recombining to form a new whole, through successively complex forms of the organic, where the individual parts gradually become so specialized that one cannot replace another and, if destroyed, cannot be re-formed from the remaining parts, until in the higher animals, and especially in man, 'alles bestimmte Form, Stelle, Zahl hat'.[25] *Steigerung* here manifests itself as increasingly complex integration, as the successive differentiation of the individual parts of an organism, and the ever more complete subordination of these parts to one dominant part or function:

> Je unvollkommener das Geschöpf ist, destomehr sind diese Teile einander gleich oder ähnlich, und destomehr gleichen sie dem Ganzen. Je vollkommener das Geschöpf wird, desto unähnlicher werden die Teile einander ... Je ähnlicher die Teile einander sind, desto weniger sind sie einander subordinirt. Die Subordination der Teile deutet auf ein vollkommneres Geschöpf.[26]

But his interest in how this more complex integration actually works, the more concrete idea of concentration and refinement, is not entirely lost even here. It clearly underlies his account of the metamorphosis of the caterpillar into a butterfly, although the word *steigern* does not actually occur,[27] and it is explicit in the following passage:

> Des Menschen Bau ist in *zartere* Ramificationen vermannigfaltiget, reich und *gedrängt* ausgestattet, bedeutende Stellen *in die Enge gezogen*, abgesonderte Teile durch Anastomose verbunden.
>
> Dem Beobachter liegt im Tiere das Tierische mit allen unmittelbaren Forderungen und Bedürfnissen vor Augen.
>
> Im Menschen ist das Tierische zu höhern Zwecken *gesteigert* und für das Auge wie für den Geist in Schatten gestellt.[28]

The difficulty about Goethe's theory of *Steigerung* is that he uses this one word to denote two slightly different things or, more precisely, two different aspects of the same thing. On the one hand it denotes one of the means whereby nature from the simplest beginnings produces the infinite variety of phenomena; it is, in other words, a *factor* in the mechanism of metamorphosis. This is unmistakably its meaning in the following passage which may be compared with those from the *Farbenlehre* concerning the union of the 'gesteigerten Pole' or 'höheren Enden' (above, p. 192):

> Unsere Vorfahren bewunderten die Sparsamkeit der Natur. Man dachte sie als eine verständige Person, die, indessen andere mit vielem wenig hervorbringen, mit wenigem viel zu leisten geneigt ist. Wir bewundern mehr, wenn wir uns auch auf menschliche Weise ausdrücken, ihre Gewandtheit, wodurch sie, obgleich auf wenige Grundmaximen eingeschränkt, das Mannigfaltigste hervorzubringen weiss.
>
> Sie bedient sich hierzu des Lebensprincips, welches die Möglichkeit enthält, die einfachsten Anfänge der Erscheinungen durch *Steigerung* ins Unendliche und Unähnlichste zu vermannigfaltigen.
>
> Was in die Erscheinung tritt, muss sich trennen, um nur zu erschei-

nen. Das Getrennte sucht sich wieder, und es kann sich wieder finden und vereinigen; im niedern Sinne, indem es sich nur mit einem Entgegengestellten vermischt, mit demselben zusammentritt, wobei die Erscheinung Null oder wenigstens gleichgültig wird. Die Vereinigung kann aber auch im höhern Sinne geschehen, indem das Getrennte sich zuerst *steigert* und durch die Verbindung der *gesteigerten* Seiten ein Drittes, Neues, Höheres, Unerwartetes hervorbringt.[29]

But on the other hand *Steigerung* also denotes the *progression* observable in the various forms of the ladder of creation. Now in order to account for the existence of *forms* at all, we have to assume a tendency in nature other than the tendency to metamorphosis and change. To be recognizable, the 'Drittes, Neues, Höheres, Unerwartetes', produced by the combined operation of *Polarität* and *Steigerung* must persist, and not at once be caught up in further transformation. This is clear from the aphorisms written in 1829 during his study of De Candolle's *Organographie végétale*, and is indispensable to a full understanding of his theory of metamorphosis:

> *gesteigerte* Gliederung, successive gegliederte *Steigerung*, dadurch Möglichkeit einer Schlussbildung . . .[30]

Steigerung in this second and wider sense itself embraces a polarity, of which metamorphosis is only one side, the other being the tendency to persist in specific form; and in *Problem und Erwiderung* (1823) Goethe does not hesitate to represent the *Specificationstrieb* and the idea of metamorphosis as opposed, albeit complementary, principles:

> Die Idee der Metamorphose ist eine höchst ehrwürdige, aber zugleich höchst gefährliche Gabe von oben. Sie führt ins Formlose, zerstört das Wissen, löst es auf. Sie ist gleich der *vis centrifuga* und würde sich ins Unendliche verlieren, wäre ihr nicht ein Gegengewicht zugegeben: ich meine den Specificationstrieb, das zähe Beharrlichkeitsvermögen dessen was einmal zur Wirklichkeit gekommen. Eine *vis centripeta*, welcher in ihrem tiefsten Grunde keine Äusserlichkeit etwas anhaben kann . . . Da nun aber beide Kräfte zugleich wirken, so müssten wir sie auch bei didaktischer Überlieferung zugleich darstellen, welches unmöglich scheint.[31]

This is not a contradiction, but a completion, of earlier statements about metamorphosis. The two components of every metamorphosis are here explicitly resolved into a polarity, but the same word is used for one of the opposing tendencies as has hitherto been used for the whole process. In a somewhat similar way the word *Steigerung* can be used both dynamically and statically: it can refer both to an aspect of the formative *process* and to the *forms* which are its result; and, in scientific contexts at least, if something is referred to as a *gesteigerte* form of something else (as for instance *Rot* is *gesteigertes Gelb*), we must assume that it has been produced, not by the mechanism of *Steigerung* alone which, left to itself, would lead to unceasing change 'ins Unendliche und Unähnlichste', but by the interaction of *Steigerung* with the *Specificationstrieb*.[32]

Any or all of this complexity of thought may colour Goethe's use of *steigern* in other than scientific contexts, at least from 1790 onwards, and increasingly as time goes on: the idea that a qualitative change can result from a difference in degree, from the intensification of original characteristics, so that what is essentially the same may appear opposed in form and function; the idea that unusually fine forms of creation result from the synthesis of intensified opposites; the idea that the evolution of higher forms is characterized by increasing subordination of the parts in a definite hierarchy. And inseparable from it all is that most fundamental law of his morphology and, indeed, of all his thinking, the law of compensation, the idea that every gain involves a corresponding loss, that all progress is achieved at the cost of some regress. Extreme specialization of organ and function, for instance, is an obvious advantage, in that it gives the higher forms of life more extensive control over their environment; but from the worm's eye view, so to speak, it represents a clear disadvantage, since it involves a corresponding loss of adaptability.[33] It is a law clearly expressed, at both the physical and the spiritual level, in his poem *Metamorphose der Tiere*, in his conversation with Eckermann on the advantages and disadvantages of every stage of life,[34] or in his aphorism on Dante: 'Metamorphose im höhern Sinn durch Nehmen und Geben, Gewinnen und Verlieren hat schon Dante trefflich geschildert'.[35]

In the following aphorisms the extension of the scientific principle of *Steigerung* to other spheres is explicit.

Die Formel der *Steigerung* lässt sich auch im Ästhetischen und Moralischen verwenden.

Die Liebe, wie sie modern erscheint, ist ein *Gesteigertes*. Es ist nicht mehr das erste einfache Naturbedürfnis und Naturäusserung, sondern ein in sich cohobirtes, gleichsam verdichtetes und so *gesteigertes* Wesen.

Es ist einfältig diese Art zu verwerfen, weil sie auch noch einfach existirt und existiren kann.

Wenn man in Küche und Keller ein *Gesteigertes* sucht und darauf ausgeht, warum soll man nicht auch diesen Genuss für die Darstellung oder für das unmittelbare Empfinden *steigern* dürfen und können?

Jeder Koch macht auf diese Weise seine Brühen und Saucen appetit-
licher, dass er sie in sich cohobirt.[36]

A cursory reading of these cryptic sentences might tempt us to equate *gesteigert* with *cohobirt*, translate it as sublimated, and have done with it. But
the two are not exactly synonymous. *Steigern* can be used for *cohobiren* because it embraces it and far more. But *cohobiren* cannot replace *steigern*;
it lacks the whole idea of an upward progression. The more completely
we have assimilated the theory of *Steigerung* in all its ramifications, the
more is this aphorism illuminated, as we find that the analogy with the
physical world holds, not just at one, but at many points. The symbolic
'Formel der Steigerung', in fact, serves us here as a mental aid in the co-
ordination of experience, and this is undoubtedly the function it fulfilled
for Goethe in the following passages, where even the most abstract use
of the term has a full-bodiedness which derives from his ever-present
awareness of a concrete physical phenomenon:

> In der Republik bilden sich grosse, glückliche, ruhig-rein tätige
> Charaktere; *steigert* sie sich zur Aristokratie, so entstehen würdige,
> consequente, tüchtige, im Befehlen und Gehorchen bewunderungs-
> würdige Männer.[37]

> . . . das Wissen, indem es sich selbst *steigert*, fordert, ohne es zu bemer-
> ken, das Anschauen und geht dahin über . . .[38]

> Es gibt eine zarte Empirie, die sich mit dem Gegenstand innigst iden-
> tisch macht, und dadurch zur eigentlichen Theorie wird. Diese *Steigerung*
> des geistigen Vermögens aber gehört einer hochgebildeten Zeit an.[39]

> Bedenkt man nun, dass wiederholte sittliche Spiegelungen das Ver-
> gangene nicht allein lebendig erhalten, sondern sogar zu einem höheren
> Leben empor *steigern*, so wird man der entoptischen Erscheinungen
> gedenken, welche gleichfalls von Spiegel zu Spiegel nicht etwa ver-
> bleichen, sondern sich erst recht entzünden . . .[40]

> Höchst willkommen war dieses Gedicht [*Die Metamorphose der Pflan-
> zen*] der eigentlich Geliebten . . . und auch ich fühlte mich sehr glück-
> lich, als das lebendige Gleichnis unsere schöne vollkommene Neigung
> *steigerte* und vollendete . . .[41]

> Der hohe Wert seines innern Vermögens hat sich durch eigentüm-
> liche Aufnahme der Aussenwelt auf einen solchen Grad *gesteigert*, dass
> man sich zusammennehmen muss um würdig zu schätzen was man
> mit Bewunderung anerkennt.[42]

Im Reich der Natur waltet *Bewegung* und *Tat*, im Reiche der Freiheit *Anlage* und *Willen*. Bewegung ist ewig und tritt bei jeder günstigen Bedingung unwiderstehlich in die Erscheinung. Anlagen entwickeln sich zwar auch naturgemäss, müssen aber erst durch den Willen geübt und nach und nach *gesteigert* werden.[43]

... das letzte Product der sich immer *steigernden* Natur ist der schöne Mensch ... indem der Mensch auf den Gipfel der Natur gestellt ist, so sieht er sich wieder als eine ganze Natur an, die in sich abermals einen Gipfel hervorzubringen hat. Dazu *steigert* er sich, indem er sich mit allen Vollkommenheiten und Tugenden durchdringt, Wahl, Ordnung, Harmonie und Bedeutung aufruft, und sich endlich bis zur Production des Kunstwerkes erhebt ...[44]

... doch ist es merkwürdig, wie von Jahrhundert zu Jahrhundert sich alles mehr begeistet und belebt, eins ins andre greift und keins ohne das andre bleiben will. Von Spinoza, der das Ganze aus Gedanke und Ausdehnung bildet, bis zu diesem Freunde, der es durch Bewegung und Willen hervorbringt, welche hübsche Filiation und *Steigerung* der Denkweisen würde sich aufzeichnen lassen![45]

Man muss etwas *sein*, um etwas zu machen. Dante erscheint uns gross, aber er hatte eine Cultur von Jahrhunderten hinter sich; das Haus Rothschild ist reich, aber es hat mehr als ein Menschenalter gekostet um zu solchen Schätzen zu gelangen. Diese Dinge liegen alle tiefer, als man denkt. Unsere guten altdeutschelnden Künstler wissen davon nichts, sie wenden sich mit persönlicher Schwäche und künstlerischem Unvermögen zur Nachahmung der Natur und meinen, es wäre was. Sie stehen *unter* der Natur. Wer aber etwas Grosses machen will, muss seine Bildung so *gesteigert* haben, dass er gleich den Griechen imstande sei, die geringere reale Natur zu der Höhe seines Geistes heranzuheben...[46]

Jeder suche den Besitz der ihm von der Natur, von dem Schicksal gegönnt ward, zu würdigen, zu erhalten, zu *steigern* ...[47]

Whereas in the scientific sphere there was no question of moral appraisement in connection with *Steigerung*—it is as neutral as any other natural phenomenon—once it is extended beyond the borders of the purely physical, the question of values inevitably creeps in (witness for instance the section of the *Farbenlehre* entitled 'Sinnlich-sittliche Wirkung der Farbe'), and then *steigern* normally carries positive associations, as it clearly does in all the above examples. Very occasionally, however, it is used with negative inflection. Not that the negative value is then inherent in the process of *Steigerung* itself. In Goethe's dynamic view of life, processes, qualities, powers of mind or body, are not good or bad in themselves; their value depends on the way they function in relation to the other tendencies of the organism, whose life is endangered if any one of them gets out of hand, if it is not kept in check by its regulative counterforce, if the natural rhythm of polarity is not maintained. There is nothing wrong with thinking, for example; but thinking without the check of its polar opposite, doing, can be dangerous:

> Denken und Tun, Tun und Denken, das ist die Summe aller Weisheit . . . Beides muss wie Aus- und Einatmen sich im Leben ewig fort hin und wider bewegen; wie Frage und Antwort sollte eins ohne das andere nicht statt finden.[48]

A healthy personality will move with ease between contemplation and activity, analysis and synthesis, the ideal and the real; however much his imagination may soar into the general, the abstract, the boundless infinity of the absolute, it will return to the limitation of the particular and the concrete—

> kehrt freilich nach einer solchen Diastole, um sich nicht zu verlieren, wieder an die Wirklichkeit zurück und verfährt wechselsweise wohl so sein ganzes Leben.[49]

The process of *Steigerung*, not in the all-embracing sense of ascending progress, but as the mechanism of concentration and refinement which is one of the factors in that progress, is no exception to this law of polarity. As we have noted many times, these two 'Triebräder aller Natur' are not to be thought of apart. Like everything else, functioning alone and unchecked, *Steigerung* becomes dangerous:

> Ein jeder Mensch wird von seinen Gewohnheiten regiert, nur wird er, durch äussere Bedingungen eingeschränkt, sich mässig verhalten, und Mässigung wird ihm zur Gewohnheit. Gerade das Entgegengesetzte findet sich bei dem Despoten; ein uneingeschränkter Wille *steigert* sich selbst und muss, von aussen nicht gewarnt, nach dem völlig Grenzenlosen streben.[50]

It is not always as easy as this to see just why the general impression is negative. The following maxim, for instance, is much more obscure:

> Der Deutsche läuft keine grössere Gefahr, als sich mit und an seinen Nachbarn zu *steigern*; es ist vielleicht keine Nation geeigneter, sich aus sich selbst zu entwickeln . . .[51]

This cannot be understood apart from the series of maxims, largely dealing with *Weltliteratur*, in which it is embedded. From these it is clear that Goethe cannot possibly be implying that the stimulus of foreign literature is in itself harmful; that would be to deny a conception which he had much at heart. If, then, the Germans are likely to be endangered by foreign influences, the cause must lie elsewhere. And here a knowledge of the principle of *Steigerung* in relation to the whole idea of metamorphosis can be illuminating. We recall the interdependence of the vertical and spiral tendencies in plant life. Is Goethe not perhaps suggesting here that the 'vertical tendency' of German literature, its solid core of continuing identity, was as yet not sufficiently developed to enable it to assimilate foreign influences without jeopardizing its own characteristic form? Certainly the following passage presents the analogous case of a poet's treatment of his literary sources in the light of that biological principle:

> Nicht allein den Stoff empfangen wir von aussen, auch fremden Gehalt dürfen wir uns aneignen, wenn nur eine *gesteigerte*, wo nicht vollendete Form uns angehört.[52]

Equal caution is required in interpreting the famous *aperçu* on Romanticism:

> Das Romantische ist kein Natürliches, Ursprüngliches, sondern ein Gemachtes, ein Gesuchtes, *Gesteigertes*, Übertriebenes, Bizarres, bis ins Fratzenhafte und Karrikaturartige.[53]

Again it is only by bearing in mind the whole complex of thought on *Steigerung* and *Polarität*, and by comparison with other pronouncements of a like nature, that we may hope to glimpse the full implications of *gesteigert* here. The following extract from a letter written about the same time makes it clear that it is not the *intensity* of imagination and feeling that Goethe deplores in the Romantics, but their failure to swing to the other pole and give form to their fantasy:

> Deswegen bringen mich auch ein halb Dutzend jüngere poetische Talente zur Verzweiflung, die bei ausserordentlichen Naturanlagen schwerlich viel machen werden was mich erfreuen kann. Werner, Öhlenschläger, Arnim, Brentano, und andere arbeiten und treiben's immerfort; aber alles geht durchaus ins Form- und Charakterlose. Kein Mensch will begreifen, dass die höchste und einzige Operation der Natur und Kunst die Gestaltung sei, und in der Gestalt die Specification, damit jedes ein besonderes Bedeutendes werde, sei und bleibe.[54]

What warps their work is not that their talents are *gesteigert*, but that they are *falsch gesteigert*;[55] in other words, *Steigerung* is not functioning properly in relation to the *Specificationstrieb*; the one tendency is over-active at the expense of the other. The converse, we may note, can also bring disaster. *Specification* without the enlivening stimulus of *Steigerung* leads up a blind alley to a dead end:

> Die Natur gerät auf Specificationen wie in eine Sackgasse: sie kann nicht durch und mag nicht wieder zurück; daher die Hartnäckigkeit der Nationalbildung.[56]

What emerges from these examples is that Goethe uses the same word *steigern* indifferently in a positive and a negative sense. It is natural and inevitable that he should do so, for what gives the mechanism of intensification positive or negative value is its normal or abnormal functioning, the criterion of 'normal' here being the properly regulated metabolism of the organism. This is, perhaps, clearest of all in the following passage, where the biological standard of reference is fully evident in the vocabulary:

> Das Ideale im Menschen, wenn diesem die Objekte genommen oder verkümmert werden, zieht sich in sich, feinert und *steigert* sich, dass es sich gleichsam übertrumpft. Die meisten Menschen im Norden haben viel mehr Ideales in sich, als sie brauchen können, als sie verarbeiten können; daher die sonderbaren Erscheinungen von Sentimentalität, Religiosität, Mysticismus und so weiter . . .[57]

It is clearly the unbalanced relation of ideal and real in romantic Northern man, with the consequent atrophy of his sensuous relation to objects, which gives *steigern* its abnormal inflexion here, its connotation of *over*-sublimated.

Most of these examples are drawn from the last two decades of Goethe's life, and it is true that at this period his whole thought was permeated by the principle of *Steigerung*. But all the same the date of an utterance is in itself no guarantee that the word has scientific colouring. There is no point at which we can say: from now onwards Goethe used it in this sense only. In the following case, for instance, it seems to bear no more than its ordinary dictionary meaning:

> die diesmal sehr *gesteigerte* Feier des 28. August (1831)[58]

But however apparently simple the thought, it is always safer to pause and ask what exactly the word means; for as soon as we try to replace it by another we usually find that something gets lost, as it is invariably lost when we translate it into another language. Even in Soret's translation of the *Metamorphose der Pflanzen*, which was sponsored and revised by Goethe himself, 'developpement progressif' loses much of the force of '*gesteigerte* Entwicklung'—loses, in fact, the whole suggestion of a process of concentration and refinement.

The date itself, then, can only suggest the likelihood that *steigern* is used with specially pregnant meaning. In order to become more certain we have to scrutinize not only the immediate but the wider context. In the case of 'ein gesteigerter Werther' a scientific association is suggested, though not proven, by the circumstances which occasioned the remark. It is recorded by Eckermann in connection with J.-J. Ampère's visit to Weimar at the end of April and beginning of May 1827.[59] According to Ampère's correspondence, he and Goethe talked of literary matters, including *Tasso*. This was only to be expected: Goethe had been following literary trends abroad with the liveliest interest, especially the reception of his own works; he had been profoundly impressed by Ampère's method of interpreting them, as indeed he was impressed by the whole critical approach of *Le Globe* and eager to be in touch with its contributors. This visit promised him a breath from a different and fresher literary atmosphere, a stimulus for which he longed: 'Wie sehne ich mich nach Wirkung in die Ferne und aus der Ferne. Der angekündigte Herr Ampère ist noch nicht erschienen', he wrote on 22 April.[60] But they also talked of the scientific discoveries of Ampère's father, André-Marie Ampère, the great physicist, whose work on electro-magnetism Goethe had been following with equal interest. 'Il m'a entretenu des découvertes de mon père, qu'il connaît très bien', Ampère wrote to Mme Récamier on 22 April; and in a letter to his father of the same date he adds the further information that Goethe possessed his electromagnetic apparatus.[61] The juxtaposition of science and literature in their conversation is significant. But no less significant is the fact that the name Ampère itself carries both kinds of associations for Goethe. How much so we may gauge from his urgent appeal to Soret to advise him on a suitable topic of conversation with which to entertain the young critic:

In Ungewissheit ob ich Sie, mein Wertester, heute Abend sehe, vermelde ich dass Herr Ampère bei mir angemeldet ist und wünschte zu hören, ob Sie etwa auch davon wissen. Auf alle Fälle frag ich an was man ihm allenfalls Freundliches erzeigte? Die kleine Maschine des magnetischen Rundstabes, um welchen sich die metallnen Eimerchen drehen,

besitze, habe aber das Experiment selbst noch niemals angestellt. Es
wäre die Frage ob man sich mit ihm darüber unterhalten sollte. Vielleicht gönnen Sie mir heute ein Viertelstündchen.

This was written as soon as the visit was announced, on 16 April, and represents therefore a fairly prompt reaction to the news. In the light of it, it
is not far-fetched to suppose that the name Ampère might well have
precipitated in Goethe's mind an *aperçu* which associated literature with
science, not difficult to imagine how it could come about that, in recalling
to Eckermann the gist of what Ampère had written about the relation
between *Werther* and *Tasso*, he should have found it natural to express
that relation in terms of *Steigerung*, so natural that he could even attribute
the *aperçu* to Ampère himself. Always assuming, of course, that what
Ampère had actually written will bear such an interpretation. And there
is another point. Such *aperçus* do not come out of the blue. They presup-
pose long rumination—'Alles wahre Aperçu kommt aus einer Folge und
bringt Folge. Es ist ein Mittelglied einer grossen produktiv aufsteigenden
Kette'.[62] It is, in short, not enough to know the precipitating factor; we
have to look at what there was suspended in solution and ready to be precipitated.

It had not needed a review of his works to bring *Werther* and *Tasso*
together in Goethe's mind. The association was of long standing, longer
even than his thought on *Steigerung*. On 30 April 1780, just at the time
when the idea of *Tasso* was beginning to stir and take shape, he re-read
his *Werther* right through for the first time since its publication.[63] And
the link remained. In the poem *An Werther* of 1824 he brought Werther's
fate into direct relation with Tasso's, and with the release that comes
from poetic utterance:

> Scheiden ist der Tod!
> Wie klingt es rührend, wenn der Dichter singt,
> Den Tod zu meiden, den das Scheiden bringt!
> Verstrickt in solche Qualen, halbverschuldet,
> Geb' ihm ein Gott, zu sagen, was er duldet.

Ampère's review, then, a couple of years later, only voiced what was
already an integral part of his own thought on its deepest level, the level
of poetic creation. But that, presumably, was one of the reasons why
Goethe valued it so highly. He was amazed at the young man's power
to read between the lines the secret connections of his different phases of
development. But it came as something of a revelation all the same—as
it always is a revelation to hear someone else make explicit what we have

long felt dimly in ourselves. As soon as he had read the first instalment of the review, he wrote:

Eine Rezension der Übersetzung meiner dramatischen Arbeiten hat mir auch viel Vergnügen gemacht. Verhalt' ich mich doch selbst gegen meine Productionen ganz anders, als zur Zeit, da ich sie concipirte. Nun bleibt es höchst merkwürdig, wie sie sich zu einer fremden Nation verhalten und zwar so spät, bei ganz veränderten Ansichten der Zeit.[64]

Ampère had, after all, brought together in the brief compass of a review the poetic fruits of a long life. The effect was not only to increase the sense of distance from his own works which Goethe already felt, but to telescope them so that they appeared as a progression, and—since they were brought into such close connection with his personal growth—as an organic progression. This feeling of progression is unmistakable in the *Trilogie der Leidenschaft* published in the next year, 1827.[65] By arranging the three poems in the reverse order of their composition, Goethe placed both *Tasso* and the *Marienbader Elegie* in the direct line of succession from *Werther;* the motto to the *Elegie*, with its preterite indicative of accomplished fact,

Gab mir ein Gott, zu sagen, was ich leide,

now followed hard upon the supplicatory imperative in the last line of *An Werther*,

Geb' ihm ein Gott, zu sagen was er duldet,

and read like a fulfilment of this prayer; the poem expressing the cathartic effect of music—now significantly called *Aussöhnung*—formed the climax and crown of the progression, and brought out both the symbolic pattern in each of the three separate experiences and the spiral movement in their recurrence.

But in his rendering of Ampère's review, which he finished about the end of 1826, Goethe gave no hint of having seen this progression in the light of his principle of *Steigerung*, neither in the phrasing of his commentary nor in his translation of the crucial passage—the translation 'durch diese harmonische Poesie hört man den Werther durch' is only intent on bringing out to the full the auditory image implied in the original 'et dans cette poésie si harmonieuse, si délicate, il y a du *Verther*'. It was in conversation with Eckermann that he put his own personal stamp upon this judgment by using the word *gesteigert*, and it would not be surprising if it were then that the scientific analogy first struck him. For it was just at that time—the last few days of 1826 and the first months of 1827—

that he was initiating Eckermann into the *Farbenlehre*, making him perform the experiments himself, and propound the principles on which it
was based. And it is as if, reflected back by another mind,[66] the great
fundamental laws common to the whole of nature became clearer to him
than ever before, burst into new life in his own mind and sent out shoots
in all directions, as he underlined the essential unity of his *Farbenlehre* and
his *Morphologie*, and went on to reveal the workings of metamorphosis,
polarity and *Steigerung* in sphere after sphere of human experience—history, art, music, literature. His sense of the all-pervadingness of these
forces is at its height:

> Sie sehen, wie alles aneinander hängt, und wie sogar ein Gesetz der
> Farbenlehre auf eine Untersuchung der griechischen Tragödie führen
> kann. (1 February)

And in trying to illuminate the composition of his own *Novelle* by the
analogy of *Steigerung* he quite evidently 'sees' the process at work:

> Ein ideeller, ja lyrischer Schluss war nötig und musste folgen; denn
> nach der pathetischen Rede des Mannes, die schon poetische Prosa ist,
> musste eine *Steigerung* kommen, ich musste zur lyrischen Poesie, ja
> zum Liede selbst übergehen. Um für den Gang dieser Novelle ein
> Gleichnis zu haben, so denken Sie sich aus der Wurzel hervorschiessend
> ein grünes Gewächs, das eine Weile aus einem starken Stengel kräftige
> grüne Blätter nach den Seiten austreibt und zuletzt mit einer Blume
> endet. Die Blume war unerwartet, überraschend, aber sie musste kom-
> men; ja das grüne Blätterwerk war nur für sie da und wäre ohne sie
> nicht der Mühe wert gewesen. (18 January)

What could be more natural at a time when his mind was continually
running on these lines than that he should see two of his most intimately
related works in this same light?

The conversation of 3 May is, as Eckermann frankly admits, a résumé
of what Goethe had said on various occasions about Ampère's review. As
it stands, it presupposes in the reader familiarity with Goethe's habit of
using *Steigerung* as an illuminating analogy; he will, it is assumed, have
been prepared for this allusiveness by the explicit detail of the preceding
conversations, and will know at once in what sense to interpret *gesteigert*.
But even so it is not altogether easy to follow Goethe's train of thought
when he attributes to Ampère the judgment that Tasso is a *gesteigerter*
Werther; for in recalling the gist of something that was so familiar to
him[67]—and probably to Eckermann too—he can afford to be careless

of logical transitions, and his recollections are inevitably coloured by thoughts which are not Ampère's at all but his own. Thus, in singling out for commendation the way Ampère had appraised his works in the light of his personal development, he evokes the analogy of organic growth:

> Als einer, der das Metier aus dem Grunde kennt, zeigt er die Ver-
> wandtschaft des Erzeugten mit dem Erzeuger und beurteilt die ver-
> schiedenen poetischen Productionen als verschiedene Früchte verschie-
> dener Lebensepochen des Dichters.

And in his subsequent summary of the effects of the Italian journey, thoughts about the cathartic effect of poetic creation, such as had found expression in the *Trilogie der Leidenschaft*, are inseparably intermingled with his memory of what was actually in the review, so that the final sentence leaps out at us with an almost inconsequent abruptness:

> Wie richtig hat er bemerkt, dass ich in den ersten zehn Jahren meines
> weimarischen Dienst- und Hoflebens so gut wie gar nichts gemacht,
> dass die Verzweiflung mich nach Italien getrieben, und dass ich dort,
> mit neuer Lust zum Schaffen, die Geschichte des Tasso ergriffen, um
> mich in Behandlung dieses angemessenen Stoffes von demjenigen frei-
> zumachen, was mir noch aus meinen weimarischen Eindrücken und
> Erinnerungen Schmerzliches und Lästiges anklebte. Sehr treffend nennt
> er daher auch den Tasso einen gesteigerten Werther.

The force of 'daher' is not immediately apparent, or not wholly apparent. Unless we are familiar enough with Goethe's thought to give full value to *gesteigert*, our attention is inclined to centre here exclusively upon the likeness between the two works. But if we turn to the original review, where the emphasis is as much on the difference as the likeness, the whole sequence of thought becomes clear. I quote from Goethe's rendering of it in *Kunst und Altertum* :[68]

> Diese beiden Stücke [*Tasso* und *Iphigenie*] sind *das Resultat einer Ver-
> einigung des Gefühls der äussern Schönheit, wie man sie in der mittägigen
> Natur und den Denkmalen des Altertums findet, von einer Seite, und von der
> andern des Zartesten und Allerfeinsten, was in dem Geiste des deutschen
> Dichters sich entwickeln mochte.* So wird im *Tasso* ein geistreicher Dialog
> angewendet, in Schattirungen, wie Plato und Euripides pflegen, eine
> Reihe von Ideen und Gefühlen auszudrücken, die vielleicht unserm
> Dichter allein angehören. . . man erkennt die Erinnerungen, die er von
> Hause mitbrachte, um sie in den poetischen Zeiten des Mittelalters und
> unter dem sanften Himmel von Italien zu verschönern . . . er selbst

spricht aus dem Munde des Tasso, und durch diese harmonische Poesie hört man den *Werther* durch.

To one who had dwelt long and continuously with the idea of metamorphosis in all its many aspects this passage must have invited translation into terms of creative synthesis, of the 'Vereinigung der gesteigerten Pole'— or 'Enden', or 'Seiten', as he had variously called them[69]—to produce 'ein Drittes, Neues, Höheres, Unerwartetes': northern imagination, at its most subtle and most finely strung, with all the inwardness and transcendency of thought and emotion which had gone to the making of *Werther*, now combined with its polar opposite, a southern feeling for the sensuous beauty of nature and antique form, to produce the strangely vibrant 'harmonische Poesie' that is *Tasso*.

What, then, seems to have happened is something like this: At a time when the relations between science and literature were running very fluid in his mind, Goethe had occasion to recall this review which he had recently translated; and the name Ampère, with its twofold associations, literary and scientific, acted as an agent which precipitated a variety of kindred ideas, long suspended in his thought, into an *aperçu* wholly characteristic of his own personal mode of organizing experience. The details of the process must necessarily remain conjectural. But what emerges as certain from a consideration of all the evidence is that

1. the word *gesteigert* is used here with that pregnant significance which derives from Goethe's scientific concept of *Steigerung*;
2. in this case there can be no question of its carrying a negative inflexion;
3. it refers to the two *works* and to the formal relation between them (as distinct from the psychology of the two *characters*)

This last point is clear enough from the conversation as recorded by Eckermann, clearer still from Ampère's review. But it is borne out by other instances in which Goethe uses *Steigerung* in connection with the formal aspect of his works. In a letter of 3 February 1826,[70] he writes that, in the new edition of his works, the first version of *Iphigenie* is destined for a volume specially designed to give the public some idea of the 'Steigerung meiner ersten Arbeiten'. His talks to Eckermann about his *Novelle* reveal something of what is implied by such formal *Steigerung*. They are all relevant—the first, of 15 January 1827, where he tells how he had originally planned it thirty years before, as an epic in hexameters, and how the change of external form, its new conception as a short story, had affected the handling of the detail; the one, already quoted, of 18 January describing the successive development of the increasingly poetic prose, until, by a contraction, sudden and unexpected, it becomes something of a qualitatively different order, viz. pure lyric poetry;[71] and the one of 31 January which tells of its final revision. This last leaves us in no doubt that formal *Steigerung* also consists in the increasing subordination of all the parts of a work to its dominant intention. The *Novelle*, we learn, was to be *gesteigert* by introducing into the exposition a detail (the roaring of the lion) which would prepare and enhance the effect of the climax.

'Diese Art zu ändern und zu bessern', sagte Goethe, 'ist nun die rechte, wo man ein noch Unvollkommenes durch fortgesetzte Erfindungen zum Vollendeten *steigert*'.

His revision of his works had, in fact, always tended in this direction: formal refinement had been achieved by concentration, by an elaboration extending to even the smallest detail of the structure, so that the finest nuance had its specialized and unalterable function in the organization of the whole. And he was well aware of it, as is clear from the following passage, with the familiar biological analogy which was never far from his thoughts:

. .. mich freut gar sehr, dass Sie den Stoff der Nausikaa gleich als tragisch erkannt . . . Ich brauche Ihnen nicht zu sagen, welche rührende, herzergreifende Motive in dem Stoff liegen, die, wenn ich sie, wie ich in Iphigenie, besonders aber in Tasso tat, bis in die feinsten Gefässe verfolgt hätte, gewiss wirksam geblieben wären.[72]

Hence in *Tasso* it is 'das Ausführliche seiner Form' that he stresses,[73] in *Egmont* the conscientious working out of the detail.[74] And long before he thought in terms of the biological analogy of *Steigerung*, he used a very similar, but mechanical, image to describe to Kestner his projected revision of *Werther*:

Ich habe in ruhigen Stunden meinen Werther wieder vorgenommen, und denke, ohne die Hand an das zu legen was so viel Sensation gemacht hat, ihn noch einige Stufen höher zu schrauben. Dabei war unter andern meine Intention Alberten so zu stellen, dass ihn wohl der leidenschaftliche Jüngling, aber doch der Leser nicht verkennt. Dies wird den gewünschten und besten Effekt tun. Ich hoffe Ihr werdet zufrieden sein.[75]

What is intended is evidently a 'screwing up' of the form through certain changes in the economy of the work, of which the 'double' view of Albert is but one. If this particular change at the same time pleases the Kestners, whose interest is naturally more personal than artistic, so much the better.

Goethe's principle of *Steigerung* has seemed generally applicable to those of his works whose *content* has some bearing on science, to *Faust II* or to the *Wahlverwandtschaften*. But his own perception of the principle at work in literary *form* is more fruitful for the development of critical method, and more in tune with his conviction that the laws of art and nature are fundamentally related. It would be as fascinating to follow the progression of form through the two versions of *Werther* to its culmination in *Tasso*, as it is to trace the *Steigerung* in the various versions of *Iphigenie*. And the advantage of using *gesteigert* in Goethe's precise sense is that it does not immediately involve us in aesthetic *judgments*. *Steigerung* is primarily a biological concept expressing the successive elaboration and complexity of living organisms. Its extension by analogy to literature can throw light on the organization of a work; it cannot automatically provide us with a standard for aesthetic evaluation. Nor would Goethe have suggested that it should. An author's work becomes different as he grows; it does not necessarily become better:

> Sein Geschriebenes, wenn es auf der Stufe recht war, wo es entstanden, wird auch ferner recht bleiben, der Autor mag sich auch später entwickeln und verändern, wie er wolle.[76]

None would deny that *Werther*, for all its symmetry, is less highly organized than *Tasso*, a work so vulnerable in its perfection that scarcely a word can be changed or moved without damaging the whole. But this is not to say that *Tasso* is the more beautiful. We shall need to know a good deal more about the laws of aesthetic response before we are able to relate the one criterion to the other.

Goethe's actual remark, then, refers to the two *works*. But the characters themselves clearly invite comparison—the *Trilogie der Leidenschaft* shows how closely linked they were in Goethe's mind—and there is no reason why the analogy of *Steigerung* should not prove illuminating here too. For this principle is wide enough to embrace the full complexity of the relation between them; there is room within it for all those paradoxes and apparent contradictions which have proved so embarrassing to critics using *gesteigert* in its ordinary dictionary sense that they have tended to ignore or suppress whatever did not fit their case. In the light of it there is no need to conclude, as many have done, that because Tasso has all Werther's sensibility and imagination in intensified form he is therefore bound to end in mental disorder. These characteristics may be intensified to the point where they become qualitatively different, and even appear as the opposite of Werther's. And this is in fact the case. In his flights of fancy Tasso goes far beyond Werther in losing touch with the reality around him; but the difference is that he sometimes goes far enough to create a new reality, a poetic world with laws of its own. He has all Werther's instability of identity, his tendency to merge with what is not himself; but with him this tendency goes to the lengths of becoming a specialized function, a power of inhabiting identities not his own. And however his imagination may soar, it does not, like Werther's, lose itself in the vague: 'er träumt nicht im allgemeinen'. However remote his visions, their expression is precise, sensuous, concrete. Even the forms of things unknown are turned to shapes and given a local habitation and a name. Werther dissolves and dissipates, but not in order to re-create. When he returns from his adventures of the spirit, it is either to kick against human limitation or to yearn in romantic impotence for patriarchal domesticity. In Tasso this rhythm of expansion and contraction takes place within the imagination itself: not only has he had the willing patience to fashion the inspired flights of his imagination into defined form in his epic poem; he has the constant urge to precipitate impression, however intense, into image, so that imagination and sensuous utterance are one, fused into inseparable unity. In short, Tasso's sensibility and imagination are akin to Werther's, but they work differently. Altogether in making any comparison of the two it is more fruitful to follow Goethe's own method, and consider the functioning, rather than the static structure, of their being, treating their characteristics not as fixed entities, but as tendencies operating within a changing complexity.

The opposite thesis that Tasso, as a poet, is 'ein höherer, ein gesteigerter Werther', and therefore necessarily more fitted to survive, is equally untenable. In the light of the principle of Steigerung his survival is by no means as certain as is often maintained. Tasso is clearly a more highly organized creature than Werther, but as such even more vulnerable. Differentiation brings loss as well as gain: the extreme specialization of his poetic function had been at the cost of his adaptation to the ordinary business of living. The survival of an organism so one-sided in its development will depend on whether the specialized function, as the regulative principle of its being, can obtain sufficient control over the environment to outweigh the effect of innumerable inappropriate responses to outward stimuli. If it can, then the highest may result; if not, then the whole organism is endangered. Whether Tasso does in fact survive can only be determined by looking at the last words, and more particularly the last word, of the play—'an dem er scheitern sollte'. To try to infer it by comparison with Werther is merely a form of pleasant speculation.

And this brings us to the crux of the matter. The tempting possibility of finding in Goethe's many obiter dicta about his works a ready-made key

212 GOETHE: POET AND THINKER

to their meaning has side-tracked criticism for far too long. His statement that they are all 'fragments of a great confession' has probably had the most lamentable effect of all. Loosely interpreted and indiscriminately applied, it has persistently diverted attention away from his poetic writings as artistic productions existing in their own right. Instead of keeping their eye firmly fixed on the text, critics have too often heeded the beckoning gleam of an idea. And the phrase 'ein gesteigerter Werther' has proved more of a will-o'-the-wisp than most, because in this case the idea itself came in such questionable shape. Hence a great deal of what passes for criticism of *Torquato Tasso* has consisted of gyratory movements vainly endeavouring to find the meaning of the play through the remark, and the meaning of the remark through the play. For to make the meaning of the remark dependent upon an interpretation of the two works, and then offer the remark as proof of the rightness of that interpretation, is plainly to argue in a circle; while to attribute some meaning to the remark, and interpret the works in the light of it, is simply to go round this same circle in reverse. In either case the critic only creates the illusion of having his interpretation confirmed by the poet by presupposing what he sets out to prove. If the remark is to be used in criticism at all, its meaning must be determined by methods suitable for determining the meaning of a word in a certain context. The two works in their turn must be interpreted by methods appropriate to literary criticism. And in bringing the results of these inquiries together we shall do well to proceed with Goethe's own scrupulous attention to the processes of thought. We must realize that his remark *proves* nothing about *Tasso*. The play is its own proof. But it evokes an illuminating analogy:

> Nach Analogien denken ist nicht zu schelten; die Analogie hat den Vorteil, dass sie nicht abschliesst und eigentlich nichts Letztes will; dagegen die Induction verderblich ist, die einen vorgesetzten Zweck im Auge trägt und, auf denselben losarbeitend, Falsches und Wahres mit sich fortreisst.[77]

It is a question of avoiding arbitrary combinations, of knowing the difference between seeing order and imposing order. Goethe himself did not take a principle of science and apply it to literature. He saw that two of his works were related in such a way that they could fall into place in a familiar pattern in his mind. And, like every good teacher, he knew that this procedure is indispensable for communication:

> Mitteilung durch Analogien halt' ich für so nützlich als angenehm; der analoge Fall will sich nicht aufdringen, nichts beweisen; er stellt sich einem andern entgegen, ohne sich mit ihm zu verbinden.

Mehrere analoge Fälle vereinigen sich nicht zu geschlossenen Reihen, sie sind wie gute Gesellschaft, die immer mehr anregt als gibt.[78]

When he used the analogy of *Steigerung* to explain the composition of the *Novelle*, Eckermann's eyes were opened—'es fiel mir wie Schuppen vom Auge'. But Goethe knew, too, that such analogies must be used with discrimination. Having connected Greek tragedy with a law of chromatics, he continues:

Nur muss man sich hüten, es mit einem solchen Gesetz zu weit treiben und es als Grundlage für vieles andere machen zu wollen; vielmehr geht man sicherer, wenn man es immer nur als ein Analogon, als ein Beispiel gebraucht und anwendet.[79]

As long as we proceed with the same caution, violating nothing, imposing nothing, proving nothing, *Steigerung* can be as fruitful a symbol to us in the ordering and communicating of literary experience as it was to Goethe himself.

XII. Unity and Continuity in Goethe

ANY truly scientific observer, Goethe declares time and time again, must prefer to order his material rather than arrange it in arbitrary combinations. The difficulty is that both methods arise from one and the same property of the human mind: its power to see relations between things. So that man's strength is at the same time his weakness. Confronted with the universe in its immensity man seeks to discover order within it. If some unity is not immediately apparent to his reason, he has no compunction in calling upon belief, prejudice, whimsical fancy, and even folly, to bring him the relief of simplification.[1]

It is something of this sort that we are apt to do when faced with the rich and varied personality of Goethe. Overwhelmed by the prodigious length of his days, by the multiplicity of his activities, by the many facets of his being, by the sovereign ease with which he moves among the forms and styles of literary tradition, it is tempting to snatch at a label with which to docket him and so, to our mental satisfaction, dispose of this embarrassing fulness of natural vitality: Goethe, the Romantic; Goethe, the Nordic poet; Goethe, the victim of Classical tyranny; Goethe, the dynamic philosopher; Goethe, the moralist—or amoralist, in our English view even the libertine; Goethe, the *Fürstendiener*; Goethe, the reactionary Philistine; Goethe, the unrepentant individualist. There is no end. But if we should resist the temptation to force him into a pattern of our own devising, are we then to fall back on a bare chronicle of his life and works? Might there not be a way of satisfying our desire for significant order without reducing his richness and variety and without doing violence to the natural rhythms of his being?

Here Goethe's own approach to the complexity of the universe may well serve as a guide. For the layman the value, and the abiding interest, of his scientific works is in their method rather than in their conclusions. In them is revealed a mind fully conscious of its own processes. Goethe knows that he is as prone as anyone to make arbitrary combinations rather than to discover order; but he is on his guard against it and aware of the necessity of scrupulously testing and retesting the validity of the method he employs. Thus it would be useless, he says in the *Vorwort zur Farbenlehre*,[2] to try to express in words the being of any phenomenon. But what we can observe is the way it behaves, and a complete account of this would presumably comprise its being. Make a survey of all a man's activities, and a picture of his character will emerge. If we follow this hint, we shall cease trying to say *what* Goethe is and concentrate instead on discovering *how* he is. In doing this we shall be adopting the methods of that science which Goethe inaugurated and for which he coined the name morphology,[3] that is, the study of forms. It was an approach which he found indispensable for the study of organic nature; for the form of a living organism is not something static which we can hold in our hands. Its very essence is movement. The form of a plant is not just the shape we see before us. It is the whole cycle from its seeding to its fading, and it is only by grasping the pattern in this movement, the law which is at work in its growth, that we can grasp the plant as a whole at all.

Might it not, then, be fruitful to approach Goethe as he himself approached natural phenomena, sharing both his patient submission to things as they are and his conviction that, however great the complexity of nature, her variety is never chaotic nor her ways arbitrary? His constant concern was to keep his thought a flexible instrument, at once active enough, and receptive enough, to perceive the unity within her variety and the continuity within her changes, and thereby to apprehend her essential forms.[4]

In a *Self-portrait* of 1797[5] Goethe speaks of his manifold activities in a way which provides a key to their hidden connections. He tells us that the 'Mittelpunkt und Base' of his existence was the 'poetischer Bildungstrieb'. *Mittelpunkt*, that is in Goethe's language the organic centre, whether in a plant, a poem, or a human being, from which everything radiates, the unity from which all variety proceeds, the focal point which, once discovered, illuminates all the parts. *Bildungstrieb*, that is the impulse to form, the urge which bids him see form and make form. This, the 'poetischer Bildungstrieb', is then the centre to which all his activities, however diverse, are ultimately related. Once this is grasped, Goethe continues, all apparent contradictions resolve themselves. It is clear that he intended the stress to be a level one, bearing as much on *Bildung* as on *poetisch*. Any occupation in which he could discover shape of some kind was a challenge and a source of satisfaction: drawing, science, statesmanship, theatre-management, mining and agriculture, all these excursions of his mind were yet related to poetry by the element of form which they contained for him. If Goethe then goes on to describe these excursions as 'false tendencies', he does not mean that they could, or should, have been avoided. For Goethe, whose realm is the present, what might have been is always an abstraction and idle speculation. Nor does he mean that they were in any sense unfruitful. They were 'false starts' in the sense that he did not become a statesman or an artist. He remained a poet. But for the kind of poet he became this roundabout way was inevitable. Goethe reminds us again and again that every step in life appears now as progress, now as regress, according to the angle from which we view it. To think of his multifarious occupations as digressions, aberrations, or vagaries, will not help us to understand him as a whole. They are rather modifications and variations of one profound and central impulse, the impulse to form, and this *Self-portrait* is illuminating just because it embraces, without obliterating, the seeming antagonisms of his being. In the light of it we can understand very well that he could say on one occasion that his scientific activities 'sprang from his inmost being',[6] on another that his real happiness had been his 'poetisches Sinnen und Schaffen'.[7] For, as he told Eckermann,[8] he really saw all his achievements as symbols, and at bottom it mattered very little whether he had made pots or pans! The important thing was that any activity should give scope for his impulse to form.

At first the impulse expressed itself unconsciously. 'Unbewusst und aus innerem Trieb'[9] he sought unceasingly to grasp the ultimate forces at work in the universe, to discover

> was die Welt
> Im Innersten zusammenhält.

Faust would force his way into the secrets of nature by a supreme effort of the will:

> Du musst! du musst! und kostet' es mein Leben!

and he vainly attempts to apprehend these processes of nature in ecstatic vision:

> *Schau'* alle Wirkungskraft und Samen.

Already the poet's intuition goes unerringly to the unity which is within, and embraces all nature's complexity:

> Wie alles sich zum *Ganzen* webt,
> Eins in dem andern wirkt und lebt!

The same intuition which enabled him to grasp the inner workings of nature permitted him to discern the inner form of a work of art. Even so complex a structure as the Strassburg minster yielded its secrets to the urgency of this intuition. Where his contemporaries perceived only arbitrary confusion and meaningless ornamentation, Goethe discovered 'a thousand harmonious details' fused with organic necessity into a related whole. By recognizing the hidden forces inherent in its structure, he was even able to complete its unfinished form in his imagination—and, to his joy, have this act of creative intuition confirmed by the discovery of the original plans.[10] And so he could write in *Von deutscher Baukunst*:[11] 'As in the works of eternal nature, everything down to the tiniest fibre, all is form—*Gestalt*—and everything contributes functionally to the whole— *alles zweckend zum Ganzen*'. The very vocabulary is reminiscent of Faust's first monologues and reveals the identity of Goethe's approach to nature and art at this period. There is, of course, some difference. Faust, after all, has his vision of the forces of nature sitting in his dim-lit study, contemplating a sign. He by-passes the outward appearances of nature to seize her mystery with the inner eye; whereas Goethe returned again and again to the minster, looked at its every detail from every angle and in every light, until his eye was weary. Yet it was only when twilight descended, blurring the details and throwing the masses into relief, that his inner eye took charge and discovered the secrets of its inner form. It was as though the spirit of Erwin von Steinbach had inclined to his pleading, as the Erdgeist had done to Faust's insistence.

How different was his relation to the outward forms and appearances of nature once he began his scientific studies in earnest. In his letters and diaries of the first ten years in Weimar we can watch the change happening. It is no longer just the elemental aspects of nature, seen through the veil of his own moods, which absorb him. Botany, geology, anatomy, zoology, they all taught him to look on even the most trivial and insignificant of natural phenomena with passionate interest. No longer is it just to pass the time, 'kalt zu seinem Zeitvertreib botanisierend',[12] as in Strassburg, that he collects stones and plants and fungi. Instead he even begs his friends to send him such specimens as were not available at home. The aim is still, as he told Frau von Stein in 1786,[13] the perception of the essential form by which nature contrives to bring forth her infinite variety. But no longer by Faust's visionary short cut. By patient and detailed study of each plant he will discover, first its individual form, then the basic form of plant life—'and, if there were time in the short space of a man's life I could extend this method to every sphere of nature'.[13] There is now no more Faustian straining of will and intuition. His mind is no less active, but it is a receptive activity. 'Everything forces itself upon me', he writes.[14] 'I no longer ponder upon it, it comes out to meet me'. This submission to the nature of the object is completed in the clear air of Italy which threw everything into sharp relief. He now felt that he was really beginning to 'see', where his whole life long he had been just 'groping about'.[15] More and more he learns to value what he possesses with his outer eye and to distrust the power of soaring and embellishing imagination to grasp essential form.

Yet there is clearly more involved than mere sense-perception when he discovers traces of the intermaxillary bone in man; or recognizes that the skull of vertebrates is a modification of the bones of the spinal column; or perceives that all the parts of the plant, except root and stem, are modifications of the leaf; thus showing that the vegetable and animal kingdoms are governed by the same principle of metamorphosis, of morphological change. Goethe called such flashes of intuition *aperçus*.[16] The term might make us think of visions such as Faust's; but there is a vast difference. An *aperçu* is not achieved by some effort of the imagination with the eye turned away from the object. It is rather a middle link in an organic succession, arising only after much observation and leading inevitably to further observation and checking.[17] An *aperçu* is the product of thought so closely permeated by sense-perceptions that, as Goethe once said, 'his perception was itself thinking and his thinking perception'.[18]

The characteristics of Goethe's scientific attempts to discover form are summed up in his *Vorwort zur Morphologie*:[19] 'to apprehend the outward, visible, and tangible parts of any living phenomenon in their relation to each other, to interpret these as indications of its inner form, thus grasping the phenomenon as a *whole—das Ganze in der Anschauung beherrschen*'. Thus intuition—the act of 'seeing-into'—has been assigned a definite place in his scientific method. It is no longer charged with emotion, but permeated by thought.

But Goethe's science does not stop short at the apprehension of forms. He penetrates into the forces which govern the forms—'les forces sous les formes', as Paul Valéry, with the perspicacity of the poet-scientist, puts it in his centenary *Discours en l'honneur de Goethe* (1932). He is as fascinated by these forces as ever he was. But from being vague pantheistic vital activities they can now be identified scientifically. He can isolate them and call them by name: *Polarität* and *Steigerung*, the two 'grosse Triebräder aller Natur', as he called them to Kanzler von Müller in 1828.[20] By a kind of symbolic extension Goethe may see these forces at work in every sphere of human life. But the important thing is that he had first perceived them sensuously as demonstrable facts of the physical world—*Polarität* in the phenomenon of the magnet, *Steigerung* as intensification and concentration in his experiments with colours and with plants. Again, we might think we had come full circle, to Faust's 'Kräfte der Natur'; and again we should be wrong. They are now '*Triebräder* der Natur'—their nature and function established by the years of observation and experiment which have intervened. It is rather full *spiral* that we have come—round to an original position at a higher level.

The changes of method in Goethe's search for form are profound and important. But the thread of continuity running through all the changes is evident in the persistence of the word *schauen*, modified into its compound *Anschauung* and into its foreign form *aperçu*. And the outward and visible signs of this continuity are the brightly-coloured threads of recurrent images which persist throughout his writings. One he was specially fond of using, he tells us in the last letter of his life,[21] was that of weft and warp—'ein Gleichnis, das ich so gern brauche'. *Weben* is the image which from the beginning comes spontaneously to his mind whenever he thinks of ceaseless activity, whether of man, nature, or art. In his vocabulary, so influenced by Luther's bible, *weben* and *leben* are synonymous, and it is natural that Gretchen's busy daily round, her 'häusliches Beginnen', should be symbolized by the picture of her at the spinning-wheel. The image of *weben* is even implicit in the 'Zäserchen' of the Strassburg minster, the tiny fibres which go to make up its fabric. Faust is lost in wonder as he contemplates the inweaving of vital processes; Werther is prostrate as he thinks of their mutually destructive aspects. Yet the image which springs to the lips of each is the same— 'Himmel und Erde und ihre webenden Kräfte'. The Erdgeist embraces both the creative and the destructive aspect, 'Geburt und Grab', in a pictorial elaboration of the whirring loom of time, weaving 'the living garment of God'. 'Poetry', Goethe says in one of his maxims,[22] 'gives intimations of the mysteries of nature and seeks to resolve them through an image.' This intimation that nature herself was the prime weaver was then confirmed by his scientific discoveries. In his *Vorwort zur Morphologie* he is still using the image 'schaffendes Gewebe' to describe the constant self-renewal of tissues in plant and animal life. And the modern scientist who has penetrated beyond Goethe to the molecular structure of tissues can find no better image to describe it than 'this gigantic textile business'. Such pregnant images as *weben* Goethe was wont to carry with him for forty or fifty years. Constantly renewed in his imagination, they took on different shape without changing their essence. In an essay of 1820, *Bedenken und Ergebung*, he takes up again those lines of the *Urfaust* where Mephistopheles mocks at the 'Gedankenfabrik' of philosophy by comparing its elaborations to those of a complicated weaving-machine. But where Mephistopheles could only mock, Goethe now reaches to the central and ultimate problem where science and philosophy meet: to the reconciliation of thought with experience, the one independent of time and space, the other confined within them. To look too closely at this problem seems to him the way that madness lies. Therefore, he says, 'let us take refuge in the sphere of poetry and sing an old song with slight variations':

> So schauet mit bescheidnem Blick
> Der ewigen Weberin Meisterstück,
> Wie ein Tritt tausend Fäden regt,
> Die Schifflein hinüber herüber schiessen,
> Die Fäden sich begegnend fliessen,
> Ein Schlag tausend Verbindungen schlägt.
> Das hat sich nicht zusammen gebettelt,
> Sie hat's von Ewigkeit angezettelt,
> Damit der ewige Meistermann
> Getrost den Einschlag werfen kann.

The older Goethe is constantly making this transition from one kingdom of the mind to another, from poetry to science, from philosphy to religion, and from each or all of these ever again back to poetry. Not, indeed, in any mystical blurring of these disciplines, not because he would confuse their separate methods, but with the single view of one who has, as he said of himself, 'separated enough to combine and combined enough to be ready to separate again'.[23] It is not that sublime sense of being one with the oneness of the universe which comes to us when we are young, not a primal unity, but the return to ultimate simplicity of one who has penetrated through to the vantage-point where all the realms of knowledge are seen as coloured reflections of the one truth which is life. He now couples in one sentence scientific and poetic aperçus. He declares that beauty is 'eine Manifestation geheimer Naturgesetze';[24] and when he now comes back to Gothic architecture he can say in a new, and fuller, sense that it is like 'the works of eternal nature'. For he is seeing it with an eye sharpened by his insight into plant morphology. His earlier intuition has been confirmed by knowledge. He now knows what he sees.[25]

The interpenetration of science and poetry comes out in the poems he wrote on scientific subjects—*Metamorphose der Tiere* or *Entoptische Farben* —or when he prefaces his *Farbenlehre* with a quotation from the Book of Job; or, most striking of all, when in a review of a scientific work he quotes from one of his most personal poems, the *Marienbader Elegie*.[26] But this interpenetration can be more intimate still. In some of his late poems where the content is remote from science there are lines so charged with the accumulation of his scientific experience that they radiate a quality unique in lyric poetry. That much-quoted line from his poem, *Urworte. Orphisch,*

Geprägte Form, die lebend sich entwickelt,

is not just a fine phrase embodying a philosophical truth about man's destiny. The secret of its perpetual power is, surely, that it mediates between the worlds of nature and of spirit. It is a perfect rounding-off for this oracular poem with its mystical and astrological symbols. But it has its roots in the natural world, and the metaphor corresponds at every point to that law of metamorphosis which is at work in every living organism. Or in the line from *Selige Sehnsucht*,

Die dich zeugte, wo du zeugtest,

the insistent repetition of *zeugen* not only serves to point the contrast between the physical begetting in 'the coolness of the love night' and the spiritual consummation of the 'Flammentod'. In its precise sequence of generation ('which begat thee, where thou didst beget') it also announces nature's indifference to the life of the individual once he has fulfilled his purpose of perpetuating his kind.

But it would be very wrong if, in our desire to see unity in Goethe, we seemed to imply that he lacked the tensions which are the source and condition of all life. The difficulty when we speak of unity is not to confuse it with simple harmony, not to imagine a uniform movement in one direction. The problem is not one that would have arisen for Goethe, since for him the idea of unity, whether in himself or in the universe, was inseparable from that of polarity. The universe is undoubtedly one; but it is equally certain that we experience it in terms of opposites: light and darkness, left and right, subject and object, body and soul, matter and spirit. For Goethe these are not mutually exclusive opposites. On the contrary, each is unthinkable without the other. They imply not dualism but duality. They are the poles of an all-embracing unity, as interdependent as the rhythm of breathing in and breathing out. And this is another image which runs through the whole length of Goethe's writings, from the fragment of a *Roman in Briefen* of 1772,[27] where it expresses the flow and recoil within the emotion of love, to a poem of the *West-Östlicher Divan* of 1814, where it is the occasion for praise of life as it is, with all its ups and downs:

Im Atemholen sind zweierlei Gnaden:
Die Luft einziehn, sich ihrer entladen.
Jenes bedrängt, dieses erfrischt;
So wunderbar ist das Leben gemischt.
Du danke Gott, wenn er dich presst,
Und dank' ihm, wenn er dich wieder entlässt.[28]

It is a commonplace that a man nowhere so clearly reveals the funda-
mentals of his being as in his style. And the sense of polarity, of opposites
within unity, so permeates Goethe's thought and feeling that it is reflected in the very structure of his language. There is his love of coupling
together in syntactical unity words which, by their meaning, pull away
from each other in different directions. An adjective will qualify a noun
of opposite meaning; the lover in *Werther* is 'der glückliche Unglück-
liche'.[29] Forty years later in the exquisite poem, *Nicht mehr auf Seiden-
blatt*, lovers everywhere and eternally are 'jene Glücklich-Unglücklichen'.
The two opposites are here brought into even closer union by the drop-
ping of the adjectival ending, and it is as if, by the use of the hyphen
which binds them, Goethe would demonstrate to us visually that these
poles, happy/unhappy, are the very condition of loving. Or, again, he
will describe his own state of mind as compounded of 'meditative carefreeness and warm coldness'.[30] In *Dichtung und Wahrheit*,[31] trying to catch
the whole of what Friederike Brion had meant for him, he writes:
'thoughtfully gay, naïve and self-aware, light-hearted and far-seeing,
qualities which seem incompatible, yet in her were united'. By paradox
he seeks to express the whole, not, as he pointed out, because truth lies
between two extremes, but because it embraces them both. At first he
seems to do it unconsciously, as when he lets his Werther say that in this
world things are rarely settled by Either/Or—'In der Welt is es sehr selten
mit dem Entweder Oder getan'[32]—but in later life it became a deliberate
method of attacking difficult problems. No words, he thinks, are delicate
and subtle enough to communicate experience, and the need for paradoxical expressions corresponds to a profound need of the human mind
to operate with antitheses if it would get at an important truth.

His linguistic use of subject and object reveals more clearly still the absence of dualism even on the deepest levels of his thought. We are apt to
think that because we say '*I* know *it*' the separation of subject and object
actually corresponds to our own experience in the act of knowledge. But
Goethe, like Coleridge, knew that this separation is merely an instrument, though a highly useful instrument, of analytical thought, and that
during the experience itself subject and object are so instantly united that
we cannot say to which of the two priority belongs.[33] '*I*' for Goethe never
has the overweening importance that it has so largely assumed in our
Western subjectivism. He can easily let the perceiving subject slip into
the role of grammatical object, and give the active part to the object perceived by turning it into the grammatical subject of the sentence. Thus,
to express his perception of the form of the plant, he will say: '*It* forces
itself upon *me* . . . *it* comes out to meet *me*.'[34] Asked how he knew that

the tower of the Strassburg cathedral had been wrongly restored, he does not say '*I* discovered it', but 'the tower told *me*'.[35] It was in this sense that he could say: 'It was not *I* made my poems, *they* made *me*.'[36] Or, of certain legendary themes that he later made into poetry: '*they* embedded themselves deep in my mind.'[37] Nothing could reflect more clearly that subject and object are but polar opposites of a single unity than the easy swing of his prose between two alternative modes of expressing the act of knowledge. And we are not surprised when he tells us that 'the elements of objects entered into his thought and were permeated by it', or when he finds the old Delphic injunction 'Know thyself!' inadequate, because, as he insists, inner and outer, self and world, are so interwoven that man can only know himself by knowing the world and by learning to look upon himself as an object.[37]

It was not, then, by the denial of tension but by his complete acceptance of tension as the very condition of existence that Goethe was able to preserve the unity of his being. It was not always so. Only gradually and with much pain and effort did he learn how to manage the tensions which at one time were dangerously insistent and threatened to destroy him as they destroyed his Werther. We can follow something of this development in his use of the two images, *Wanderer* and *Hütte*, which pursue him throughout his life, and represent the two poles of self-realization and self-limitation. Where at first he is flung helplessly from one extreme to the other he learns eventually to accept these alternations as part of the larger rhythms of universal polarity.[38]

The rich texture of Goethe's thought and the variety of his achievement are undoubtedly due to his willingness to accept polarity as an integral part of his mental processes. He moved freely between the poles of reflection and imagination, analysis and synthesis, and learned to exploit each to the full. It is often maintained that Goethe neglected analysis. But though it is true that as a poet he naturally inclined more to synthesis, to expressing things as wholes, yet he knew very well that outside poetry analysis is inevitable, that language by its very nature imposes it, and he was ready enough to accept analysis as a means to knowledge. Indeed, he claims that he himself had always moved from synthesis to analysis and back again, and, in an essay of 1829, *Analyse und Synthese*, he calls them the complementary methods of science, the one being unthinkable without the other. But he felt that, flushed with the success of its analytical technique, science too often tended to neglect synthesis altogether. Hence his insistence that the results of analysis to be valid must constantly be referred back to the living whole; and hence also his belief that it must be possible to perfect an alternative technique which begins with the whole and proceeds to the parts. There must be a way, he told Schiller,[39] of apprehending the form of a living whole and of working from this whole to the parts, 'aus dem Ganzen in die Teile strebend'.

All his life he was concerned with this truth that the whole is more than and different from the sum of its parts, and it is generally accepted that here he was anticipating the findings of *Gestalt*-psychology. In the Leipzig poem, *Die Libelle*, the idea is already implicit. In an attempt to catch the secret of the dragon-fly's form in its play of changing colours the hasty youth holds it in his hand, only to find a dull uniform blue. Mephisto gibes at the scientist who reduces everything to its parts, thus losing the vital spirit which holds them together. The *Philosophische Studie* of 1784 expresses the same thought in terms of Spinozian philosophy: 'in every living organism the parts are so inextricably combined with the whole that they can only be grasped in and with the whole.'[40] Goethe then repeats the thought with scientific precision in his *Considerations on Morphology* of 1795, where he shows that we do, in fact, always apprehend things as wholes.[41] It was consequently vain for Professor Wagner to attempt to realize synthetic man by putting the parts together in his laboratory. Homunculus is made, but before he can come into being he must first go through all the forms of creation.

Only the artist can catch form out of flux, create permanence out of change, 'Dauer im Wechsel', as Goethe himself caught the changing forms of human life in the imperishable distichs of the *Römische Elegien* or in the plastic scenes of *Hermann und Dorothea*. But outside of art the only way that man can satisfy the longing of his mind for permanence is to accept change and seek to discover the continuity running through it. This conception of form as a complexity which is constantly changing (he more often uses the word *Gestalt* in a dynamic rather than a static sense), is perhaps Goethe's most valuable contribution to thought, and it is only the nostalgic desire of the human mind for permanence which prevents us from seeking the dynamic form in his own development, which makes us long to hold him fast at one particular stage and regret that he ever passed beyond it. If he had only continued in his early *Sturm und Drang* manner! cries the one. Why did he waste his time and our patience with these dabblings in science? cries the other. What a pity he did not settle down with Friederike or Lili to a life of respectable domesticity! His contemporaries showed similar unwillingness to see that life must go on and that with it a man's style must change. They too found it hard to accept the new where they expected the old and familiar. 'Because my seven brothers did not in the least resemble sister Iphigenie, they were badly received', he writes of a novel he had tried out on his friends.[42]

And to Eckermann[43] he complained that people had never really been satisfied with him as he was. 'They always wanted me different from what it had pleased God to make me. Nor were they really satisfied with the works I produced.' But, Goethe protests, art, like nature,[44] must be treated with the respect due to its inevitable and unalterable form. There it stands, 'ein unveränderliches Factum', as much a hard fact of existence as any actual event—'Das Gedichtete behauptet sein Recht, wie das Geschehene'.[45]

Goethe thought of his own life and works as inevitable, as a natural growth. And, just as he rejoiced in nature as it is, and in the unfailing return of the seasons, neither wanting spring to be red for a change[46] nor to pluck roses in April,[47] so he accepted each season of his own life as it came with whatever advantages and disadvantages it brought.[47] And when we cling, as so many of us are tempted to cling, to the young and spontaneous Goethe, captivated by the poignancy and freshness of his first sensations, we are doing violence to the form of his being by seeking to arrest his development at a given stage. Surely the way to get the best out of him is to take him as he is and not as we would have him be.

And are we even sure that the Goethe we cling to and admire is always as 'spontaneous' as we think he is? Who would not be sorry to lose this lovely image: 'Wie die Natur sich zum Herbste neigt, wird es Herbst in mir und um mich her. Meine Blätter werden gelb, und schon sind die Blätter der benachbarten Bäume abgefallen'? And yet it is from the second, carefully revised version of *Werther*,[48] completed on the eve of his Italian journey in 1786, a product of self-criticism both personal and artistic. And the image itself is obviously inspired by a re-reading of *Macbeth*. The other great works of his 'spontaneous' youth, *Götz* and *Faust*, he never thought worth publishing in their first form at all. And who would recognize from this first quatrain in the *Urfaust* the ballad we know and love so well?

> Es war ein König in Tule
> Einen goldnen Becher er hett
> Empfangen von seiner Bule
> Auf ihrem Todtesbett.

Who would not agree that the familiar wording is a great improvement? And yet it first appeared in this form in 1790, after Goethe's return from Italy. Many of the poems we associate with Friederike and Lili we quote in a form which is not that of their first inspiration. Thus when we read the young, spontaneous, Goethe we are often in fact reading works produced by a certain measure of reflection.

It would in any case be false to draw a hard and fast distinction between the spontaneous and the reflective Goethe as though they represented rigid opposites. Reflectiveness and spontaneity, conscious and unconscious, are for him like any other pair of opposites, the two poles of a unity between which he is constantly moving. But it is not just a question of oscillation. There is also an upward movement at work, and it can happen that each of the opposites becomes intensified and that they then unite to produce what Goethe called 'ein Drittes, Neues, Höheres, Unerwartetes'.[49] The poem *Um Mitternacht* of 1818 must have come into being by some happy mating of this kind. Here is a poem as spontaneous in effect as one could wish, and as spontaneously composed. Goethe held it specially dear because it came to him 'unexpectedly at the midnighthour'.[50] Yet how much of conscious reflection has coupled in the creative darkness of the unconscious with ancient and more recent experience to merge at last in images so perfectly articulated that there is no separating sound and sense.

> Um Mitternacht ging ich, nicht eben gerne,
> Klein kleiner Knabe, jenen Kirchhof hin
> Zu Vaters Haus, des Pfarrers; Stern am Sterne,
> Sie leuchteten doch alle gar zu schön;
>   Um Mitternacht.
>
> Wenn ich dann ferner, in des Lebens Weite,
> Zur Liebsten musste, musste, weil sie zog,
> Gestirn und Nordschein über mir im Streite,
> Ich gehend, kommend Seligkeiten sog;
>   Um Mitternacht
>
> Bis dann zuletzt des vollen Mondes Helle
> So klar und deutlich mir ins Finstere drang,
> Auch der Gedanke, willig, sinnig, schnelle
> Sich ums Vergangne wie ums Künftige schlang;
>   Um Mitternacht.

If we ask what the poem is 'about', we have to reply that it is not about any or all of these separate experiences of the midnight sky, but about the moment when their symbolic quality is recognized. This illuminating moment of recognition embraces within itself past and future and is therefore eternal. This meaning is not communicated to us in the form of discursive statement. The images speak to us directly, and it is only by brooding on them that the full meaning of the poem emerges. Yet the thought of making the moment eternal by recognizing its significance had long been the subject of Goethe's conscious reflection and, in a later philosophic poem, *Vermächtnis*, he will express this idea in conceptual form:

> Dann ist Vergangenheit beständig,
> Das Künftige voraus lebendig—
> Der Augenblick ist Ewigkeit.

But in the poem *Um Mitternacht*, this reflection is so completely dissolved in images that scarcely a trace of the conceptual remains. Image has become thought, and thought image.

In Goethe the traffic between the conscious and the unconscious is not only in one direction. From early Weimar days he was increasingly interested in his own psychological processes, in the periodic cycle of his creativity, and anxious, through understanding, to obtain some measure of control. The last letter of his life opens up immense vistas of the possibility of integrating elements of the unconscious into consciousness, and elsewhere[51] he speaks in terms of the highest praise of a certain condition of 'bewusste Bewusstlosigkeit', conscious unconsciousness—another of these paradoxes by which he attempts to express the inherent unity of what we experience as opposites.

The advantage of studying Goethe in the way that he himself studied organic nature is that any mental image we may form of him never hardens and becomes static. It can go on growing in our minds as it assimilates new facts and new aspects we may discover about him. They modify, widen, or enrich the picture without overthrowing its fundamental form. And at the risk of sounding paradoxical we may say that the most marked characteristic of this fundamental form is his own concern with form. His pursuit of form is the pivot of his being, the unifying principle of all his activities. He sought it constantly in his life as he had found it in nature. His eye was so trained to perceive it that he could catch experience taking shape even as he was still experiencing. He is happy when he can write from Italy that his 'journey is taking on shape'—'meine Reise nimmt eine Gestalt'—[52] that is, he is beginning to see its full significance. It was still easier to see it in retrospect, and *Dichtung und Wahrheit* is an attempt to see his life, not as he had lived it in terms of time and space, but in terms of significance. The motto which he prefixed to the Second Part,[53] 'What one longs for in youth, turns up in old age in plenty', is the recognition of pattern in his life, and of the fulfilment of his destiny in accordance with the laws of organic growth and change.

From Goethe much indeed may be learnt; much of his practical wis-

dom is still relevant for us today. But the most vital and fruitful things
he can teach us are truths concerning forms, forms which each in his own
generation must fill with new content. He can teach us that the very forms
in which we experience the world are the forms of change and polarity,
but that within the change there is continuity, and that, embracing
polarity there is unity. In one of the loveliest poems of the *West-Östlicher
Divan* Goethe invests his beloved with all the infinite variety, with all the
ceaseless change, of nature. As always in his later poetry, she is at once
herself and the symbol of everything else. The metrical structure of the
ghazel—in which the same rhyme is used throughout, though with slight
variations, in the second line of each couplet—brings a sense of continuity
into the very form of the poem. It is characteristic of Goethe's unity of
being that it should be in a pure love lyric that he gives most perfect expression to his deep sense of the unity and continuity of the universe:

> In tausend Formen magst du dich verstecken,
> Doch, Allerliebste, gleich erkenn' ich dich;
> Du magst mit Zauberschleiern dich bedecken,
> Allgegenwärt'ge, gleich erkenn' ich dich.
>
> An der Cypresse reinstem, jungem Streben,
> Allschöngewachs'ne, gleich erkenn' ich dich;
> In des Kanales reinem Wellenleben,
> Allschmeichelhafte, wohl erkenn' ich dich.
>
> Wenn steigend sich der Wasserstrahl entfaltet,
> Allspielende, wie froh erkenn' ich dich;
> Wenn Wolke sich gestaltend umgestaltet,
> Allmannigfalt'ge, dort erkenn' ich dich.
>
> An des geblümten Schleiers Wiesenteppich,
> Allbuntbesternte, schön erkenn' ich dich;
> Und greift umher ein tausendarm'ger Eppich,
> O Allumklammernde, da kenn' ich dich.
>
> Wenn am Gebirg der Morgen sich entzündet,
> Gleich, Allerheiternde, begrüss' ich dich;
> Dann über mir der Himmel rein sich ründet,
> Allherzerweiternde, dann atm' ich dich.
>
> Was ich mit äusserm Sinn, mit innerm kenne,
> Du Allbelehrende, kenn' ich durch dich;
> Und wenn ich Allahs Namenhundert nenne,
> Mit jedem klingt ein Name nach für dich.

NOTES

Abbreviations:

Goethe's works are referred to throughout according to the easily accessible Jubiläums-Ausgabe (Stuttgart and Berlin, 40 vols. + *Registerband*), here abbreviated as JA. In the case of writings which do not appear there, the reference is either to the Weimar Ausgabe (or Sophienausgabe, as it is alternatively known, Weimar, 133 vols.), abbreviated as WA, or to the Gedenkausgabe (Zürich, 1949, 24 vols. + *Ergänzungsband*), abbreviated as GA. Other abbreviations used are:

SA   = *Schillers Sämtliche Werke.* Säkular-Ausgabe (Stuttgart, 16 vols.).

GLL = *German Life & Letters*

MLR = *Modern Language Review*

PEGS = *Publications of the English Goethe Society*

GR   = *Germanic Review*

The MOTTO of the book is taken from *Wilhelm Meisters Lehrjahre*, VIII, 5; JA, XVIII, 312.

I. THE LIVING GOETHE. By L. A. Willoughby. GLL, II (1949), 277 ff. An enlarged version of the talk broadcast to England from Frankfurt a.M. on the 200th anniversary of Goethe's birth, 28 August, 1949 (*The Listener*, XLII, 351 ff.).

1. *Ephemerides*, 1770. *Der Junge Goethe*, ed. Max Morris, 1909 f., II, 33 and VI, 146.
2. *Fragment über die Natur*, 1781-2; JA, XXXIX, 5.   3. 12.IV.1829.
4. In conversation with Riemer, early in 1807.   5. Ibid., 3.II.1807.
6. It is the theme of *Wilhelm Meisters Wanderjahre*, as its sub-title, 'Die Entsagenden', implies.
7. In conversation with Eckermann, 20.II.1831, and *passim*.
8. *Maximen u. Reflexionen*; JA, XXXVIII, 263.
9. Letter to Lavater, 20.IX.1780.   10. *Urworte. Orphisch*.
11. In conversation with F. v. Müller, 17.V.1829.
12. Letter to F. H. Jacobi, 6.I.1813.
13. *Wilhelm Meisters Wanderjahre*, II, 9; JA, XX, 25.
14. 4.II.1829.   15. E.g. to J. H. Meyer, 8.II.1796.

II. GOETHE'S POETRY. By Elizabeth M. Wilkinson. GLL, II (1949), 316 ff.

1. *The Name and Nature of Poetry*, Cambridge, 1933, p. 47.   2. JA, XL, 7 ff.
3. Letter to Godwin, 22. IX. 1800.
4. *Coleridge on Imagination*, London, 1934, p. 215.
5. *Buch der Freunde. Ges. Werke*, XV (*Aufzeichnungen*), 47.
6. But where, in these precise terms?
7. Cf. p. 218 and Note 18.
8. Cf. p.136.   9. *Venezianische Epigramme*, 29.

10. Cf. Goethe's own appreciation of Herder's way of reading aloud in *Dichtung u. Wahrheit*, II, 10; JA, XXIII, 254 f.

11. *Alexis und Dora*: I, 30.

12. H. Loiseau. Collection Bilingue des Classiques Étrangers. Éditions Montaigne, Paris, 1931.

13. Sir Charles Sherrington, *Goethe on Nature and on Science*, Cambridge, 1942, p. 23.

14. *The Colloquial Element in English Poetry*, Newcastle on Tyne, 1947.

15. *Works*, II (1910), 202.

III. 'WANDRERS STURMLIED'. A Study in Poetic Vagrancy. By Elizabeth M. Wilkinson and L. A. Willoughby. GLL, I (1948), 102 ff.

1. It is worth noting that a volume of the popular *Insel-Bücherei* should be devoted to *Wanderlieder* and that the old *Wandervogel Bewegung* has been revived.

2. In the *Nordische Miscellen*, 1810.   3. III, 12; JA, XXIV, 89.

4. Cf. Paul Reiff, 'Pindar and Goethe', *Mod. Lang. Notes*, XVIII (1903), 171.

5. Cf. Von der Hellen; JA, II, 290.

6. Cf. B. Litzmann, *Goethes Lyrik*, Berlin, 1903, 160.

7. Jacobi to Goethe, 26.VIII.1774.   8. Goethe to Jacobi, 31.VIII.1774.

9. III, 1; JA, XX, 51 ff.

10. Cf. W. F. Michael, 'Zur Interpretation von Goethe's "Wandrers Sturmlied"', GR, XIX (1944), 177.

11. III, 10. Professor Hermann Weigand drew our attention to this passage, and pointed out that Goethe had introduced Jung-Stilling to Fielding's novels in Strassburg days (Max Morris, *Der junge Goethe*, II, 101).

12. Of the kind suggested in the essay on 'Wiederholte Spiegelungen', p. 160 f. above.

13. The notable exception is H. Trevelyan, *Goethe and the Greeks*, Cambridge, 1941, p. 82.

14. Cf. J. Boyd, *Notes to Goethe's Poems*, Oxford, 1944, I, 28.

15. Cf. G. v. Loeper, *Goethes Gedichte*, II, 322, and Max Morris, *Der junge Goethe*, VI, 187.

16. Leipzig, 1771. II, 116.

17. *Werke*, ed. Suphan, I, 310.

18. Letter of July, 1772.

19. Cf. R. M. Meyer, 'Studien zu Goethes Wortgebrauch', *Archiv für das Studium der neueren Sprachen*, XCVI (1896), 7 ff., although Meyer sees no special significance in the use of the word in *Wandrers Sturmlied*.

20. After a masterly exposition of the possible ways of taking *Neidgetroffen*, H. Weigand ('Wandrers Sturmlied—"Neidgetroffen"', GR, XXI (1946), 170) rejects the possibility of Apollo's *Neid* being directed to the cedar, on the grounds that such an ambivalent feeling of admiration and hostility as this would imply, while appropriate enough in a Greek poem, is out of place in this 'German poem of simple, strong and straightforward emotions'. It must be directed to the apathy of the poet; and to make this possible Weigand suggests that we read *Neid* in its now obsolete sense of 'anger', a purely negative feeling of hostility. But ambivalence is not incompatible with strong feeling. Far from being confined to sophisticated complexity, it is characteristic of feeling at its most primitive level. Nor is the feeling in *Wandrers Sturmlied*, though strong enough, either simple or straightforward. Moreover in a poem so saturated with Greek

images and myths a conception as familiar as the envy of the gods is not far-fetched. *Neidgetroffen* even has a translated ring about it. To see how close was the association in Goethe's mind between the cedar and the conception of hybris we have only to look at the series of *Parabeln* written in these early years (JA, XXXVI, 106.), where again and again this finest of the forest trees is struck down in its glory and pride.
21. For a similar use of the image of lens and focus in connection with artistic form cf. *Aus Goethes Brieftasche*, JA, XXXVI, 116.
22. *Biographia Literaria*, Ch. I.   23. Letter to Schiller, 7.XII.1796.
24. Cf. L. Spitzer ('Nochmals: Zur Interpretation von "Wandrers Sturmlied" ', GR, XX (1945), 161), who interprets the end as ironical criticism of the *Genie-gedanke*.
25. Late in 1771, undated.   26. Letter to Schiller, 31.I.1798.
27. *Wilhelm Meisters Lehrjahre*, IV, 20; JA, XVII, 326.
28. *Über die Galgenlieder*. Berlin, 1921, p. 13.   29. JA, XXXVIII, 255.

IV. THE RELATION OF FORM AND MEANING IN 'EGMONT', By Elizabeth M. Wilkinson. PEGS, XVIII (1949), 149 ff.

1. *Tel Quel*, Paris, 1941, I, 180.
2. Or anastomosis, as Goethe would call it, i.e. 'intercommunication between two vessels, channels, or branches, by a connecting cross branch' (OED). Cf. *Die Metamorphose der Pflanzen*, VIII, § 62 ff.
3. Letter to Boisserée, 4. XII. 1817. Cf. p. 209 and Note 74.
4. Cf. p. 88.   5. Cf. p. 91 f. and p. 126 f.
6. Walter Pater, *The School of Giorgione*.
7. *Über Egmont, Trauerspiel von Goethe*; SA, XVI, 180.
8. In *Dichtung u. Wahrheit*, IV, 20; JA, XXV, 124 f.
9. Cf. Goethe in conversation with Eckermann, 19.II.1829.
10. Such as that for the BBC's highly successful production, with Stephen Murray as Egmont, in 1949. Cf. E. M. Wilkinson, 'Goethe's *Egmont* Might Have Been Written for Us', *The Radio Times*, 22.IV.1949.
11. Cf. *Dichtung u. Wahrheit*, IV, 20; JA, XXV, 124.
12. *Über Egmont*, ed. cit., p. 190.   13. Conversation with Eckermann, 18.I.1827.
14. Cf. p. 191 f.   15. 18.I.1825.
16. Cf. E. M. Wilkinson, *Goethes Trilogie der Leidenschaft*. Freies Deutsches Hochstift: Reihe d. Vorträge und Schriften, No. 18. Fft. a.M., 1957.
17. JA, XXXIX, 94.

V. 'TORQUATO TASSO'. The Tragedy of the Poet. By Elizabeth M.Wil-kinson. PEGS, XV (1946), 96 ff. German version in *Das deutsche Drama*, hrsg. v. Benno von Wiese. I (1959), 193 ff.

1. *Maximen u. Reflexionen*; JA, XXXV, 303. Cf. p. 181 above.
2. *Dichtung u. Wahrheit*, III, 12; JA, XXIV, 81.
3. E.g. Gustav Freytag, *Die Technik des Dramas*, Leipzig, 1876, pp. 59, 60, and Margaret Kennedy, *The Outlaws on Parnassus*, London, 1958, p. 161.
4. To Haydon, 10.V.1817.
5. *Noten und Abhandlungen zum Divan*; JA, V, 212: 'Die Besonnenheit des Dichters bezieht sich eigentlich auf die Form, den Stoff gibt ihm die Welt nur allzu freigebig, der Gehalt entspringt freiwillig aus der Fülle seines Innern; *bewusstlos* begegnen beide einander, und zuletzt weiss man nicht, wem eigentlich

der Reichtum angehöre. Aber die Form, ob sie schon vorzüglich im Genie liegt, will erkannt, will bedacht sein ...'
6. *Zahme Xenien*; JA, IV, 59. 7. Conversation with Eckermann, 6.V.1827.
8. *Dichtung u. Wahrheit*, III, 11; JA, XXIV, 9. 9. To Hugo Heller in 1908.
10. Keats to Haydon, 10.V.1817. 11. To Frau von Stein, 11.III.1781.
12. *Dichtung u. Wahrheit*, III, 15; JA, XXIV, 232.
13. Ibid., III, 13; JA, XXIV, 166 f.
14. *Maximen u. Reflexionen*; JA, XXXV, 309. 15. Esp. in Bks. 11-16.
16. JA, XXIV, 156 f. Cf. letter to Frau von Stein, 11.III.1781.
17. Cf. p. 163 f. 18. Keats to Benjamin Bailey, 18.VII.1818.
19. Cf. *Dichtung u. Wahrheit*, III, 15; JA, XXIV, 228, 260.
20. Cf. L. A. Willoughby, 'Wordsworth and Germany', *Fiedler Studies*, Oxford, 1938, pp. 442-5, and E. M. Wilkinson, 'Coleridge und Deutschland', *Forschungsprobleme d. vergl. Literaturgesch*. II, Tübingen, 1958, p. 19 f.
21. *Venezianische Epigramme*, 76. Cf. 29. 22. *Wordsworth, The Prelude*, V.
23. Keats to Benjamin Bailey, 14.VIII.1819. 24. JA, II, 90.
25. *Requiem für Wolf Graf von Kalckreuth*.
26. To Herder, 2.III.1789. For different interpretations of this much discussed word cf. E. L. Stahl, 'Tasso's Tragedy and Salvation', *German Studies presented to L. A. Willoughby*, Oxford, 1952.
27. For a discussion of the many interpretations see W. Rasch, *Goethes Torquato Tasso. Die Tragödie des Dichters*, Stuttgart, 1954. Cf. R. Peacock, *Goethe's Major Plays*, Manchester, 1959, p. 115 f.
28. Goethe to Karl August, 28.III.1788: 'Wer selbst auf dem Punkte der Existenz steht, um welchen der Dichter sich spielend dreht, dem können die Gaukeleien der Poesie, welche aus dem Gebiet der Wahrheit ins Gebiet der Lüge schwankt, weder genug thun ... noch ... ergötzen.' Cf. to Fr. Oeser, 13.II.1769, to Kestner, Oct. 1774, and *Ital. Reise*, 19.IX.1786.
29. An even earlier preoccupation with waves and storm in 1074 ff. Cf. above pp. 125 ff.
30. The term is A. E. Housman's in *The Name and Nature of Poetry*, Cambridge, 1933, p. 41.
31. Rilke, *Requiem für Wolf Graf von Kalckreuth*. 32. 10.VIII.1789.
33. To Richard Woodhouse, 27.X.1818.

Bibliography: I was esp. indebted to A. Metz, 'Die Tragödie in Goethes "Tasso" ', *Preussische Jahrbücher*, CXXII (1905); O. Pniower, *Dichtungen und Dichter*, Berlin, 1912; W. E. Delp, 'Goethe's *Tasso* in the Light of Chekhov', *Comparative Literature Studies*, XII (1944). More recent works are listed at the end of the German trsl. of this article in *Das deutsche Drama*, ed. cit.

VI. GOETHE'S 'FAUST'. A Morphological Approach. By L. A. Willoughby.

Adapted from 'Faust als Lebensorganisation', read at the Bicentenary Celebrations of the Johann Wolfgang Goethe Universität, Frankfurt am Main, 27 August, 1949, and published in *Goethe und die Wissenschaft*, Fft:a.M., 1951, pp. 35 ff.

1. Cf. conversation with Eckermann, 10.I.1825.
2. Ibid., 22.III.1824 (of nature); 3.I.1830 (of *Faust*).
3. Ibid., 6.V.1827. 4. 19.VIII.1806; *Goethes Gespräche*, ed. Biedermann², I, 427.
5. 20.VI.1831. 6. Cf. pp. 49, 215.
7. *Maximen u. Reflexionen*; JA, XXXV, 305.

NOTES

233

8. *Kampagne in Frankreich*; JA, XXVIII, 122.
9. *Von deutscher Baukunst* (1773); JA, XXXIII, 9.
10. Cf. W. Robson-Scott, 'Goethe and the Gothic Revival', PEGS, XXV (1956).
11. *Aus Goethes Brieftasche* (1776); JA, XXXVI, 116.
12. Letter to F. H. Jacobi, 21.VIII.1774.
13. A term Goethe was to reject (Eckermann, 20.VI.1831) as far too mechanical for designating the processes of either art or nature. How could it possibly be maintained, he asked, that Mozart had 'composed' *Don Juan*.
14. *Gespräche*, ed. cit., p. 428. 15. Ibid., p. 429. 16. Ibid., p. 427.
17. Cf. p. 24 and Note 5. 18. From the poem *Allerdings*.
19. Cf. p. 59 and Note 2. 20. Letter to Knebel, 21.II.1821.
21. *Dante*; JA, XXXVIII, 63. 22. Cf. p. 95 f. and Note 3.
23. Cf. 'Sphinx-Natur, ein Ungeheur, / Schreckt sie dich mit hundert Brüsten.' WA, I, 4, p. 137.
24. We have only to think of what happens to the word *Bild* in *Iphigenie*. Cf. S. P. Jenkins, 'The Image of the Goddess in *Iphigenie auf Tauris*', PEGS, XXI (1952).
25. *Aus Goethes Brieftasche*; JA, XXXVI, 115. Cf. above pp. 140 ff., 174 ff.
26. Cf. *Urfaust and Faust, Ein Fragment*, ed. L. A. Willoughby, Oxford, 1943, pp. xxiv ff.
27. Does this not perhaps offer support for Barker Fairley's contention that Goethe's genius was primarily lyrical? Cf. his *Goethe As Revealed in his Poetry*, London, 1932, and *Goethe's 'Faust'*. Six Essays, Oxford, 1953.
28. Goethe's *Faust*, ed. G. Witkowski, Leipzig, 1929[8], II, 248.
29. Cf. pp. 179, 225 below and Notes thereto.
30. For a more recent discussion of such problems, cf. E. Grumach, 'Prolog und Epilog im Faustplan von 1797', *Goethe. Neue Folge des Jahrbuchs der Goethe Gesellschaft*, XIV–XV (1953).
31. To Luden, *Gespräche*, ed. cit., p. 430.
32. Cf. E. M. Wilkinson, 'The Theological Basis of Faust's *Credo*', GLL, X (1957).

VII. ON THE STUDY OF GOETHE'S IMAGERY. By L. A. Willoughby.

Annual Bulletin of the Modern Humanities Research Association, No. 21, pp. 11 ff. Presidential Address, delivered on 6 January, 1949.

1. *Dichtung u. Wahrheit*, II, 7; JA, XXIII, 77.
2. 'The Image of the Horse and Charioteer in Goethe's Poetry', PEGS, XV (1946), 47 ff.
3. Cf. conversation with Eckermann, 20.XII.1829.
4. *Zur Farbenlehre*, § 751; JA, XL, 87. 5. 10.V.1806.
6. Letter of 27.III.1801.
7. *Contributions to Analytical Psychology*, London, 1928, p. 248.
8. *Shakespeare's Imagery*, Cambridge, 1935, p. 4.
9. *Archetypal Patterns in Poetry*, London, 1934, p. 89.
10. *Das Bild in der Dichtung*, Marburg, II (1939), p. 457.
11. *The Poetic Image*. The Clark Lectures. London, 1947, p. 22.
12. Coleridge to Godwin, 22.IX.1800.
13. [*Polarität*]; WA, II, 11, p. 165. 14. 8.III.1781.
15. *Invektiven. Voss contra Stolberg*; JA, IV, 149.

16. 17.III.1787; JA, XXVI, 246.
17. *Dichtung u. Wahrheit*, II, 10; JA, XXIII, 280.
18. His letters between 1772 and 1774 are frequently concerned with the problem of expressing thought directly, as it is felt and lived.
19. *Dichtung u. Wahrheit*, II, 6; JA, XXIII, 11.
20. Cf. our joint article, 'The Blind Man and the Poet' in *Essays Presented to W. H. Bruford*, London, 1962.
21. JA, II, 223.
22. Letter of 21.VI.1771. Cf. L. A. Willoughby, 'The Image of the "Wanderer" and the "Hut" in Goethe's Poetry', *Études Germaniques*, VI (1951), 207 ff.
23. Letter to Lavater, 6.III.1776.   24. Letter to Merck, 8.X.1775.
25. *Die Leiden des jungen Werther. Ihr geistesgeschichtlicher Hintergrund*. Fft.a.M., 1938.
26. 18.VIII.1823.
27. Cf. E. M. Wilkinson, *Goethes Trilogie der Leidenschaft*. Freies Deutsches Hochstift: Reihe der Vorträge und Schriften, No. 18. Fft.a.M., 1957.
28. VI, 9; GA, VIII, 849.   29. I, 23; GA, VIII, 578.   30. JA, XI, 215.
31. 5.VII.1827.   32. 22.X.1828.   33. Letter to Salzmann, 28.XI.1771. Cf. *Werther*, 19. VI. 1771; JA, XVI, 29.
34. *Faust II*, 6992.

VIII. THE POET AS THINKER. By Elizabeth M. Wilkinson. *German Studies Presented to L. A. Willoughby*, Oxford, 1952, pp. 217 ff.

1. To Kanzler v. Müller, 24.V.1828. WA, II, 11, p. 10; JA, XXXIX, 349.
2. *Maximen u. Reflexionen*; JA, XXXV, 307.   3. Ibid.; JA, XXXVIII, 271.
4. From the poem *Vermächtnis*. But compare the corrective complement—'only what is true is fruitful'—in *Naturphilosophie* (1827); JA, XXXVIII, 118.
5. *Maximen u. Reflexionen*; JA, XXXIX, 58.   6. Ibid.; JA, XXXIX, 67.
7. This came out very clearly, for instance, in J. Z. Young's Reith Lectures, *Doubt and Certainty in Science : a Biologist's Reflections on the Brain*, Oxford, 1951.
8. One of Coleridge's formulations of the doctrine: *Biographia Literaria*, Ch. XII.
9. *Einwirkung der neueren Philosophie* (1820); JA, XXXIX, 30.
10. Goethe to Schiller, 6.I.1798.
11. *Älteres, beinahe Veraltetes. Aus den Heften 'Zur Naturwissenschaft'* (1823); JA, XXXIX, 61 f.
12. *Der Versuch als Vermittler von Objekt und Subjekt* (1792); JA, XXXIX, 20.
13. JA, XXXIX, 67. Cf. his account of a debate in the French Academy of Sciences between Cuvier and Saint-Hilaire on the principles of zoology; JA, XXXIX, 218 ff.
14. *Bedeutende Fördernis durch ein einziges geistreiches Wort* (1823); JA, XXXIX, 49.
15. Ibid., p. 48.
16. Cf. Agnes Arber, *The Natural Philosophy of Plant Form*, Cambridge, 1950, p. 210.
17. 6.I.1798.
18. Review of E. Stiedenroth's *Psychologie zur Erklärung der Seelenerscheinungen* (1824); JA, XXXIX, 373.
19. Cf. Otto Regenbogen, 'Goethes Pindar-Erlebnis' in *Griechische Gegenwart. Zwei Vorträge über Goethes Griechentum*, Leipzig, 1942.
20. *Aus Goethes Brieftasche*; JA, XXXVI, 115 f. Cf. p. 175 above.
21. Ibid., 115 f.

22. Cf. the section 'Alchimisten' in the *Geschichte der Farbenlehre* (JA, XL, 181), which might well serve as a commentary on his own youthful remarks.
23. *Maximen u. Reflexionen*; JA, XXXV, 317 f. Cf. p. 175 above.
24. To Goethe, 23.VIII.1794.
25. *Dichtung u. Wahrheit*, III, 12; JA, XXIV, 81. Cf. p. 76 above.
26. Susanne Langer, *Philosophy in a New Key*, Pelican edition, p. 79.
27. Ibid., p. 33.
28. A confusion fostered by Sir Charles Sherrington, among others, in *Goethe on Nature and on Science*, Cambridge, 1942.
29. On p. 134. 30. 19.II.1802. 31. Op. cit., p. 210.
32. 'Goethe und die mathematische Physik. Eine erkenntnistheoretische Betrachtung' in *Idee und Gestalt*, Berlin, 1924. According to Cassirer (p. 74) Schelling's natural philosophy is exactly the hybrid affair that Goethe's is often accused of being, and entirely lacks the latter's strictness and self-consistency of method.
33. Goethe to Herder, July, 1772.
34. *Der Gestaltkreis*, Stuttgart, 1950[4], p. 149 f. Cf. Note 11 above.
35. *Vorwort zur Farbenlehre*; JA, XL, 63.
36. 'Bei Betrachtung der Natur im grossen wie im kleinen hab' ich unausgesetzt die Frage gestellt: Ist es der Gegenstand oder bist du es, der sich hier ausspricht?' (*Maximen u. Reflexionen*; JA, XXXIX, 74.)
37. *Metamorphose der Tiere*. Cf. B. Hassenstein, 'Goethes Morphologie als selbstkritische Wissenschaft und die heutige Gültigkeit ihrer Ergebnisse', *Goethe, Neue Folge d. Jahrbuchs der Goethe-Gesellschaft*, XII (1950), 354.
38. Cf. O.Walzel, JA, XXXVI, p. lxxiv. 39. On p. 138 (Note 17).
40. Susanne Langer, op. cit., p. 73. 41. Cf. p. 168.
42. *Betrachtung über Morphologie überhaupt*; JA, XXXIX, 133-7 and 368.
43. As, for example, in his review of Stiedenroth's *Psychologie zur Erklärung der Seelenerscheinungen*; JA, XXXIX, 373.
44. Cf. p. 76 (Note 2) and p. 143 (Note 25).
45. *Die Wahlverwandtschaften*; JA, XXI, 174.
46. *Maximen u. Reflexionen*; JA, XXXIX, 112. 47. To F. H. Jacobi, 6.I.1813.
48. JA, XXXIX, 34-6.
49. Ibid., p. 342 f. Cf. the reply (*Erwiderung*) by the professor of botany, E. H. F. Meyer; GA, XVII, 179 ff., esp. 184.

IX. LITERARY RELATIONS IN THE LIGHT OF GOETHE'S PRINCIPLE OF 'WIEDERHOLTE SPIEGELUNGEN'. By L. A. Willoughby. *Comparative Literature*, I (1949), 309 ff.

1. Cf. p. 197 f. 2. *Die Metamorphose der Pflanzen*, § XVII.
3. 26.II.1824. 4. 15.IX.1773. 5. 24.VI.1783. 6. JA, XXV, 221 f.
7. *The Future in Education*, Cambridge, 1941.
8. See E. Beutler [ed.], *Goethes Rede zum Schäkespears Tag. Schriften der Goethe-Gesellschaft*, L (1938), 10.
9. *Annalen*; JA, XXX, 398. Cf. the poetic version of his theory, *Entoptische Farben* (JA, II, 257), written for a lady of his acquaintance.
10. *Ital. Reise*; JA, XXVI, 96.
11. *Bezüge nach aussen* (1828); JA, XXXVIII, 137. 12. *Annalen*; JA, XXX, 43.
13. *Aus Goethes Brieftasche*; JA, XXXVI, 116.
14. *Dichtung u. Wahrheit*, III, 11; JA, XXIV, 20.
15. Ibid., Vorwort; JA, XXII, 4-6. 16. Ibid., III, 11; JA, XXIV, 19.

17. In *Protestantismus und Literatur*, Leipzig, 1922. Cf. K. Dockhorn in *Wandlung* (1948), p. 301.
18. *Goethe's Knowledge of English Literature*, Oxford, 1932, p. 105.
19. *Von Deutscher Baukunst*; JA, XXXIII, 4.
20. E. Beutler, 'Von deutscher Baukunst', *Goethe*, VI (1941), 232.
21. JA, XXII, 296.   22. *Dichtung u. Wahrheit*, II, 6; JA, XXIII, 17.
23. *Ennead*, I, i, 9.   24. *Wilhelm Meisters Lehrjahre*, VI; JA, XVIII, 96.
25. GA, V, 544; cf. JA, XIII, 292.   26. JA, XVI, 6.
27. Cf. J. M. Thorburn, *Art and the Unconscious*, London, 1928, p. 89.
28. JA, XXXVIII, 282.   29. JA, XXXVI, 209.   30. JA, XVIII, 251.
31. JA, XIX, 123.   32. JA, XVIII, 166.   33. JA, XVI, 289.
34. *Mit einem gemalten Bande*.   35. *Dichtung u. Wahrheit*, IV, 18; JA, XXV, 84.
36. From Cyprian. Cf. J. G. Robertson, *Goethe and Byron*, PEGS, II (1925), p. 34.
37. JA, XIX, 262.   38. JA, XXIII, 17; XXIV, 224.
39. Cf. Zimmermann to Frau v. Stein, 22.X.1775; GA, XVIII, 1030.
40. 5.XII.1772.   41. To Frau v. Stein, 9.IX.1783.
42. To Frau v. Stein, 20.I.1787.   43. JA, XI, 332.   44. JA, IV, 252.
Bibliography: Konrad Burdach, 'Goethes West-östlicher Divan', *Goethe-Jahrbuch*, XVII (1896), 16* ff.; Ruprecht Matthei, 'Neues von Goethes entoptischen Studien', *Goethe*, V (1940), 71; Ernst Beutler, 'Lili. Wiederholte Spiegelungen', *Essays um Goethe* (Wiesbaden, 1947), II, 1 ff.

X. GOETHE'S CONCEPTION OF FORM. By Elizabeth M. Wilkinson. Annual Lecture on a Master Mind. Henriette Hertz Trust of the British Academy. Read 11 July, 1951. *Proceedings of the British Academy*, XXXVII, 175 ff.

1. *Maximen u. Reflexionen* (ed. Günther Müller, Stuttgart, 1943), 895. The reader is here referred to this particular edition because its arrangement of Goethe's 1,200 odd aphorisms so clearly exhibits that 'polar' movement of his thought which I am at pains to bring out in the opening pages of this essay.
2. *Maximen*, ed. cit., 1056, 1058.   3. Ibid., 606.   4. Ibid., 1174.   5. Ibid., 926.
6. Ibid., 888.   7. Ibid., 1040, 1041.   8. Ibid., 934.   9. Ibid., 985.
10. Ibid., 873.   11. Ibid., 875.   12. Ibid., 82.   13. Ibid., 1183.
14. Ibid., 1177.   15. In *Attitudes toward History*, New York, 1937.
16. This is how S. E. Hyman (*The Armed Vision*, New York, 1948, p. 357 f.) explains Kenneth Burke's choice of the word 'comic' to describe this attitude of ambivalence.
17. I borrow this phrase from J. Bronowski's review of Viscount Samuel's *Essay in Physics*, *The Observer*, 15.IV.1951.
18. Walter de la Mare and Dr. Martin Johnson. Their exchange of ideas, lasting over a period of years, was discussed by the latter in a broadcast on 13.II.1951 (Third Programme).
19. I.e., at the time of writing. Cf. *Aspects of Form*. A Symposium, ed. L. L. Whyte, issued on the occasion of this Exhibition. London, 1951.
20. *Maximen*, ed. cit., 1020.   21. Ibid., 1109.
22. *Goethes Morphologische Schriften*, ed. Wilhelm Troll, Jena, 1926; *Goethes naturwissenschaftliche Schriften*, ed. Rudolf Steiner, Dornach, 1926; *Goethes Schriften über die Natur*, ed. Günther Ipsen, Leipzig, 1928; *Goethes naturwissenschaftliche Schriften*, ed. Waldemar v. Wasielewski in vol. 36 of Goethe's *Werke*, Berlin (Bong), 1929.
23. See, f.i., *Maximen*, ed. cit., 1042–84, the remarks with which he prefaced his

Theory of Colour, or his short essays on scientific method, e.g. *Der Versuch als Vermittler von Objekt und Subjekt, Erfahrung und Wissenschaft, Erfinden und Entdecken.*
24. *Goethe's Botany. Chronica Botanica*, Waltham, Mass., X, 2 (1946).
25. *The Natural Philosophy of Plant Form*, Cambridge, 1950.
26. *Maximen*, ed. cit., 885.
27. In conversation with J. Falk, 28.II.1809.
28. *Goethe on Nature and on Science*, Cambridge, 1942, p. 23.
29. *Dichtung u. Wahrheit*, IV, 16; JA, XXV, 10.
30. The poem *Um Mitternacht*. Cf. p. 226 below and Note 50.
31. 1.XII.1831.
32. Cf. p. 227.
33. 26.III.1780.
34. In a letter to v. Humboldt of 17.III.1832, which is a commentary on the conscious commanding of inspiration referred to in his earlier letter of 1.XII. 1831.
35. *Aus Goethes Brieftasche*; JA, XXXVI, 115.
36. *Maximen*, ed. cit., 769. Cf. p. 141 above.
37. *Versuch einer allgemeinen Vergleichungslehre* (1792); JA, XXXIX, 130.
38. *Vorträge über die drei ersten Capitel des Entwurfs einer allgemeinen Einleitung in die vergleichende Anatomie* (1796); ibid., 163.
39. In the section headed 'Die Absicht eingeleitet'; ibid., 252.
40. *Versuch einer allgemeinen Vergleichungslehre*; ibid., 130.
41. 'Die Absicht eingeleitet'; ibid., 251.
42. Ibid., 252. 43. E.g. *Vorträge über vergleichende Anatomie*; ibid., 170.
44. His conception of the scope and function of morphology is set out in his *Betrachtung über Morphologie überhaupt* (1795); ibid., 133 ff.
45. *The Natural Philosophy of Plant Form*, ed. cit., p. 209.
46. *Maximen*, ed. cit., 1168.
47. Cf. *Erste Bekanntschaft mit Schiller. 1794*; JA, XXX, 391.
48. Letter to Zelter, 30.X.1808.
49. Cf. p. 225 and Note 45.
50. With H. Luden, 19.VIII.1806. 51. VIII, 7; JA, XVIII, 352.
52. JA, XXXIV, 17. Cf. too his poem *Permanence in Change*, discussed on pp. 12, 182 and 224.
53. For a fuller discussion of this problem see E. M. Wilkinson—' "Form" and "Content" in the Aesthetics of German Classicism', *Stil- und Formprobleme in der Literatur*. Vorträge des VII. Kongresses der Internationalen Vereinigung für moderne Sprachen und Literaturen in Heidelberg 1957. Heidelberg, 1959.
54. *Maximen*, ed. cit., 536-7. 55. K. L. v. Knebel, 21.II.1821.
56. *Maximen*, ed. cit., 36.
57. Cf. L. A. Willoughby, 'Goethe Looks at the English', MLR, L (1955), esp. p. 482.
58. For details see the notes to the poem *Dauer im Wechsel* in Emil Staiger's edition of Goethe's *Gedichte* (Zürich, 1949), II, 463 f.
59. *Dichtung u. Wahrheit*, III, 11; JA, XXIV, 34.
60. *Maximen*, ed. cit., 561-3.
61. *Dichtung u. Wahrheit*, II, 10; JA, XXIII, 257 f. I hope that this paraphrase catches the gist and tone of a passage too long to quote in full.
62. *Vorwort zur Farbenlehre*; JA, XL, 61 ff.
63. Ibid., p. 63. Cf. *Vorwort zur Morphologie*. 'Die Absicht eingeleitet'; ibid., 252.
64. *Wilhelm Meisters Lehrjahre*, VIII, 7; JA, XVIII, 352.

XI. 'TASSO—EIN GESTEIGERTER WERTHER' IN THE LIGHT OF
GOETHE'S PRINCIPLE OF 'STEIGERUNG'. By Elizabeth M. Wilkinson.
MLR, XLIV (1949), 305 ff. Reprinted in *Goethe. Neue Folge des Jahrbuchs der
Goethe-Gesellschaft*, XIII (1951), 28 ff.
1. 3.V.1827.   2. 29. IV. and 20.V.1826.
3. V, 3 (1826) and VI, 1 (1827); JA, XXXVIII, 23 ff.
4. This was first observed by J. G. Roberston in his edition of *Torquato Tasso*,
Manchester, 1918, p. L. But the error persisted as late as 1947 in G. Lukács,
Goethe und seine Zeit, p. 28.
5. 'Studien zu Goethes Wortgebrauch', *Archiv f. d. Studium d. neueren Sprachen*,
XCVI (1896); 'Wort und Bedeutung in Goethes Sprache', *Litterarhist. Forschungen*, XX (1901).
6. *Die Metaphysik Goethes*, Berlin, 1932.   7. WA, II, 11, p. 10; JA, XXXIX, 349.
8. Letter to Auguste v. Stolberg, 13.II.1775.   9. 17.III.1832.
10. Cf. pp. 146 f. and 223.
11. *Über die Einteilung der Farben und ihr Verhältnis gegen einander* (1793); WA, II,
5, I, p. 95 f.
12. *Zur Farbenlehre. Didaktischer Teil* (1807) § 518; WA, II, 1, p. 211 f.
13. Ibid. § 519.   14. Ibid. § 517.   15. Ibid. § 523.   16. Ibid. § 794.
17. Ibid. §§ 739, 745.   18. *Vorarbeiten zur Morphologie*; WA, II, 7, p. 12.
19. *Versuch, die Metamorphose der Pflanzen zu erklären* (1790), § 27; JA, XXXIX,
266 f.
20. *Über die Spiraltendenz der Vegetation* (1831); WA, II, 7, p. 344 f.
21. Cf. Agnes Arber, *Goethe's Botany, Chronica Botanica*, X, 2 (1946), 75.
22. WA, II, 13, p. 18.   23. *Tag- und Jahreshefte* (1812); JA, XXX, 269.
24. 'Über die Gesetze der Organisation überhaupt', i.e. § III of *Vorträge
über die drei ersten Capitel des Entwurfs einer allgemeinen Einleitung in die vergleichende
Anatomie*; JA, XXXIX, 171 ff.
25. Ibid., 177.
26. *Zur Morphologie*. Vorwort. 'Die Absicht eingeleitet ; JA, XXXIX, 252.
27. 'Über die Gesetze der Organisation überhaupt'; JA, XXXIX, 175.
28. 'Von den Vorteilen der vergleichenden Anatomie', i.e. § I of *Erster Entwurf
einer allgemeinen Einleitung in die vergleichende Anatomie* (1795); JA, XXXIX, 138.
29. [*Polarität*]; WA, II, 11, p. 165 f.
30. *Zur Morphologie*. 'Aphoristisches'; WA, II, 6, p. 353.
31. *Zur Morphologie*; JA, XXXIX, 343.
32. Cf. *Zur Farbenlehre. Didaktischer Teil*, § 531; WA, II, 1, p. 216.
33. Cf. *Vergleichende Anatomie* (JA, XXXIX, 145) and *Vorarbeiten zur Morphologie*
(WA, II, 7, p. 14).
34. 12.IV.1829. Cf. p. 225.
35. *Maximen u. Reflexionen*; JA, XXXVIII, 255.
36. Conversation with Riemer, 24.III.1807.
37. *Noten u. Abhandlungen zum Divan*; JA, V, 173.
38. *Zur Morphologie*. 'Vorarbeiten zu einer Physiologie der Pflanzen'; WA, II,
6, p. 302.
39. *Maximen u. Reflexionen*; JA, XXXIX, 70.
40. *Wiederholte Spiegelungen*; JA, XXV, 222.
41. 'Verfolg' [*der Geschichte meines botanischen Studiums*]; WA, II, 6, p. 143.
42. Letter to Reinhard, 26.XII.1824.
43. *Maximen u. Reflexionen*; JA, XXXIX, 62.

44. *Winckelmann*; JA, XXXIV, 17.
45. Letter to Reinhard, 13.II.1812. *Filiation* bears a similar relation to *Steigerung* as does *cohobiren*. It too is from the Low Latin, was used by the alchemists, and is still used in science, to denote successive filial generation. No more than *cohobiren* has it such a full meaning as *Steigerung*: it lacks the element of intensification and refinement. Even together the two do not give the whole meaning suggested by the much more frequent *Steigerung*, since neither bears the image of ascending progress; but to people familiar with the general trend of his thought Goethe sometimes uses one of these words to call up the whole complexity of associations, e.g. to Eckermann, 4.I.1827: 'Es geht durch die ganze Kunst eine Filiation. Sieht man einen grossen Meister, so findet man immer, dass er das Gute seiner Vorgänger benutzte und dass eben dieses ihn gross machte. Männer wie Raffael wachsen nicht aus dem Boden.'
46. To Eckermann, 20.X.1828.
47. *Wilhelm Meisters Wanderjahre*, I, 6; JA, XIX, 76.
48. Ibid., II, 9; JA, XX, 25.
49. 'Verfolg' [*der Geschichte meines botanischen Studiums*]; WA, II, 6, p. 226.
50. *Noten u. Abhandlungen zum Divan*: JA, V, 283.
51. *Maximen u. Reflexionen*; JA, XXXVIII, 278.
52. *Zur Naturwissenschaft*. 'Meteore des literarischen Himmels. Plagiat'; JA, XXXIX, 41.
53. Conversation with Riemer, 28.VIII.1808.
54. Letter to Zelter, 30.X.1808.
55. Cf. letter to Zelter, 20.X.1831, where Goethe speaks of Adam Müller as a 'recht hübsches, aber falsch gesteigertes Talent'.
56. *Maximen u. Reflexionen*; JA, XXXVIII, 254.
57. Conversation with Riemer, [?] VIII. 1808.
58. Letter to Reinhard, 7.IX.1831.
59. See Goethe's diary from 16 April onwards. According to the editor of Ampère's correspondence, it was in a letter to Reinhard that Goethe attributed to Ampère the remark that Tasso was 'ein *gesteigerter* Werther' (*André-Marie Ampère et Jean-Jacques Ampère. Correspondance et Souvenirs de 1805 à 1864*. Recueillis par Madame H. C. Paris, 1875, I, 440, fn.). I have been unable to find such a letter, although Baldensperger (*Bibliographie Critique de Goethe en France*, Paris, 1907, p. 55) refers to one written to Reinhard on 12.V.1827, which is not to be found in the standard collections. It is most likely a slip for 12.V.1826—a letter to Reinhard of this latter date certainly mentions Ampère's review.
60. Draft of a letter to C. G. D. Nees von Esenbeck.
61. *Correspondance*, ed. cit., pp. 441 ff.
62. *Maximen u. Reflexionen*; JA, XXXIX, 60. Cf. p. 218 above.
63. Cf. *Tagebuch*, 30.III and 30.IV.1780.
64. To Reinhard, 12.V.1826.
65. For further details cf. E. M. Wilkinson, 'Goethe's *Trilogie der Leidenschaft*' (cf. p. 231 above, Note 16).
66. Cf. p. 154 f. above.
67. It must have been very familiar; for, according to J.-J. Ampère (*Correspondance*, ed. cit. p. 441), Goethe lost the manuscript of the second part of his translation, i.e. the part containing the reference to Tasso and Werther, and therefore had to translate it a second time.
68. JA, XXXVIII, 30 f. Italics mine.   69. See above, pp. 192, 196.

70. To C. M. Engelhardt.
71. *Steigerung* is used in precisely this sense in his discussion of lyrical passages in Manzoni's *Graf Carmagnola* (1821); JA, XXXVII, 181.
72. Letter to S. Boisserée, 4.XII.1817.
73. Conversation with Eckermann, 10.I.1825.   74. *Ital. Reise*, 3.XI.1787.
75. Letter to Kestner, 2.V.1783.   76. Conversation with Eckermann, 17.II.1831.
77. *Maximen u. Reflexionen*; JA, IV, 231.   78. Ibid.; JA, XXXIX, 87.
79. Conversation with Eckermann, 1.II.1827.

XII. UNITY AND CONTINUITY IN GOETHE. By L. A. Willoughby. The Taylorian Lecture. Read on 25 November, 1946. Oxford, 1947. Reprinted as 'Einheit und Zusammenhang bei Goethe' in *Goethe, Jb. d. Goethe Gesellschaft*, X (1947), 149 ff.

1. Cf. esp. his essays, *Der Versuch als Vermittler von Objekt und Subjekt* and *Bedenken und Ergebung*; JA, XXXIX, 20, 35.
2. JA, XL, 61.
3. *Vorwort zur Morphologie*. 'Die Absicht eingeleitet'; JA, XXXIX, 251.
4. Ibid., 249, 252. Cf. *Maximen u. Reflexionen*: ibid., 103.
5. JA, XXV, 277.   6. *Kampagne in Frankreich*; JA, XXVIII, 155.
7. In conversation with Eckermann, 27.I.1824.   8. Ibid., 2.V.1824.
9. *Anschauende Urteilskraft*; JA, XXXIX, 34.
10. *Dichtung u. Wahrheit*, III, 11; JA, XXIV, 63.   11. JA, XXXIII, 9.
12. *Von deutscher Baukunst*; JA, XXXIII, 4. Cf. letter to Frau v. Stein, 31.X.1778.
13. 9.VII.1786.   14. To Frau v. Stein, 20-23.XII.1786.
15. Ibid., 25.I.1787; 19.I.1788.   16. *Dichtung u. Wahrheit*, IV, 16; JA, XXV, 20.
17. *Maximen u. Reflexionen*; JA, XXXIX, 60.
18. *Bedeutende Fördernis durch ein einziges geistreiches Wort*; JA, XXXIX, 48.
19. JA, XXXIX, 251.
20. Letter of 24.V.1828. WA, II, 11, p. 10; JA, XXXIX, 349.
21. 17.III.1832.   22. JA, XXXIX, 114.   23. JA, XXXIX, 350.
24. *Maximen u. Reflexionen*; JA, XXXV, 305.
25. *Von deutscher Baukunst* (1823); JA, XXXV, 236 f. Cf. *Dichtung u. Wahrheit*, II, 9; JA, XXIII, 202-6.
26. *Maximen u. Reflexionen*; JA, XXXVIII, 263.   27. GA, IV, 263.
28. JA, V, 7.   29. JA, XVI, 105.   30. To Sophie v. Laroche, 1.IX.1780.
31. III, 11; JA, XXIV, 9.   32. JA, XVI, 47.
33. *Biographia Literaria*, Ch. XII. Cf. JA, XXXIX, 29 f., 48.
34. To Frau v. Stein, 9.VII; 24.XI; 20.XII.1786.
35. *Dichtung u. Wahrheit*, III, 11; JA, XXIV, 63.
36. *Kampagne in Frankreich*, XXVIII, 25.
37. *Bedeutende Fördernis durch ein einziges geistreiches Wort*; JA, XXXIX, 48 f.
38. Cf. L. A. Willoughby, ' "Wanderer" and "Hut" ', *Études Germaniques*, VI, 219.
39. *Erste Bekanntschaft mit Schiller*. 1794; JA, XXX, 391.   40. JA, XXXIX, 7.
41. Ibid., 135.   42. *Kampagne in Frankreich*; JA, XXVIII, 154.   43. 4.I.1824.
44. *Kampagne in Frankreich*; JA, XXVIII, 122.
45. Letter to Reinhard, 31.XII.1809.
46. *Dichtung u. Wahrheit*, III, 13; JA, XXIV, 158.
47. In conversation with Eckermann, 27.IV.1825; 12.IV.1829.
48. Letter of 4.IX.[1772]; JA, XVI, 87.

49. [*Polarität*]; WA, II, 11, p. 165 f.
50. JA, XXXVII, 221; cf. XXX, 316.
51. In his review of Fr. Rochlitz' *Für Freunde der Tonkunst* (1824); JA, XXXVII, 282.
52. To Frau v. Stein, 18.IV.1787.
53. Its significance is discussed by Goethe towards the end of II, 9; JA, XXIII, 206 f.

INDEX

II IDEAS, IMAGES & KEY WORDS